HONG KONG'S FINANCIAL INSTITUTIONS
AND MARKETS

HG5802
H66
1986

Hong Kong's Financial Institutions and Markets

EDITORS
Robert Haney Scott   K.A. Wong   Yan Ki Ho

CONTRIBUTORS
Simon S.M. Ho   Yan Ki Ho   Dan L. Hsu   Robert Haney Scott
Elbert Y.C. Shih   Lawrence S.T. Tai   K.A. Wong

With a Foreword by Q.W. Lee

NO LONGER THE PROPERTY
OF THE
UNIVERSITY OF R.I. LIBRARY

HONG KONG
OXFORD UNIVERSITY PRESS
OXFORD NEW YORK MELBOURNE

14702042

Oxford University Press

Oxford New York Toronto
Petaling Jaya Singapore Hong Kong Tokyo
Delhi Bombay Calcutta Madras Karachi
Nairobi Dar es Salaam Cape Town
Melbourne Auckland

and associated companies in
Beirut Berlin Ibadan Nicosia

© Oxford University Press 1986

First published 1986
Second impression 1986

All rights reserved. No part of this publication may be reproduced,
stored in a retrieval system, or transmitted, in any form or by any
means, electronic, mechanical, photocopying, recording or otherwise,
without the prior permission of Oxford University Press

ISBN 0 19 583958 7 (cloth)
ISBN 0 19 583957 9 (limp)

OXFORD is a trade mark of Oxford University Press

Printed in Hong Kong by Ko's Arts Printing Co., Ltd.
Published by Oxford University Press, Warwick House, Hong Kong

Foreword

THE emergence of Hong Kong as a major international financial centre is the culmination of three decades of rapid development by the territory's financial system. Such development has been marked by a number of crises, constant adaptation to the demands of a rapidly expanding manufacturing economy and keen competitive pressure. As a financial centre, Hong Kong has now reached a level of sophistication at which important new questions are being asked about the range of services to be offered for the rest of this century, its relations with the world economy and the appropriate system of supervision to maintain public confidence in the integrity of its financial institutions.

The banking sector's own expansion began with the establishment of Hong Kong as a major export centre. The territory's industrialization accelerated sharply in the mid-1950s, creating new demands for commercial banking services. As manufacturers began to boost their sales in overseas markets, their need for additional financial resources outstripped their ability to raise equity capital. The banks filled this gap with various types of credit facility.

The 1960s can best be described as a period of consolidation for the local banking industry. The sharp increase in business was accompanied by certain unhealthy practices and excessive competition which highlighted the need for more effective supervision of bank operations. The territory's banking legislation was overhauled; an interest rate agreement was established; and a moratorium was imposed on the issue of new bank licences. These measures gave the banks a breathing space in which to consolidate and to attain more mature management standards.

By the end of the 1960s, Hong Kong's economic base had broadened considerably. The financial sector had begun to market its services to the rest of the Asia-Pacific region and has subsequently become a major earner of foreign exchange in its own right. The significance of the financial sector's contribution to the economy as a whole was enhanced by the increased attention which the international financial community accorded to this region in the 1970s, and the marked rise in the general prosperity of the key economies in the Asia-Pacific region during that decade.

Hong Kong has special advantages which enabled it to respond to these banking opportunities. Hong Kong is ideally located as a communications centre and as a base to serve much of Asia and the Pacific. It is in the right time zone to supplement both New York and London. The community could offer adequate numbers of professionals of all types, whose training and expertise matched international standards. Well-trained and highly motivated executives and clerical staff were available to work in an expanding banking industry. The Government imposed no controls on capital movements; exchange controls were non-existent, taxes and other constraints were kept to low levels.

Hong Kong provided an attractive business environment which few places could match. The world's leading banks responded by setting up representative offices and deposit-taking companies and buying into local banks. During the 1970s, this international presence had indeed strengthened Hong Kong's role as a financial centre. When the moratorium on new bank licences was relaxed in 1978, many of these overseas financial institutions upgraded their representation to serve not only the domestic market but also their customers throughout Asia and the Pacific. Within the territory, the demand for more sophisticated financial services increased as domestic financial markets developed. A wholesale money market emerged, and a variety of new financial instruments was introduced.

Hong Kong's role as an international financial centre has been reinforced by the expansion of China's commercial and financial ties with the rest of the world. Since 1978, the country has embarked on a programme of economic reforms which has achieved impressive results in modernizing agriculture and industry. The reform programme has included special measures to promote foreign trade as well as direct foreign investment. China looks to capital and credit facilities from abroad as an important source of development finance. As a financial centre, Hong Kong is ideally placed — politically, geographically, and culturally — to act as bridge between China and the world's business and financial communities.

During the 1980s, the financial sector has been faced with new challenges. The deposit-taking companies have been reorganized in the wake of new regulations to improve the specialization of different types of financial institution. The banks have been given a strengthened statutory organization to improve the industry's control of its own affairs.

In the early 1980s, world trade was hit by the worst recession in half a century. Banks all over the world came under pressure from a spate of bad loans. Within Hong Kong, doubts about the political future caused considerable uncertainty about both the currency and investment prospects. At the same time, key sectors of the economy, such as real estate, suffered a severe downturn.

The Sino-British Joint Declaration of 1984 resolved the political uncertainty for Hong Kong. But in common with other major financial markets, Hong Kong must now tackle several critical issues. The growing internationalization of banking services, the launching of financial futures, the authorization of banks to engage in brokerage, and the concept of banks as providers of comprehensive financial services on a global basis have led to discussion and debate about new internal management systems for financial institutions and to an overhaul of the supervisory systems for the sector as a whole.

If Hong Kong is to continue to make progress as a financial centre, it is important that the quality of analysis and discussion about current issues and future trends be maintained at the highest level. The freedom with which professional bankers, government officials, academic economists and a profusion of other commentators have expressed themselves has always been a significant factor in the creative development of the financial sector. The essays presented in this volume are a further contribution to the task of mobilizing a wide spectrum of Hong Kong's expertise for the enhancement of the role which financial institutions can play in the further progress of the territory's economy. Each essay represents an individual viewpoint and personal research designed to add to our understanding of the way in which the financial sector functions. A community better informed about the way its financial services are provided should be in a strong position to meet the challenges of the future with confidence and creativity.

Q.W. LEE
Chairman, Hang Seng Bank
Hong Kong
September 1985

Preface

EVERYONE agrees: Hong Kong is unique — unique in its history, its culture, and its future. However, Hong Kong's economic development has followed a classical pattern. Vestiges of the cottage-industry methods of production that prevailed before the industrial revolution may be found in Hong Kong even today as many small producers often pool their efforts to supply large buyers with wholesale quantities of textiles. Beside them one finds modern mass-production techniques used in producing watches and toys. But economic history shows that industrial capitalism is followed by financial capitalism as financial management evolves into a centrepiece of control.

In a closed society and a closed economy financial controls usually lead to restraints because of an undue concentration of economic power in the hands of a few. But this is not Hong Kong's situation. Its Government has opened the door to competition in finance, and the plethora of financial institutions and markets now operating in Hong Kong provide adequate testimony to the Government's concern for fostering a business climate appropriate to the continuation of economic growth. A modern business-oriented exchange economy simply cannot exist without a well-developed financial structure.

We have tried to put together in one volume a brief description of Hong Kong's financial markets and institutions as they exist today in the hope that it will be useful to those who work in these markets as well as to students and to newcomers to Hong Kong. We have also included some commentary on the usefulness of financial institutions and some analysis of controversial issues such as the appropriateness of the activities of the Hong Kong Association of Banks and the linked exchange rate system. That is, we have sought first to describe the structure of financial institutions and markets, second to explain the reasons for their existence — their usefulness — and third to discuss various policy issues concerning their regulation and control.

As time marches on toward the date of the return of Hong Kong to China, these financial institutions and markets will continue to develop. Hong Kong will continue to strengthen its position as an international financial centre. This development is, surely, in the spirit of the Sino-British Joint Declaration. And if, as expected, Hong Kong's financial institutions and markets remain free for another 50 years after 1997, they will surely serve China well.

If this book leads to greater understanding of the role of these institutions and provides but a portion of a platform for the continued discussion of policy issues, we will have served our purpose.

We wish to thank especially Dr Philip Fu, whose encouragement helped strengthen our efforts. We are also indebted to Joannie Shearer, Nancy Chung, Yvonne Kwok, and the editorial staff of Oxford University Press for their several and significant contributions in support of our efforts.

ROBERT HANEY SCOTT, K.A. WONG, AND YAN KI HO

Contributors

Professor Robert Haney Scott
Professor of Economics and Finance, Schools of Business Administration, University of Washington, Seattle, USA. Formerly Visiting Professor of Finance, Department of Accounting and Finance, The Chinese University of Hong Kong.

Dr K.A. Wong
Senior Lecturer, School of Management, National University of Singapore. Formerly Lecturer, Department of Accounting and Finance, The Chinese University of Hong Kong.

Dr Yan Ki Ho
Lecturer, Department of Accounting and Finance, The Chinese University of Hong Kong.

Mr Simon S.M. Ho
Lecturer, Department of Accounting and Finance, The Chinese University of Hong Kong.

Mr D.L. Hsu
Lecturer, Department of Accounting and Finance, The Chinese University of Hong Kong.

Dr Elbert Y.C. Shih
Lecturer, Department of Accounting and Finance, The Chinese University of Hong Kong.

Dr Lawrence S.T. Tai
Lecturer, Department of Accounting and Finance, The Chinese University of Hong Kong.

Contents

Tables

Figures

1. Commercial Banking

LAWRENCE S.T. TAI

SINCE the end of the Second World War, Hong Kong has developed from an entrepôt to an industrial economy. During the process of transformation there has been a huge demand for banking services. At the same time, the growth in national income and in saving by individuals has led to a rapid expansion of bank deposits. Foreign capital in the form of portfolio and direct investment has also entered Hong Kong, primarily because of its political stability, its low tax rates, and the low level of government intervention in commercial affairs. Thus, domestic commercial banks have experienced a period of rapid growth, and foreign banks have also found Hong Kong an attractive place in which to set up branches or representative offices.

The Growth of Commercial Banking in Hong Kong

The Number of Banks and Branches

An obvious indication of the level of banking activity is the number of banks. In 1954 there were 94 licensed banks in Hong Kong. The number of banks declined to 73 in 1969, mainly as a result of a banking crisis in 1965, when a series of runs on many banks continued for nearly a year.[1] In 1966 the Government imposed a moratorium on the issue of new bank licences.[2] The number of banks rose from 73 to 74 in 1972 and remained at this figure until 1977. The moratorium was lifted in March 1978 and this action led to an influx of new banks. During a 17-month period, 41 new licences were issued. But the Government decided to reimpose the moratorium in August 1979 and temporarily suspended the issue of bank licences for a period of six months. The moratorium was again lifted in May 1981 and in 1984 there were 140 banks. New banks are currently allowed to apply for licences, but they must meet more stringent asset and capital requirements than before.

Despite the decline in the number of licensed banks during the period 1954–71, the number of branches and the total number of bank offices increased. The number of branches jumped from only 3 in 1954 to 1,407 in 1984 while the total number of bank offices rose from 97 to 1,547 during the same period. Table 1.1 shows the number of licensed banks, the number of branches, and the total number of bank offices for selected years between 1954 and 1984.

The increase in the number of banks and branches provides only one dimension of banking growth in Hong Kong. Much more important than this indicator are the changing assets and liabilities of the banking system.

Table 1.1 Banks and Banking Offices

Year End	Number of Licensed Banks	Number of Branches	Total Offices
1954	94	3	97
1959	82	13	95
1964	88	204	292
1969	73	289	362
1974	74	557	631
1979	105	906	1,011
1984	140	1,407	1,547

Source: Hong Kong Monthly Digest of Statistics (Hong Kong, Census and Statistics Department), various issues; and *Hong Kong Annual Report* (Hong Kong, Hong Kong Government Printer), various issues.

The changes in assets and liabilities reflect the growth and internationalization of the financial sector.

The Growth in Bank Assets

Commercial bank assets in Hong Kong may be divided into five basic categories: cash, amount due from banks abroad, loans and advances, investments, and other assets. Table 1.2 shows the distribution of bank assets for selected years from 1961 to 1984.

Although the cash in banks increased more than 16 times, or at an annual rate of 12.9 per cent, as a proportion of total assets cash declined from 2.4 to 0.3 per cent. The item 'amount due from banks abroad', which consists of demand and time deposits in foreign countries, has expanded rapidly. It grew at an annual rate of 26.8 per cent, and its relative share in total assets rose from 23.1 per cent in 1961 to 46.4 per cent in 1984, reflecting the banking system's increasing use of foreign balances both as earning assets and as liquid assets.

Table 1.2 The Distribution of Bank Assets (per cent per annum)

	1961	1965	1969	1973	1977	1981	1984
Cash	2.4	2.0	2.0	1.4	0.9	0.7	0.3
Amount due from banks abroad	23.1	26.3	32.1	26.9	34.0	34.9	46.4
Loans and advances	39.3	45.5	47.7	57.8	55.5	47.6	40.4
Investments	3.9	4.8	4.0	4.9	3.9	8.8	7.0
Other assets	31.3	21.4	14.2	9.0	5.7	8.0	5.9
Total	100.0	100.0	100.0	100.0	100.0	100.0	100.0

Source: Hong Kong Annual Digest of Statistics (Hong Kong, Census and Statistics Department), 1983 and *Hong Kong Monthly Digest of Statistics* (Hong Kong, Census and Statistics Department), various issues.

Another asset item that has shown enormous growth is 'loans and advances'. This item represents the bulk of the finance used by current business operations in Hong Kong. It increased from HK$2,334 million in 1961 to HK$286,277 million in 1984, representing an annual growth of 23.3 per cent. Its relative share in total assets rose from 39.3 per cent to 40.4 per cent, but reached its highest level, 57.8 per cent, in 1973. These data provide an indication of Hong Kong's rapid rise as a financial centre. Table 1.3 provides a detailed breakdown of the types of loans and advances extended by banks to customers, as at 31 December 1984. Over 60 per cent of the total comprised non-trade financing loans for use in Hong Kong.

Investments grew at an annual rate of 26.2 per cent and, as a proportion of total assets, they increased from 3.9 per cent in 1961 to 7.0 per cent in 1984.

Table 1.3 Bank Loans and Advances to Customers Analysed by Purpose (in HK$ million as at 31 December 1984)

	HK$	Foreign Currencies	Total
To finance imports to, and exports and re-exports from, Hong Kong	19,983	10,073	30,056
To finance merchandising trade not touching Hong Kong	206	3,459	3,665
Other loans for use in Hong Kong	142,631	33,600	176,231
Other loans for use outside Hong Kong	2,391	62,982	65,373
Other loans where the place of use is not known	1,609	9,344	10,953
Total loans and advances	166,820	119,458	286,278

Source: Hong Kong Monthly Digest of Statistics (Hong Kong, Census and Statistics Department), January 1985.

The Growth in Bank Liabilities

On the liabilities side, the most notable feature is the remarkable growth of the item 'amount due to banks abroad'. It increased 1,000 times, or at an annual rate of 35.1 per cent. This item jumped from only 6.2 per cent of total liabilities at the end of 1961 to 50.3 per cent at the end of 1984. The significance of this increase is that it reflects not only Hong Kong's growing importance as a financial centre, but also the banking system's evolving method of managing its sources of funds. Traditionally banks have relied on asset management to meet their liquidity needs; there is a growing trend to turn more to liability management as a means of raising funds. Simultaneously, the relative share of deposits in total liabilities has declined from 56.3 to 39.9 per cent, and this indicates that the banking system has become less dependent on deposits from the public. (See Table 1.4.)

Table 1.4 The Distribution of Bank Liabilities (per cent per annum)

	1961	1965	1969	1973	1977	1981	1984
Deposits	56.3	65.2	74.4	65.1	52.8	32.0	39.9
Amount due to banks abroad	6.2	7.5	11.2	22.1	36.7	52.2	50.3
Other liabilities	37.5	27.3	14.4	12.8	10.5	15.8	9.8
Total	100.0	100.0	100.0	100.0	100.0	100.0	100.0

Source: Hong Kong Annual Digest of Statistics (Hong Kong, Census and Statistics Department), 1983 and *Hong Kong Monthly Digest of Statistics* (Hong Kong, Census and Statistics Department), various issues.

The capital of the banking system is not shown separately in the balance sheet of banks but is included in the item 'other liabilities'. Since capital comprises the major part of this item, the whole item can be considered as a surrogate for the capital of the banking system. During the period 1961–84, such liabilities increased 57 times, or at an annual rate of 19.2 per cent. Their relative share, however, declined from 37.5 to 9.8 per cent, implying a higher leverage for the capital structure of the banking system.

Although the banking system has become less dependent on deposits as a source of funds, bank deposits have shown phenomenal growth in the past two decades. They increased from HK$3,367 million at the end of 1961 to HK$296,103 million at the end of 1984, representing an annual growth of 21.5 per cent. It is, therefore, appropriate to give a brief description of the changing composition of bank deposits.

Despite the fact that there is an upward trend in the growth of bank deposits in Hong Kong, the trend has not been uniform. Growth was relatively slow during the 1950s, as compared to the 1970s and early 1980s. The growth in national income and increased saving by individuals, together with increasing inflows of deposits from foreign (especially South-east Asian) countries, have led to the rapid expansion of deposits.

Savings and time deposits have increased more rapidly than have demand deposits, thus altering the composition of commercial bank deposits. In 1954 demand deposits accounted for 77.5 per cent of total deposits and savings and time deposits for 22.5 per cent, while in 1984 these percentages were 7.9 and 92.1 respectively (see Table 1.5). Rising interest rates partially account for this development. Another factor is the change in payment technology; this, combined with increasing income, implies that deposits are regarded more as a store of value than as a medium of payment. Since demand deposits are a more volatile form of bank deposit, the structural shift may reflect, *inter alia*, the growing confidence of both residents and non-residents in Hong Kong's banking system.

The Foreign Currency Liabilities of the Banking Sector

The net spot foreign currency liabilities of the banking sector have been decreasing since the end of September 1983. As a result of the stabilization of the exchange value of the Hong Kong dollar in October 1983, bank

Table 1.5 The Distribution of Bank Deposits (per cent per annum)

Year End	Demand Deposits	Savings Deposits	Time Deposits	Total Deposits
1954	77.5	9.5	13.0	100.0
1959	58.6	18.0	23.4	100.0
1964	34.1	23.1	42.8	100.0
1969	30.2	27.4	42.4	100.0
1974	26.3	27.9	45.8	100.0
1979	20.0	48.9	31.1	100.0
1984	7.9	27.4	64.7	100.0

Source: *Hong Kong Monthly Digest of Statistics* (Hong Kong, Census and Statistics Department), various issues.

customers began to switch their foreign currency deposits (mainly United States dollar deposits) into Hong Kong dollar deposits. As shown in Table 1.6, at the end of December 1984 the net foreign currency liabilities of the banking sector were reduced to − HK$4.3 billion, compared with HK$20.5 billion at the end of September 1983. The confidence of the public was restored by the signing of the Sino-British agreement on the future of Hong Kong in December 1984, and this helped to decrease the net spot foreign currency liabilities of the banking sector.

The Structure and Regulation of the Commercial Banking System

The Banking Ordinance, Chapter 155 of the Laws of Hong Kong, defines banking business as either '(a) receiving from the general public money on current, deposit, savings or other similar account repayable on demand or within less than three months or at call or notice of less than three months; or (b) paying or collecting cheques drawn by or paid in by customers, or both'.[3] This definition of banking business is quite broad and thus allows licensed banks in Hong Kong to carry on mixed banking.

By way of contrast, the legal definition of a commercial bank in the United States is an institution that accepts deposits and makes commercial loans. Some institutions, however, accept deposits but do not make commercial loans; and they are thus able to avoid many government regulations. These institutions are now referred to by the unfortunate phrase 'non-bank banks'.

The Structure of the Banking System

The commercial banks in Hong Kong are often classified, according to their national origins, into three major groups: British, Chinese, and non-British foreign banks.[4]

The British banks are unquestionably the leaders in the banking sector, due to their long history in Hong Kong and their close relationship with the

Table 1.6 The Balance Sheet of the Licensed Banks (in HK$ million as at 31 December 1984)

	HK$	Foreign Currencies	Total
Liabilities			
Amount due to banks and deposit-taking companies in Hong Kong	79,622	81,860	161,482
Amount due to banks abroad	8,586	364,415	373,001
Deposits from customers	158,005	138,099	296,104
Negotiable certificates of deposit outstanding	4,838	6,765	11,603
Other liabilities	44,846	16,534	61,380
Total liabilities	295,897	607,673	903,570
Assets			
Notes and coins	2,340	–	2,340
Amount due from banks and deposit-taking companies in Hong Kong	74,877	120,447	195,324
Amount due from banks abroad	13,808	315,018	328,826
Negotiable certificates of deposit held:			
Issued by banks in Hong Kong	1,661	1,349	3,010
Issued by deposit-taking companies	212	63	275
Issued by banks outside Hong Kong	–	8,090	8,090
Loans and advances to customers	166,820	119,457	286,277
Bank acceptances and bank bills of exchange held	1,052	9,109	10,161
Floating-rate notes and commercial paper held	1,064	10,976	12,040
Treasury bills, securities, shareholding and interests in land and buildings	13,309	2,243	15,552
Other assets	16,470	25,206	41,676
Total assets	291,613	611,958	903,571

Notes: Number of reporting licensed banks: 140.
Average liquidity during month: 49.6%.

Source: Hong Kong Monthly Digest of Statistics (Hong Kong, Census and Statistics Department), January 1985.

Government. In the absence of a central bank in Hong Kong, two of these banks, the Hongkong and Shanghai Banking Corporation and the Standard Chartered Bank, on occasion perform some of the functions that a central bank might be expected to perform in other economies. They are also note-issuing banks.

Although the Chinese banks form a very large section of the commercial banks in Hong Kong, they are by no means a homogeneous group. They can be divided into four sub-groups. The first is the Bank of China Group, comprising 13 banks affiliated to Beijing. It is a highly cohesive banking group operating under the leadership of the Bank of China. A second sub-group may be called the Overseas Chinese banks. These banks were established by Chinese domiciled outside China and Hong Kong. A third sub-group consists of local banks, other than Overseas Chinese banks, which are incorporated in Hong Kong. A fourth sub-group comprises banks that are tightly held family businesses managed by traditional methods.

The third major group of banks is the non-British foreign banks. These are mainly branches of American, European, and Asian banks. This group of banks has been steadily increasing in number. The large number of foreign banks indicates the growing importance of Hong Kong as an international financial centre. Of the 140 licensed banks operating at the end of 1984, 96 were foreign banks incorporated outside Hong Kong. In addition, there were 112 representative offices of foreign banks.[5]

Since a large number of local Chinese banks have been acquired by foreign banks or holding companies with controlling or minority equity interests, the above classification of banks into three main groups according to national origins has become less clear. Hence, licensed banks in Hong Kong may best be differentiated as note-issuing banks and other ordinary banks. In the absence of a central bank, the responsibility for issuing notes is delegated to commercial banks. As mentioned above, there are two note-issuing banks in Hong Kong: the Hongkong and Shanghai Banking Corporation and the Standard Chartered Bank.

Inter-bank Competition

Competition among banks is very intense in Hong Kong. Banks must acquire sufficient deposits and earning assets to survive and grow. Inter-bank competition in Hong Kong is primarily aimed at the acquisition of more deposits. There are two forms of competition: price and non-price competition. Price competition refers to the offering of attractive rates on time deposits while non-price competition mainly takes the form of setting up more branches, operating longer working hours, and providing free services.

1. Price Competition.   Competition for the acquisition of time deposits was very intense during the period 1958–65 and it led to an interest rate 'war' which peaked in 1963.[6] Many local banks raised their interest rates to attract depositors. To curb the cut-throat competition which ensued, an interest rate agreement was established in July 1964 by the Hong Kong Exchange Banks Association. The interest rate agreement was to be followed by all licensed banks. Under the agreement licensed banks were divided into five categories. The first category comprised the foreign banks and the other four categories comprised the local banks, classified by size. Each category had an interest rate ceiling on time deposits. The rate offered by the foreign banks was the basic rate, while those offered by local banks were successively higher than the basic rate, by uniform increments of 0.25 per cent. The interest rate agreement could be altered at any time by the Exchange Banks Association. In general, no interest was to be paid on demand deposits and there was a uniform rate on savings deposits.

As an aftermath of the 1965 banking crisis the Government imposed a moratorium on bank licences in 1966. This move denied newcomers entry to the Hong Kong banking market. In order to boost the status of Hong Kong as a financial centre, the moratorium was relaxed in March 1978. This initiated a large influx of foreign banks and the Government had to reimpose the moratorium.

In April 1981 the Government made three significant changes to the banking system. First, the Hong Kong Association of Banks was established, replacing the Exchange Banks Association. Second, foreign banks were again allowed to apply for new bank licences in May 1981. Third, a three-tier banking structure was established.

2. The Role of the Hong Kong Association of Banks.   The Hong Kong Association of Banks (HKAB) is a statutory body which was established by ordinance in 1981, replacing the former Hong Kong Exchange Banks Association. Membership of the HKAB covers all licensed banks. The Hongkong and Shanghai Banking Corporation shares with the Standard Chartered Bank the chairmanship of the HKAB, on a two-year rotating basis. These two note-issuing banks, together with the Bank of China, are the three permanent members of a Committee of twelve. The other nine banks on the Committee are elected members, of which four are elected by locally incorporated banks and five by banks incorporated outside Hong Kong. In addition, there is a Consultative Council of twenty banks, which is intended to form a link between the individual members of the Association and the Committee which runs the HKAB.

The HKAB has a specific role in the administration of the interest rate agreement, which it took over from the Exchange Banks Association. This agreement regulates the maximum rate of interest that may be paid by licensed banks for time deposits with a maturity of not more than 12 months. The HKAB also operates the Bankers Clearing House.

3. The Three-tier Banking Structure.   The three-tier banking system, which was established in 1981, divided the existing depository financial institutions into three categories: licensed banks, licensed deposit-taking companies, and registered deposit-taking companies. The interest rate agreement was changed to suit the new banking structure. Licensed banks were still subject to the interest rate agreement established in 1964, except for deposits with maturities over 15 months. Deposit-taking companies were not allowed to take demand deposits.

Licensed banks were divided into two main groups. The first group comprised foreign banks and those domestic banks that had been acquired by foreign banks or holding companies with at least 25 per cent equity interests, while the second group consisted of local Chinese banks and the Bank of China Group. The interest rate ceiling of the first group was 0.5 per cent less than that of the banks in the second group.

Licensed deposit-taking companies were only allowed to take deposits of HK$500,000 or more, on which there were no maturity restrictions. The interest rate agreement did not apply to such large deposits. Licensed deposit-taking companies were established to allow large institutions that engaged in merchant banking activities to carry on their business without affecting the general banking business of accepting routine deposits and the cheque clearing activities of the general public.

Registered deposit-taking companies were only allowed to take deposits of

HK$50,000 or more which had maturities of three months or longer. The interest rate agreement did not apply to these deposits. (These institutions play a role that is somewhat similar to that of savings or thrift institutions in other economies.) The objective of the HK$50,000 deposit limit is, according to the Government, to debar small savers from depositing in DTCs, which are supposed to be more risky institutions. The process of inflation has weakened the protection afforded by this measure. The Financial Secretary therefore announced in his budget speech on 27 February 1985 that the deposit limit was to be raised to HK$100,000 as from 1 March 1986.

The interest rate agreement was further revised in February 1982. Licensed banks were no longer subject to the agreement on interest rates for deposits of HK$500,000 or more with maturities of less than three months. The effect of the relaxation of the agreement on the market values of banks with publicly traded stocks was studied by Ho (1985). His results indicate that the liberalization did not affect the value of the banks. However, he favours a gradual removal of the interest rate agreement.

4. Non-price Competition.   With respect to non-price competition, the establishment of bank branches seems to be a powerful tool. Before 1967 there was no legislative control over the establishment of branches. Competition to form branches began in 1959 and gathered momentum in the 1960s. To stop reckless branch formation, the Banking Ordinance was amended in 1967, requiring banks to obtain prior approval from the Banking Commissioner for the opening of branches.

There are other methods of non-price competition. Many local banks operate longer working hours than foreign banks, and their management is more accessible to their customers. Highly personalized service is one of the main reasons for the survival of the smaller banks.

In recent years commercial banks in Hong Kong have also begun to compete in offering electronic banking services to the public. The speed of technological developments is forcing banks to make decisions on which their future competitiveness will depend. In 1980 the Hongkong and Shanghai Banking Corporation and the Standard Chartered Bank initiated the changes by setting up Automated Teller Machine (ATM) systems. Many other banks followed. At present, the largest competing ATM systems are that operated by the Hongkong and Shanghai Banking Corporation (which is linked with the ATMs of its subsidiary Hang Seng Bank); and Joint Electronic Teller Services Ltd. (JETCO), which was formed jointly by the Bank of East Asia, the Bank of China Group, Chekiang First Bank, Shanghai Commercial Bank, and Wing Lung Bank, and is steadily recruiting more members, including Chase Manhattan Bank.

The introduction of Electronic Funds Transfer at Point Of Sale (EFTPOS) will further increase pressure on banks by opening the possibility of competition from department stores and supermarket chains.

While some banks are concentrating on automating their retail operations, a few have been competitive in offering electronic banking services to their corporate clients. A good example of competition in this area is the introduction of an electronic corporate cash management system.[7] Chase

Manhattan Bank and Citibank are now the leaders in providing this service to corporate customers. The Bank of America and the Hongkong and Shanghai Banking Corporation will provide stiff competition for the corporate electronic banking services.

Although electronic banking can be applied on many levels, most banks will have to choose a specialized field because few have the resources to cover all areas. There is no doubt that large banks, and banks which have sharing agreements, have a competitive advantage in electronic banking services. Nevertheless, in order to survive, smaller banks are fighting to keep up with their larger and wealthier competitors.

Concentration in Banking

The growth of commercial banks in Hong Kong has been accompanied by a noticeable trend towards concentration. Many local Chinese banks have been acquired by foreign banks or financial corporations. The origin of this trend can be traced back to the 1965 banking crisis. Because of the crisis, local Chinese banks that were having liquidity problems had to seek new capital from the large banks. A total of 18 such bank acquisitions occurred in Hong Kong.[8] Probably the most significant event was the acquisition of a majority interest in Hang Seng Bank by the Hongkong and Shanghai Banking Corporation.

In terms of its branch network, at the end of 1984 the Hongkong Bank Group (comprising the Hongkong and Shanghai Banking Corporation, Hang Seng Bank, and Wayfoong Finance Company) was the largest banking group in Hong Kong, with over 380 offices. The Bank of China Group, with over 250 offices, was the second largest banking group.[9]

The Regulation of Commercial Banks

Commercial banks in Hong Kong are well regulated and closely supervised, for a number of reasons. Firstly, it is necessary to protect the safety of depositors. Since demand deposits comprise a significant part of the money supply, the failure of a commercial bank can severely disrupt the economy. Another reason for regulating commercial banks is to limit particular kinds of lending which could also have adverse effects.

The development of banking regulation also reflects an attempt to avoid the disturbing effects that past events have had on commercial banking in Hong Kong. The most dramatic incident was the banking crisis in 1965. This crisis, together with other less serious incidents, constituted sufficient evidence of managerial and structural deficiencies in the banking system. Since then, the Banking Ordinance has been amended many times with the object of maintaining the confidence and stability of the banking system.

Licensed banks in Hong Kong operate subject to the provisions of the Banking Ordinance, Chapter 155 of the Laws of Hong Kong. The Banking Ordinance was enacted in 1964 and various amendments have been made since then. The current Banking Ordinance provides, inter alia, for minimum holdings of liquid assets and capital and limitations on holdings of certain classes of assets such as shares, land, and advances to directors and employees. The following are some of the current statutory requirements for licensed banks in Hong Kong.

A bank must maintain a minimum holding of specified liquid assets, equal to 25 per cent of its deposit liabilities. In addition, 15 per cent of its deposit liabilities must be held in 'super liquid assets'. Liquid assets are assets that are due in, or realizable up to, seven days; super liquid assets are realizable immediately (demand or 24-hour money). The deposit liabilities which comprise the minimum level of 25 per cent of liquid assets include the required super liquid assets. The minimum requirement rule is designed to ensure that the banking system has adequate liquidity to meet withdrawal demand. As shown in Table 1.6, the average liquidity of all licensed banks during December 1984 was 49.6 per cent, which was well above the 25 per cent requirement.

A local corporation is not granted a bank licence in Hong Kong if its issued and paid-up share capital is less than HK$100 million. After commencing operations, a bank is required to maintain an aggregate of paid-up capital and reserves of not less than HK$200 million. This requirement is designed to ensure that banks have adequate capital as a basis for operations and for the protection of depositors.

The limitation on ownership of corporate shares by licensed banks is 25 per cent of the paid-up capital and reserves of the bank, while the limitation on holdings of interest in land is also 25 per cent of the paid-up capital and reserves of the bank.

The limitation on total advances extended by licensed banks to any one person, firm, corporation or company, or to any group of companies or persons is also 25 per cent of the paid-up capital and reserves of the bank.

The object of these rules is to avoid undue concentration and to reduce the risk to depositors of losses. Loans to directors and employees are also closely regulated. The aggregate amount of unsecured advances extended by a licensed bank to its directors, the relatives of directors, and their related companies is limited to 10 per cent of the paid-up capital and reserves of the bank, while the aggregate amount of unsecured advances granted to any employee is limited to an amount equivalent to one year's salary.

Banks are also prohibited from making loans secured by their own stock. The reason for this law is obvious — it would not be in the public's interest if bank owners were permitted to borrow from the bank the equity that is necessary for the protection of depositors. Banks are also required to submit to the Commissioner of Banking a monthly return of assets and liabilities, a quarterly return on loan categories and external positions, and an annual audited balance sheet and profit and loss account. The supervision and regulations of the banking industry are far from perfect. The DTC crisis in late 1981 and early 1982 and the government take-over of the Hang Lung Bank illustrate this well. With the help of the Bank of England, the supervision and regulations of the Hong Kong banking system will undergo tremendous changes. Such changes will include more stringent capital and liquidity requirements, more reporting information from banks and their auditors, and greater powers for the Banking and DTC Commissioners to enable them to adopt a more flexible method of supervision.

Fig. 1.1 A Sample Bank Balance Sheet (Stage 1)

Assets (HK$)		Liabilities (HK$)	
2. Vault cash	+ 100	1. Mr A's demand	
3. Loan to Mr B	+ 80	deposit	+ 100
4. Vault cash*	− 80		

Note: *The cash remaining is HK$20.

The Expansion of the Money Supply

The process by which the supply of money expands within an economy is very complex, but may be understood by examining its early stages, using an analogy with general banking procedures at the personal level. When an individual deposits currency in a cheque account in a bank, the form of his or her money changes from cash to demand deposit money. But another change also takes place. It is a change that many people do not recognize: the bank now has additional cash reserves on the basis of which it can create additional demand deposit money. It is possible to observe this money creation process by constructing a bank's balance sheet and examining the changes that take place. A simplified sample bank balance sheet is shown in Fig. 1.1.

Entry 1 in the balance sheet shows the increase in the holdings of demand deposits by an individual (Mr A). Double-entry accounting requires a second entry on the balance sheet on the asset side. Entry 2 shows an increase in vault cash of HK$100.

The cash itself may have been issued by the Government and spent by the Government in order to buy the services it needs. Individuals are paid this currency and it remains in public hands. But, having been paid, some individuals (represented in this example by Mr A) deposit part of their new cash holdings in banks.

Now that the bank holds an extra sum of cash, its managers recognize that it need not hold the entire amount in reserves against the possibility of withdrawal. This is because, after some people have withdrawn their money, others will redeposit it. Thus banks need only hold a fraction of their outstanding demand deposit liabilities in the form of cash. Banking systems are sometimes called fractional reserve banking systems.

For the sake of simplicity, we may assume that the managers of this bank decide that they can lend HK$80 of the HK$100 deposited and keep HK$20 in reserves. We may also assume that a second individual, Mr B, takes his loan in the form of HK$80 in cash. Entry 3 shows the loan that Mr B signs. It is an asset of the bank. And entry 4 shows that the bank's cash position is reduced by HK$80. Thus, there remains HK$20 in vault cash as reserves against the outstanding deposit of HK$100.

At first glance this appears to be simply a case of the bank lending money that has been deposited with it. This is often the banker's view. Indeed, it is appropriate for him as a manager to view it in this way, because his bank earns interest on the loan and profit for the bank. Also, he can only lend more and expand the bank's earnings if more people deposit more money in the bank (assuming the percentage held as reserves is constant).

But, from the point of view of the public, this loan of HK$80 also represents the creation of HK$80 in new money — money that did not exist before the loan was made. Mr A still has HK$100 in deposit money, as he did before he deposited his cash, but now Mr B also has HK$80 in cash. Thus the money supply is greater, by HK$80, than it was before Mr A made his deposit. The net effect is as if the bank had created HK$80 worth of Mr A's deposit money on the basis of HK$20 of Mr A's cash, and had lent the remaining HK$80 of Mr A's cash.

The money creation process has begun, but it does not stop here. Again let us assume, for the sake of simplifying the example, that this bank is the only bank in the country. Let Mr B buy something from a third person, Mr C, using the HK$80, and assume that Mr C deposits this extra cash in the bank. Again, the changes are recorded on the bank's balance sheet (see Fig. 1.2).

Entries 1 and 2 reflect the cash deposit of Mr C. Entries 3 and 4 reflect the bank's loan to a fourth person, Mr D, of 80 per cent of the cash deposit, that is, HK$64. If Mr D withdraws cash then the vault cash is reduced by HK$64 and this leaves HK$16 in vault cash in the bank, or 20 per cent of the additional demand deposit of HK$80. Another HK$64 of money has been created.

The process continues as Mr D spends the HK$64 and the person receiving the HK$64 places it in the bank. The bank lends 80 per cent of this, or HK$51.20, and retains HK$12.80 in reserves. Thus, another HK$51.20 in deposit money is created. The process continues until, when the entire HK$100 cash remains as vault cash, the total of deposit money equals HK$500. Of this HK$500, some HK$400 has been created by the bank, and the other HK$100 represents the original deposit.

Even without the assumption, made for the sake of simplicity, that there is only one bank, the result for the banking system as a whole is the same. The only change would be the necessity to trace the successive redeposits of cash from bank to bank.

Fig. 1.2 A Sample Bank Balance Sheet (Stage 2)

Assets (HK$)		Liabilities (HK$)	
2. Vault cash	+ 80	1. Mr C's demand	
3. Loan to Mr D	+ 64	deposit	+ 80
4. Vault cash	− 64		

If the managers of a bank decide that it is appropriate to maintain vault cash at the level of 20 per cent of deposits, to ensure that the bank can meet its obligations, a simple formula can be employed to describe the situation. Let reserves of vault cash be R and deposits be D. Then $R = rD$ where $r = R/D$. Where $r = 20$ per cent, $R = 0.20D$ or $D = R/r = 5R$. That is, when managers decide on a figure of 20 per cent, then deposit money will be five times vault cash.

The figure of 20 per cent has been chosen to simplify arithmetical procedures. Actual reserve figures are much smaller, perhaps only 5 or 6 per cent. Similarly the fivefold multiplier effect given in the example ($1/r = 5$) is also much larger than it is in reality. The multiplier effect is in fact smaller because, as business expands with the increased volume of lending and the money creation by banks, some businesses need to hold more cash than they did before. Therefore, the full amount of HK$100 is not added to the reserves. There is a cash drain from banks into currency in circulation and this drain holds the actual expansion of deposits to a level about twice that of the increase in vault cash. This process is explained in greater detail in Chapter 3. It is sufficient to note here that the true value of r varies as bankers exercise their judgement about making loans. Also governments may impose legal requirements in relation to r. Thus r should not be viewed as a constant, although it appears to be a constant in the simple formula. Instead it should be viewed as a variable which is set by the preferences of the managers of banks and the institutional constraints under which they operate.

Demand Deposit Expansion in Hong Kong

The money creation process described above applies in general to banking practice in all countries, including Hong Kong. However, in Hong Kong as elsewhere, the process has evolved with some unique attributes. Currency consists of coins and paper money. Sometimes the paper money is issued by the Government in the form of an 'I Owe You' (IOU). And sometimes banks are authorized to issue their own paper notes. These banknotes payable are the 'paper' part of the circulating medium. As noted earlier, in Hong Kong two banks issue notes that are legal tender — the Hongkong and Shanghai Banking Corporation and the Standard Chartered Bank. (Legal tender means that if a debtor tenders this money to a creditor to discharge a debt, the creditor has a legal obligation to accept it.)

For banks other than the note-issuing banks, the process described above applies. They must hold vault cash reserves in the form of currency, which consists of coin issued by the Government and notes issued by the two note-issuing banks.

For the note-issuing banks, however, the process is somewhat different. Again, a look at bank balance sheet changes is helpful. Fig. 1.3 shows various accounting entries which describe how banknote issues enter into circulation. We may assume that the bank has already made a loan to Mr A and has given him a demand deposit account. We assume that Mr A wants to withdraw cash. Entry 1 shows that his demand deposit is reduced. Having

Fig. 1.3 A Sample Balance Sheet of a Note-issuing Bank

Assets (HK$)		Liabilities (HK$)	
3. Exchange Fund certificates of indebtedness	+ 100	1. Demand deposits	− 100
		2. Notes payable	+ 100
		4. Exchange Fund deposits*	+ 100

Note: *At present these are denominated in United States dollars.

issued its notes to Mr A, the bank has an outstanding liability in the form of notes payable, and this is shown as entry 2.

A further facet of the note-issuing process involves the Exchange Fund. The Government established the Exchange Fund 50 years ago. The Fund has several responsibilities, one of which is to issue Certificates of Indebtedness (CIs) that are designed to 'back' a bank's note issues with gold or foreign exchange. Originally, a note-issuing bank was required to give its foreign exchange asset holdings directly to the Fund, but now the procedure is for the Fund to issue a CI to the bank, whereupon the bank gives to the Fund a United States dollar account containing the equivalent of HK$100, converted at the fixed rate of HK$7.80 to US$1, or about 13 United States cents for every HK$1.

The accounts of the Exchange Fund also show the second pair of entries that appear in the balance sheet of a note-issuing bank (see Fig. 1.4). Entries 3^1 and 4^1 are equivalent to entries 3 and 4 on the balance sheet of the note-issuing banks. Entry 3^1 shows a CI as a liability now outstanding, and an asset in the form of a United States dollar account in the bank.

The Exchange Fund is required to hold at least 105 per cent of the value of its holdings in various foreign currencies or gold, as backing for its CI issues, and hence for the circulating banknote issues. Since the Fund has accumulated earnings in the past, its actual holdings are far in excess of the required amount, although, as its accounts are not published, the precise amount is not generally known. Therefore the Fund may, or may not (at its discretion), buy some other kind of United States dollar assets or other assets with its new dollar account. If it should buy United States dollar assets

Fig. 1.4 Sample Balance Sheet Entries Showing the Exchange Fund's Issue of a Certificate of Indebtedness

Assets (HK$)		Liabilities (HK$)	
4^1. US dollar deposits	+ 100	3^1. Certificate of Indebtedness	+ 100

directly from the banks themselves, this process would involve additional accounting entries. These are shown in Fig. 1.5. Entry 5 shows that the Fund's account with the note-issuing bank has fallen, and entry 6 shows that the bank's holdings of United States dollars has also dropped. The two entries are matched on the Exchange Fund's balance sheet as shown.

In a very basic way, therefore, money in Hong Kong is created when the note-issuing banks, having a sufficient supply of United States dollar assets in their portfolios, decide to make loans in Hong Kong dollars. They create deposits in the process and, when the borrower withdraws cash, the banks issue their notes and are prepared to deliver part of their United States dollar assets to the Fund as backing for the outstanding issue of notes. Therefore these banks, in a sense, hold fractional reserves to meet withdrawals by the Exchange Fund in the form of United States dollar assets.

The other banks in the system (those which do not issue notes) also have the right to exchange their United States dollar assets for notes of the note-issuing banks at the rate of HK$7.80 for every United States dollar. Thus their reserves consist of vault cash and/or available United States dollars. On the basis of these kinds of reserves, which they hold as a fraction of outstanding demand deposit liabilities, the banks in Hong Kong create additional money in Hong Kong. This process and its management are examined further in Chapter 3.

Some Implications of the Process of Note Issue

The Exchange Fund does not pay interest to the banks on the CIs which it issues to them. However, the Fund becomes the owner of interest-earning assets in the form of, say, foreign currency deposits at the note-issuing banks or United States Treasury bills (T-bills). These earnings represent seignior-

Fig. 1.5 The Exchange Fund's Purchase of United States Dollar Assets as Shown on the Balance Sheets of a Note-issuing Bank and the Exchange Fund

(a) Note-issuing Bank		
Assets (HK$)		Liabilities (HK$)
6. US dollar assets − 100		5. Exchange Fund deposits − 100

(b) Exchange Fund		
Assets (HK$)		Liabilities (HK$)
5¹. US dollar deposits − 100		
6¹. US dollar assets + 100		

age, for the Fund specifically, and for the Hong Kong Government generally.

The note-issuing banks must hold certain minimum holdings of coins, but they need not hold vault cash reserves to meet withdrawals, because they have the authority to issue their own notes. Having made a loan, they earn interest on it. If borrowers withdraw cash, the banks may be required to turn some of their interest-earning United States dollar assets over to the Fund, and these earning losses may partially offset the earnings from loans. It is only a partial offset, however, because most of the deposit money remains in the system. Less than half of the amount of a deposit created by a loan is ever withdrawn in cash. Therefore money can expand to the point that bank managers feel is prudent, as they review the adequacy of their voluntary reserve position. Under this system, the more plentiful a bank's reserves of United States dollar assets, the more likely the bank will be to extend loans. If Hong Kong's manufacturers earn more United States dollars from their sales abroad, they may deposit these with local banks in exchange for Hong Kong dollars. If they do this, the banks will feel more comfortable making loans and presumably the money supply will increase. But this takes us into monetary policy in Hong Kong, which is the subject of Chapter 3.

Notes

1. For an excellent review of the causes and consequences of the crisis, see Jao (1974), pp. 244–50.
2. The only exception was the issue of a licence to Barclays Bank International in 1972.
3. Banking Ordinance, 1964, p. 5.
4. This classification is based on Jao (1974), pp. 37–40.
5. *Hong Kong Annual Report* 1985, p. 91.
6. For more details, see Jao (1974), pp. 52–5.
7. For a detailed description of the competition in this area, see South China Morning Post (1984), p. 8.
8. See Jao (1984), p. 129.
9. *Hong Kong Economic Yearbook*, 1984.

References

Effros, Robert C., *Emerging Financial Centers: Legal and Institutional Framework* (Washington, DC, International Monetary Fund, 1982).

Greenwood, John G., 'How to Rescue the HK$: Three Practical Proposals', *Asian Monetary Monitor*, September–October 1983.

Ho, Y.K., 'The Hong Kong Financial Institutions and Markets', in Y.K. Ho and C.K. Law (eds.), *The Hong Kong Financial Markets: Empirical Evidences* (Hong Kong, University Publisher and Printer, 1983), pp. 11–38.

_____ 'Interest Rate Cartel and Depositors' Income — The Hong Kong Experience', mimeographed, 1985.

Hong Kong Economic Yearbook (Hong Kong, Economic Information Agency Ltd.), various issues.

Hong Kong Government, *Hong Kong Annual Report* (Hong Kong, Hong Kong Government Printer), various issues.

_____ Census and Statistics Department, *Hong Kong Annual Digest of Statistics* (Hong Kong, Hong Kong Government Printer), various issues.

_____ *Hong Kong Monthly Digest of Statistics* (Hong Kong, Hong Kong Government Printer), various issues.

Jao, Y.C., *Banking and Currency in Hong Kong: A Study of Post-War Financial Development* (London, Macmillan Press, 1974).

_____ 'Hong Kong as a Regional Financial Centre: Evolution and Prospects', in C.K. Leung, J.W. Cushman and Gungwu Wang (eds.), *Hong Kong: Dilemmas of Growth* (Canberra, Australian National University Press, 1980) pp. 161–94.

_____ 'The Financial Structure', in David G. Lethbridge (ed.), *The Business Environment in Hong Kong* (Hong Kong, Oxford University Press, second edition, 1984), pp. 124–79.

Kwong, Winston P.C., 'The Regulatory Environment in the Banking Sector in Hong Kong', *The Hong Kong Manager*, January 1984, pp. 6–11.

Lee, S.Y. and Jao, Y.C., *Financial Structures and Monetary Policies in Southeast Asia* (London, Macmillan Press, 1982).

Lethbridge, David G. (ed.), *The Business Environment in Hong Kong* (Hong Kong, Oxford University Press, second edition, 1984).

McCarthy, Ian S., 'Financial System of Hong Kong', in Robert C. Effros, *Emerging Financial Centers: Legal and Institutional Framework* (Washington, DC, International Monetary Fund, 1982), pp. 95–114.

South China Morning Post, *Banking, Finance and Investment Review 1984* (Hong Kong, South China Morning Post, 1984).

2. Deposit-taking Companies and Merchant Banking

D.L. Hsu

CHAPTER 1 described the structure of commercial banking in Hong Kong, and analysed the role which commercial banks play in the process of money creation. Nearly as important to Hong Kong's financial system is the group of about 350 deposit-taking companies (which are commonly referred to as DTCs). Most of these companies engage in what might be called merchant banking and, indeed, the merchant banks in Hong Kong operate with licences which are issued by the Hong Kong Government in accordance with the regulations of the Deposit-taking Companies Ordinance 1976. There are, in addition, a few other financial organizations which perform some merchant banking functions but without holding DTC status.

In Hong Kong, as elsewhere, commercial banks engage in nearly all facets of merchant banking, along with their normal commercial banking activities. But merchant banks, while usually accepting deposits, do not normally engage in the activities that are generally the exclusive province of commercial banks.

The regulation of financial institutions in a number of countries, including Hong Kong, has created some anomalies among such institutions. The existence of these anomalies has been confirmed by recent developments in the United States. The legal definition of a commercial bank in the United States is an institution that both accepts deposits and makes commercial loans. The regulations which implement this definition have led to the formation of companies that do one activity, but not both. Thus, if a firm accepts deposits but does not engage in commercial lending, it can theoretically avoid the regulations that are generally applied to commercial banks. Others can make commercial loans without accepting deposits and again escape the regulations. Firms that have opted to engage in just one of these activities are now called 'non-bank banks'. This is, of course, a contradiction of terms, which has arisen from inadequate specification in the regulations. Some writers now use the term 'limited-service banks'. Needless to say, the United States Congress is, at the time of writing, actively considering additional regulations to correct these anomalies.

This chapter discusses the characteristics and activities of DTCs and the extent to which they overlap with those of the commercial banks. It also describes the regulations which cover the operations of DTCs in Hong Kong. Finally, some of the many activities of merchant banks are described briefly.

Deposit-taking Companies

Finance companies accept deposits, raise money from financial markets, and provide financial services. Finance companies were first established in Hong Kong during the 1960s.

After the 1965 banking crisis (see Chapter 1), the Hong Kong Government introduced a moratorium on the issue of new banking licences. International banks that wished to establish their business in Hong Kong were denied entry to the financial market-place, except as finance companies. These finance companies expanded their business rapidly, having the backing of their parent banks — whose creditworthiness was unquestionable.

The Banking Ordinance (1964) and other regulations covering the operations of licensed banks prevented them from carrying on any non-banking activities or engaging in high-risk business. Bank interest rates were set by the Exchange Banks Association (EBA) in 1964 and were compulsory for all banks. Some banks began losing large customers to finance companies which paid higher returns. In order to diversify into these financial areas that were closed to them, the commercial banks began to set up their own finance companies. (Most finance companies during the 1960s were wholly owned subsidiaries of established licensed banks.)

Finance companies which were subsidiaries of banks were able to pay higher rates of interest than their parent banks, and were able to provide new financial services, thus enabling the banks to satisfy the demands of their customers.

During the period of rapid economic growth in Hong Kong in the 1970s, finance companies' operations expanded at an accelerating pace, mainly as a result of the stock-market boom. In 1973, it was estimated that there were about 2,000 finance companies. Finance companies were either affiliated to banks or not affiliated to banks. Finance companies affiliated to banks were almost exclusively subsidiaries of large and well-established banks with experience in domestic and overseas corporate finance, underwriting, and even loan syndications. On the other hand, finance companies which were not affiliated to banks were locally oriented, had relatively small capitalization and engaged principally in domestic financial operations.

Regulation of DTCs

Prior to 1970, finance companies, including those now known as merchant banks, were registered under the Companies Ordinance with the Hong Kong Registrar General's Department. They were subject to the same financial regulations concerning their operations and structure as any other company, with the exception of credit unions, pawnbrokers and banks.

With the rapid growth in the number of finance companies engaging in borrowing and lending operations, some observers became concerned that these companies might cause economic disorder. The Hong Kong Government eventually took steps to regulate all deposit-taking finance companies. In April 1976, the Deposit-taking Companies Ordinance came into effect. In regulating DTCs and strengthening their financial position the Ordinance protected investors who invested in finance companies. The Ordinance empowered the Commissioner of DTCs, who is also the Commissioner of Banking, to supervise incorporated companies. The provisions of the Ordinance allowed finance companies (now called DTCs) to carry on banking business.

In order to qualify for registration, DTCs had to meet the following conditions: (a) a specified minimum issued capital and a specified minimum paid-up capital; (b) a specified maximum lending limit to any one customer; and (c) a minimum deposit. Many DTCs were unable to meet these requirements, and were forced out of business. Fewer than 200 were registered under the Ordinance in 1976.

However the DTCs increased rapidly during the late 1970s. This growth led to the reconstruction of the banking sector through the introduction, in May 1981, of the three-tier financial system. This divided deposit-taking institutions into three tiers: banks, licensed DTCs and registered DTCs. Since the introduction of this 'three-tier' financial system, local financial markets have experienced many changes in their financial activities.

The main characteristics and activities of registered DTCs and licensed DTCs are described below.

1. Registered Deposit-taking Companies.   Literally, a registered DTC is a company registered under section 10 of the Deposit-taking Companies Ordinance. Registered DTCs are only allowed to accept deposits with a maturity of three months or more. The minimum deposit they can accept is HK$50,000. (This figure will be increased to HK$100,000 in March 1986.) The minimum paid-up capital for registered DTCs was originally set at HK$10 million. At the end of 1983, there were 319 registered DTCs, while there were 311 at the end of 1984. During 1984, some registrations were revoked and some new registrations were approved.

Any company applying for registration as a DTC must be incorporated, either in Hong Kong or outside Hong Kong, with an issued share capital of not less than HK$10 million, of which at least 50 per cent must be held by a bank that is recognized and properly supervised in the country in which it is incorporated.

Any company which complies with the minimum requirements of the Deposit-taking Companies Ordinance has the right to be registered. If the management of a registered DTC is unfit, the authority will revoke its registration. If a DTC applying for registration is not well managed, its application will not be approved.

2. Licensed Deposit-taking Companies.   By definition, a licensed DTC is one that has received a licence under section 16A of the Deposit-taking Companies Ordinance. The Ordinance states that any applicant for a licence must be a registered DTC which has operated actively for at least three years; it must have an issued share capital of not less than HK$100 million and a paid-up share capital of not less than HK$75 million. A company which applies for a licence must be in reputable ownership; it must be in good standing in Hong Kong and in the international money market; and it must have substantial assets and a record of steady growth and normal operation

for at least three years.[2] Moreover, the company must have proper management. A company applying for a licence, which is a subsidiary of a licensed bank in Hong Kong, must have a separate management structure at its executive level. Licensed DTCs may accept deposits of any maturity in minimum amounts of HK$500,000 each. (In March 1986, the minimum deposit amount will increase to HK$1 million.)

At the end of 1983, there were 30 licensed DTCs. During 1984, the numbers increased to 33.

With effect from 1979, all DTCs were required to maintain a minimum holding of specified liquid assets. This liquidity ratio is based on the size of deposit liabilities during a month and the company's holdings of specified liquid assets. As at the time of writing, the Hong Kong Financial Secretary has set the minimum percentage of the liquidity ratio at 30 per cent on deposits of seven days or less and 15 per cent on all other time deposits.

Other statutory restrictions which apply to all DTCs include the following:[3]

(a) The aggregate amount of a loan or advance granted to any one customer is restricted to 25 per cent of the net worth of the DTC.

(b) The aggregate amount of all unsecured facilities granted to the directors of a DTC and their relatives should not exceed 10 per cent of the net worth of the company.

(c) The aggregate amount of any unsecured facilities granted to any employee of a DTC should not exceed one year's salary for such an employee.

(d) The maximum limit on investing in another company or in the share capital of other companies is 25 per cent of the net worth of the DTC.

(e) The maximum limit of investment in real estate property is 25 per cent of the net worth of the DTC.

There are at least two reasons for imposing ratios and lending rules related to a firm's capital base. The first is that the Government may desire to protect innocent or ignorant depositors. Depositors can be certain that their deposits are, to a great extent, safe when deposited with a licensed DTC — at least safer than they would be without the Government's regulation. In this regard, the Government attempts to be paternalistic and rejects the doctrine of *caveat emptor*.

Restrictions on lending to one director or one employee are also designed to prevent the misuse of privilege which might lead to losses for depositors. But restrictions on the extent of lending in the area of real estate property and in the shares of company stock are designed to limit the extent to which financial institutions can control real estate property or corporations. It is generally believed that the concentration of financial power may lead to illiquid bank assets and high-risk operations and lead to a potential breakdown in the competitive economic system.

Balance Sheet Analysis

A balance sheet describes a firm's financial position. From the items listed as liabilities on the balance sheet one obtains an impression of the sources of funding for the firm's activities, and from the items listed as assets one can infer the types of product the firm produces.

Table 2.1 presents the composite balance sheet of the DTCs in Hong Kong as compiled by the Monetary Affairs Branch of the Hong Kong Government. The year 1981 was the first year in which comparable statistics were made available. As a composite, this table indicates the lending and borrowing activities of the DTC industry as a whole. The table shows that DTCs play an important role in the process of savings and investment. The main sources of funds for the DTCs (the liabilities) in 1981 were: funds from domestic banks, 21 per cent; funds from overseas banks, 40 per cent; while 27 per cent of funds were deposits from customers. This funding pattern changed very little in 1984: 29 per cent of funds were from domestic banks; 39 per cent were from overseas banks; just under 20 per cent were from the general public. It is clear from these percentages that the DTCs, on average, do not have a wide deposit base of funding from the public. A small public deposit base has advantages and disadvantages.[4]

The primary use of funds, as shown under 'assets' in Table 2.1, was for loans and advances to customers. This use accounted for nearly 44 per cent of total assets in 1981. However in 1984 this use declined to just under 37 per cent.

Table 2.2 provides a partial analysis of the use of the loans and advances made by DTCs. However the breakdown into categories of use is incomplete, as the table deals only with foreign trade-related loans and with the 'location' of loans (either inside Hong Kong or outside Hong Kong). In 1981, 2 per cent of loans by DTCs were for the purpose of financing imports, exports, and re-exports from Hong Kong, whereas a sizeable 47 per cent of loans were for use outside Hong Kong. The figures for 1984 were much the same: nearly 2 per cent of loans were for financing imports, exports, and re-exports from Hong Kong, and 57 per cent were for use outside Hong Kong. These figures indicate the relative importance of foreign loan activities to the DTCs.

Table 2.3 shows the industrial sectors in which the loans and advances made by DTCs for use in Hong Kong were used in 1981 and 1984. In 1981, 24 per cent of loans were used in building, construction, and property development projects; while in 1984, just under 20 per cent of loans were used for this purpose. The percentage of loans used by individuals to purchase residential property in 1981 was nearly 36 per cent; in 1984, this figure had decreased to 24 per cent. Only 9 per cent of loans were used for transport, and 4 per cent for manufacturing industry in 1981; the corresponding figures for 1984 were 14.8 per cent for transport and 4 per cent for manufacturing industry. It would be very useful to have a similar breakdown by sector of use for the largest category of loans made by DTCs — those for use outside Hong Kong.

Competition with Banks

The loans and advances made by the DTCs for use in Hong Kong are applied to similar uses to the loans and advances made by the banks in Hong

Table 2.1 The Balance Sheet of All Deposit-taking Companies 1981 and 1984 (in HK$ million as at 31 December each year)

| | 1981 | | 1984 | |
	Total	%	Total	%
Liabilities				
Amount due to banks and deposit-taking companies in Hong Kong	46,062	21.09	107,191	29.28
Amount due to banks abroad	87,730	40.16	143,454	39.19
Deposits from customers	59,167	27.09	72,283	19.74
Negotiable certificates of deposit outstanding	1,430	0.65	3,197	0.87
Other liabilities	24,048	11.01	39,963	10.92
Total liabilities	218,436	100.00	366,089	100.00
Assets				
Notes and coins	8	—	7	—
Amount due from banks and deposit-taking companies in Hong Kong	57,596	26.37	71,347	19.49
Amount due from banks abroad	38,944	17.83	85,535	23.37
Negotiable certificates of deposit held:				
Issued by banks in Hong Kong	1,578		3,889	
Issued by deposit-taking companies	380	3.56	986	5.48
Issued by banks outside Hong Kong	5,825		15,188	
Loans and advances to customers*	95,742	43.83	134,772	36.81
Bank acceptances and bank bills of exchange held	783	0.36	816	0.22
Floating-rate notes and commercial paper held	4,465	2.04	24,409	6.67
Treasury bills, securities, shareholding, and interests in land and buildings	4,061	1.86	10,850	2.96
Other assets	9,055	4.15	18,289	5.00
Total assets	218,436	100.00	366,089	100.00

Notes: *See Table 2.2.
　　　Number of deposit-taking companies: 1981, 350; 1984, 344.
　　　Average liquidity during a month: 1981, 46.0%; 1984, 43.8%.

Source: Monetary Affairs Branch, Hong Kong Government.

Kong. There is, therefore, direct competition between the banks and the DTCs. This competition is likely to be greatest in the sectors in which most loans from DTCs are used — transport and building. Competition in the manufacturing and trade sectors is likely to be less.

DTCs cannot of course offer their customers all the facilities and services which banks offer. For example they cannot offer cheque accounts. The deposit accounts of the DTCs therefore compete only with the savings and time deposits of the banks.

Table 2.2 Loans and Advances to Customers Analysed by Purpose 1981 and 1984 (in HK$ million as at 31 December each year)

	1981		1984	
	Total	%	Total	%
To finance imports to, and exports and re-exports from, Hong Kong	2,167	2.26	2,411	1.79
To finance merchandising trade not touching Hong Kong	891	0.93	783	0.58
Other loans for use in Hong Kong*	40,034	41.81	44,675	33.15
Other loans for use outside Hong Kong	45,225	47.24	77,417	57.44
Other loans where the place of use is not known	7,425	7.76	9,487	7.04
Total loans and advances	95,742	100.00	134,772	100.00

Note: *See Table 2.3.
Source: Monetary Affairs Branch, Hong Kong Government.

As noted earlier in this chapter, the DTCs expanded in response to the fixed interest rate on bank deposits which the Exchange Banks Association imposed in 1964. Rather than lose customers to finance companies whose interest rates were not fixed, the banks established their own subsidiary DTCs. The requirements of the Deposit-taking Companies Ordinance regarding minimum deposits and minimum maturities prevented the smaller (registered) DTCs from competing with the banks for the small deposits of customers. Some of the operations of the DTCs were in fields closed to the banks. The larger deposit requirements and the absence of a limit on maturities also permitted the larger (licensed) DTCs to carry on

Table 2.3 An Analysis of DTC Loans and Advances for Use in Hong Kong 1981 and 1984 (in HK$ million as at 31 December each year)

	1981		1984	
	Total	%	Total	%
Manufacturing	1,761	4.40	1,853	4.15
Agriculture and fisheries	8	0.02	10	0.02
Transport and transport equipment	3,830	9.57	6,613	14.80
Electricity, gas, and telephones	235	0.59	654	1.46
Building, construction, and property development	9,619	24.03	8,782	19.66
Wholesale and retail trade	2,799	6.99	2,220	4.97
Mining and quarrying	17	0.04	2	—
Private purchases by individuals	14,366	35.88	10,821	24.22
Miscellaneous	7,399	18.48	13,719	30.71
Loans and advances for use in Hong Kong	40,034	100.00	44,675	100.00

Source: Monetary Affairs Branch, Hong Kong Government.

merchant banking operations (such as daily and weekly transfers of funds) without the restrictions which limited the banks.

The future of DTCs depends on a continuing process of adjustment. The keen competition among DTCs and between DTCs and commercial banks has reduced the ability of DTCs to attract deposits. As a result, some DTCs have failed. This in turn has led to a certain public lack of confidence in some DTCs, and their businesses have therefore deteriorated. Moreover, the Government has tightened supervision of DTC operations, some DTCs have had their registration or licence revoked and some DTCs have had to reorganize their liabilities and restructure their organization.

Nevertheless, some bank-affiliated DTCs, which have support from their parent holding banks or other banks, have had no difficulties in attracting deposits from the general public, in obtaining finance through the capital or money markets, in granting loans to support industrial projects, and in operating efficiently. These DTCs are likely to continue to operate efficiently and economically.

However, registered DTCs that attempt to compete with the banks for small deposits are at a severe disadvantage. The owners of these DTCs have stated that they are unable to compete and that they want the Government to set the rules to provide what they call a 'level playing field'. The three-tier banking system and the role of the Hong Kong Association of Banks are discussed further in Chapter 3.

Merchant Banking

It is impossible to present a precise and narrow definition of a merchant bank because merchant banking activities are extensive and varied, and because the managers of merchant banks may choose to specialize to a greater or lesser extent. Furthermore, the activities of merchant banks often overlap with those of commercial banks. So, if it is true that merchant banks are what merchant banks do, then a definition would include a long list of specialized activities, and a typical merchant bank would engage in only a part of the list.

For example, a Hong Kong merchant bank recently advertised that the scope of its business included the following: acting as both broker and dealer in a large variety of securities and money market instruments, underwriting the debt issues of business and government, providing research services and investment advice on economic, financial and corporate affairs, foreign exchange trading, deposit taking, loan syndication, and commercial lending when secured by deposits or marketable securities. To this list could be added other activities such as mergers, acquisitions, divestitures, interest rate swaps, leveraged buy-outs, and so forth. The income of merchant banks is largely in the form of fees.

Since it is impossible to examine all of these activities in the space of this chapter we will discuss only a few.

Mergers, Acquisitions and Divestitures

The role of merchant banks in the fields of mergers, acquisitions, and divestitures may be illustrated by a number of examples.

Corporations are constantly expanding and contracting. In order to do so, they often engage the services of merchant banks. For example, the managers of a large chain of hotels may feel that they could benefit by expanding the number of locations in which they operate. It may be expensive in monetary terms and costly in terms of time to build additions to their chain, and relatively much more efficient to buy into an existing chain. Therefore they seek the advice of a merchant bank regarding opportunities, finance, and so on. The merchant bank seeks out the existing opportunities for expansion, prepares detailed industry information, analyses the terms of financing, finds additional financing when necessary, arranges for all the necessary documentation, and presents the plans to the merging parties. The bank's fee is often in the form of a charge for expenses and a percentage of the overall financing package.

Another illustration of merchant banking activities may be found in the field of acquisitions. A rapidly expanding company may wish to invest in another company, but may not wish to assume operating control of this company. However, by acquiring a sizeable minority position in the ownership of the second company, the expanding company may achieve some co-ordination of markets, while leaving the existing management in control.

Again, a company may want to sell a subsidiary or a division. Its managers seek assistance from a merchant bank in finding an appropriate buyer and arranging the presentation of the necessary information to a potential buyer.

An illustration is provided by the following example, which is based on a genuine case, although some of the details have been changed to preserve anonymity. The owner of 20 per cent of the stock in a large American company was, for reasons unrelated to the business itself, looking for an investor. The company had a large wholesale operation in the fruit business and had also diversified into the hotel business. A merchant bank was asked to look for an investor who would want a seat on the board of directors. The firm's shares were traded on the New York Stock Exchange for US$32 per share, and the total transaction was likely to cost US$65 million. The merchant bank contacted a potential Hong Kong buyer and asked to be retained as an exclusive financial adviser. The bank asked for reimbursement of out-of-pocket expenses and a fee of 1 per cent of the purchase price if the transaction was satisfactorily completed.

Syndicated Loans

A syndicated loan is one in which a group of banks or other investors pool their resources to provide financing. Projects requiring very large investments always require syndication because nearly all lenders prefer not to take risks. To avoid risk one should not place 'all one's eggs in one basket'. It is customary (and appropriate) for a merchant bank to take a piece of a loan, rather than the entire financing package of a large project.

An example based on a genuine case illustrates the process of a syndicated loan and some of the problems that may be encountered. (Again, some identifying details have been changed.)

A paper manufacturing company in Malaysia had a well-planned scheme for expansion. It had received support from an American company that had decided to engage in a joint venture with the Malaysian company. Three American banks with offices in Hong Kong were asked to provide interim financing for the project. These banks jointly offered to fund 3-year notes which were to be readjusted each quarter at a rate of 0.5 per cent above the Hong Kong Inter-bank Offering Rate (HIBOR). The notes were accompanied by a letter of intent from the American company to back the notes with its credit rating. After the expansion was under way the Malaysian economy faltered. After two years the Malaysian company was unable to meet the repayment terms of the agreement. The American company also had difficulties and would not stand behind its pledge. The three banks met regularly to decide how to proceed.

The problems that occurred in this case were financial difficulties which the borrowing groups faced and, as a result of which, questions of credit backing were raised. Letters of intent to back are not legally binding in the United States but, if a large company does not live up to its moral agreement, it will have difficulty borrowing again without signing legally binding documents and paying higher interest rates.

Interest Rate Swap Agreements

One new activity in which merchant banks have begun to engage is arranging interest rate swap agreements. Although this is a new activity which accounts for only a small part of the efforts of merchant banks, it is worth examining briefly as it illustrates how merchant banks direct their efforts towards problem-solving in the area of finance, making use of innovative techniques. (The subject of interest rate swap agreements is also discussed briefly in Chapter 6 in the context of risk reduction.)

Interest rate swap agreements were first introduced in the Eurobond market in early 1982. They were extensively promoted in 1983 in the United States by the Student Loan Marketing Association, which is known as 'Sallie Mae' (see below).[5]

An interest rate swap agreement is an agreement between two parties to trade each other's interest payment liabilities. The most common form of swap agreement involves one firm's trading the interest payments on its debt for the interest payments that must be made by the other firm that is party to the agreement. Firms wishing to enter an interest rate swap agreement ask merchant banks to arrange a swap.

Interest rate swap agreements between DTCs are quite frequent. In accepting deposits, DTCs in effect borrow from the public. The background to a swap agreement could be as follows. One DTC may have short-term liabilities of, say, six months or one year. The interest cost of these liabilities fluctuates from one period to the next. The DTC may wish to acquire an asset that has a life of 10 years. For example, it may wish to make a 10-year mortgage loan at a fixed interest rate. If the DTC makes this loan, it incurs a certain amount of risk. The yield on the 10-year asset is fixed, but the costs of the funds which the DTC borrows from year to year may rise above the yield on the fixed-rate asset. If these costs rise, the DTC stands to lose.

The maturity of this DTC's liabilities is short and, as a result, interest costs are subject to great variability. The maturity of assets, often in the form of home mortgages, is long and interest receipts are therefore 'locked in'. But institutions such as DTCs cannot easily enter the long-term debt market in order to match the maturity structure of their liabilities with the maturity structure of their assets and so ensure steady returns — a step that would be necessary if interest payments and receipts were to be matched.

There are, however, organizations which experience problems the opposite of those faced by the DTCs: the costs of their liabilities are fixed and the revenues from their assets are variable. Such an organization is Sallie Mae. Sallie Mae can readily issue 10-year bonds (in the United States). Its credit rating is very high because it is backed by the United States Treasury. The 10-year bonds issued by Sallie Mae are liabilities that carry a fixed interest cost. But Sallie Mae's revenues from its assets are variable.

If Sallie Mae and the DTC described above could agree to swap their interest rate liabilities (Sallie Mae's fixed-rate liabilities for the DTC's variable-rate liabilities) both parties would benefit. Both would be protected from risk — the DTC's risk that its interest costs could rise, and Sallie Mae's risk that its interest revenues could decline.

Fig. 2.1 provides a diagrammatic representation of an interest rate swap agreement based on the above description of an agreement between Sallie Mae and a DTC. The arrows in the figure show that Sallie Mae gives its fixed interest costs to the DTC and accepts the DTC's variable interest costs in exchange.

After trading variable costs for fixed costs the two entities have matching assets and liabilities — Sallie Mae has variable returns and variable costs, while the DTC has fixed costs to match its fixed returns. In this example the principal value of the interest rate swap is to reduce risk, that is, to reduce

Fig. 2.1 An Interest Rate Swap Agreement

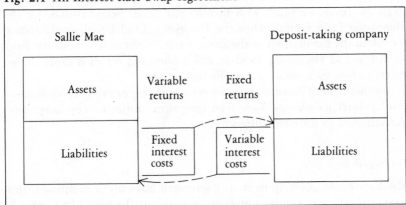

the extent to which a firm might profit or lose from unanticipated changes in interest costs.

From Fig. 2.1, it is clear that the two institutions could have traded the returns from their assets rather than the returns from their liabilities.

The concept of an interest rate swap, as shown in the above example, is straightforward, but many details have not yet been explained. For example, Sallie Mae has acquired variable interest costs, but in what respects, and by how much, do the interest rates that it pays vary? Sallie Mae has made swaps worth approximately US$100 million and has agreed to pay interest at a rate equivalent to 25 basis points above the United States Treasury bill (T-bill) yield, averaged over six months. Other indices besides the T-bill yield are also used for the purpose of determining interest rates.

The role of the merchant banks in arranging interest rate swap agreements differs according to the circumstances and needs of the parties involved. Merchant banks sometimes simply agree to convert a fixed-rate debt into a floating-rate debt for an organization. An organization may not even need to know the identity of the other party involved. That is, the merchant bank may match the parties and arrange for each to deal directly with the bank. The bank in turn would make the necessary payments between the two parties. The bank usually charges a fee of about 0.5 per cent of the face value of the agreement at the time the swap agreement is executed.

Merchant banks can also bring together organizations which can borrow on different terms from the money markets. One institution may be able to borrow cheaply in a fixed-rate market while another may be able to borrow cheaply in a floating-rate market. If such institutions can be brought together and can agree to swap their interest rates, both might be able to realize greater profits.

An example of such an interest rate swap agreement was that between the Bank of Tokyo's Hong Kong branch and the Hongkong Land Group, in which a newly raised Hong Kong dollar fixed-rate CD was swapped for variable-rate funds. In March 1985, one of the merchant banks in Hong Kong, Schroder Asia, arranged for the Bank of Tokyo in Hong Kong to borrow certificates of deposit worth HK$100 million at a fixed rate of 11 per cent for the first three years and a floating rate of 0.25 per cent above HIBOR for the final year. At the same time, the Bank of Tokyo arranged to swap the fixed-rate funds with floating-rate funds below HIBOR for the Hongkong Land Group. Thus the Hongkong Land Group could reduce its risk to the fluctuations in the interest rate. Nevertheless, both the Bank of Tokyo and Hongkong Land in effect borrowed for each other in the market where each could obtain the best terms.

Another kind of financial swap agreement that is growing in importance involves foreign exchange. In such an agreement, institutions exchange debt denominated in different currencies.

Leveraged Buy-outs

Merchant banks also help to arrange leveraged buy-outs of companies. In a leveraged buy-out, a buyer simply arranges to buy the stock of a company.

Although the concept is simple, the arrangements to be made can become quite complex and require co-ordination by a merchant bank.

To finance the purchase of stock in a company, the buyer borrows money and pledges some of the company's assets as collateral for the loan. The effect of this kind of transfer of ownership on the firm's balance sheet is to raise the ratio of debt to equity. Such a change in this ratio increases the leverage of the shareholders. This explains the term 'leveraged buy-out'.

It has been estimated that in the United States during the year 1983 company ownership worth about US$10 billion changed hands through leveraged buy-outs. However, of a total of approximately 300 buy-outs in 1983, about half were essentially divestitures — that is, they were initiated by sellers who wanted to obtain liquidity, rather than by buyers who wanted to take over a company.[6]

A company in which the ratio of debt to equity is already high is not a suitable target for a leveraged buy-out. Moreover, the managers of a company with a large equity position could, if they wished, expand the company by issuing additional debt against the firm's assets. But the decision to expand or not is very complicated. Certainly expansion for its own sake is not regarded as desirable.

Quite often the managers of a subsidiary company may want to buy the equity of the subsidiary and become independent of the parent company. They obtain funds to do this by investing some of their own funds and borrowing the rest.

Those who wish to undertake leveraged buy-outs can also borrow from a number of lenders, including pension funds, insurance companies, venture capitalists, or banks (although not all of these sources are available in Hong Kong).

This brief description of some aspects of a leveraged buy-out shows the need for the co-ordination of many complex factors, such as the terms of the loan, the mortgage of assets, and the terms of the purchase of stock from the current owners. Furthermore, the documents must all be signed and settled almost simultaneously. Thus it is clear that the merchant bank's role in making and following up all these arrangements is considerable.

Summary and Conclusion

In this chapter we have described the history, development, and functions of DTCs and merchant banking in Hong Kong, since they commenced operating in the early 1960s, in a section of the financial markets which commercial banks could not enter.

Since 1976, the DTCs have been under the control of the Commissioner of DTCs, who is also the Commissioner of Banking. In 1981 the three-tier financial system of banks, licensed DTCs, and registered DTCs was introduced. This system strengthened the financial position of registered DTCs. The operations of all DTCs are severely regulated.

The assets of DTCs consist mainly of loans and advances that assist the development of local business, and amounts due from banks and other DTCs domestically and abroad. The liabilities consist mainly of borrowings from banks and DTCs locally and abroad. Deposits from the general public comprise only 20 per cent of the total liabilities.

Before the signing of the Sino-British agreement on the future of Hong Kong, in December 1984, there was some financial instability in Hong Kong. As a result of this, and also because of changes in the regulation of DTCs in 1984, there have been some heavy flows of funds from DTCs to commercial banks.

Merchant banking operations in Hong Kong cover a wide range of activities, which assist the development of money and capital markets and support the growth of businesses. Despite frequent changes in the operational environment, merchant banking has shown its importance to the Hong Kong economy. Merchant banks have introduced many financial facilities to Hong Kong and have expanded Hong Kong's financial expertise in the international markets, in such operations as interest rate swaps and leveraged buy-outs. Moreover, merchant banks are efficient in managing investment portfolios and have made significant contributions to foreign exchange markets. However, merchant banking is still not familiar to or accepted by many people in Hong Kong. Therefore merchant banks should publicize their services in order to attract more potential customers.

A survey of merchant banks and finance companies in Asia contains a number of interesting comparative figures.[7] In January 1983, it found, Hong Kong had about 230 merchant banks and finance companies, Indonesia had 10, Malaysia 50, the Philippines 13, Singapore 58, and Thailand 111. In terms of asset size, Hong Kong's Wardley Ltd. was Asia's biggest merchant bank with assets of about US$3 billion.

In addition, at the time of writing, Hong Kong had about 350 deposit-taking companies that engage in one or more of the financial activities described above. For an economy with a population of about six million, such figures are very high. In a relative sense — relative to population and gross domestic product, Hong Kong may be the most highly concentrated financial centre in the world. But of course it serves an area much larger than that confined within Hong Kong's geographical boundaries.

Notes

1. For an excellent discussion of the development of merchant banking activities and their current operations in Asia see Skully (1980) and Skully (1983).
2. See Kwong (1984), pp. 6–11.
3. Deposit-taking Companies Ordinance, 1984, Chapter 328.
4. An example of a disadvantage is provided by the case of the financial difficulties faced by Continental Illinois Bank in the United States in early 1984. This bank, which had a record of careful management, was damaged by rumours because it had funded its loans largely through inter-bank and overseas borrowings and less extensively through its small depositors. The State of Illinois does not allow branch banking. So, to expand, Continental Illinois used its credit in world financial markets. But these markets are fickle. Huge withdrawals of funds can occur readily

when a rumour is started. On the other hand, growth through the expansion of small customer deposits is a slow and cumbersome process.
5. See an excellent description by Stieber (1983), pp 78–81, and Rose (1982).
6. See Ferenbach (1984).
7. Financial Editor (1984), pp 67–81.

References

Chang, L.W., 'The Adjustment and Prospects of Hong Kong DTCs', *Economic Reporter*, 13 December 1982, pp. 7–8.
Effros, Robert C. (ed.), *Emerging Financial Centers* (Washington, DC, International Monetary Fund, 1982), pp. 95–114.
Ferenbach, Carl, 'In Praise of the Leveraged Buyout', *Asian Wall Street Journal*, 1–2 June 1984, commentary page.
Financial Editor, 'Capital Adequacy and Liquidity', *Asian Finance*, 15 February 1984, pp. 67–81.
Fung, K.H., 'The Operations and Prospects of Hong Kong DTCs', *Economic Reporter*, 1 January 1982, pp. 52–3.
Ho, Y.K., 'The Critique on the Hong Kong Banking Structure', *Economic Digest*, 14 September 1981, pp. 8–11.
_____ 'The Financial Structure and Monetary Policy in Hong Kong', *Hong Kong Economic Weekly*, 1 February 1982, pp. 25–7.
_____ 'Financial Institutions, Markets, and Policies in Hong Kong', in J.Y.S. Cheng (ed.), *Hong Kong in the 1980s* (Hong Kong, Summerson Eastern Publishers Ltd., 1982), pp. 60–80.
_____ 'Some Suggestions to Improve the Hong Kong Financial Control', *Economic Reporter*, No. 1759, pp. 5–6.
Ho, Y.K. and Law, C.K. (eds.), *Hong Kong Financial Markets: Empirical Evidences* (Hong Kong, University Publisher and Printer, 1983).
Jao, Y.C., 'How to Prevent a Run on a Bank', *Asian Banking*, January 1983, pp. 30–1.
_____ 'The Financial Structure' in David Lethbridge (ed.), *The Business Environment in Hong Kong* (Hong Kong, Oxford University Press, second edition, 1984), pp. 124–79.
_____ 'How to Solve the Financial Crisis in Hong Kong', *Hong Kong Economic Journal Monthly*, Vol. 6, No. 12.
Kwong, P.C.W., 'The Regulatory Environment in the Banking Sector in Hong Kong', *Hong Kong Manager*, January 1984, pp. 6–11.
Lee, P.N., 'DTCs in the Gap', *Hong Kong Economic Weekly*, 21 June 1982, p. 28.
Martin, Colin, 'Inter-Bank Squeeze: Crisis Time for Hong Kong's DTCs', *Asian Money Manager*, December 1982, pp. 2–4.
Rose, Sanford, 'Swapping Away Asset–Liability Problems', *American Banker*, 19 November 1982.
Skully, Michael T., *Merchant Banking in the Far East* (London, Financial Times Business Publishing, second edition, 1980).
_____ *Merchant Banking in ASEAN* (Kuala Lumpur, Oxford University Press, 1983).
Stieber, Sharon, 'Rate Swaps Stabilize Costs, Aid in Quest for Profitability', *Savings and Loan News* (United States Savings and Loan League), March 1983, pp. 78–81.
'Tough Times for Local Banks', *South China Morning Post*, 3 January 1983.

3. Monetary Policy in Hong Kong

ROBERT HANEY SCOTT

IT might be expected that the descriptions of commercial and merchant-banking operations in Hong Kong, which are contained in the preceding chapters, would be followed by a chapter on central banking. But since Hong Kong has no central bank, a description of the methods of money supply control comes under the general heading of monetary policy.

The Absence of a Central Bank

In the history of money, central banking is a newcomer on the scene. The Bank of England, established in 1694, was formed as a private bank and only slowly assumed the responsibilities which are usually delegated to central banks in modern times. It was established as the government's bank and was not originally charged with responsibility for controlling the money supply as central banks are today.

In colonial times, even though banknotes circulated widely, gold and silver continued to provide the principal medium of exchange, as they had since ancient times. Some of the Spanish, French, Portuguese, Dutch, and English colonies were established principally to obtain gold and silver ores which were valued so highly because of their purchasing power. To be useful, of course, gold and silver ore must be refined so that coins can be minted. The cost of the minting process is called brassage. Any profit made from minting is called seigniorage. Colonial governments were authorized to receive seigniorage from the production of money, and the expenses of government were often paid for nearly as much through seigniorage as through taxation.

In colonial times, coins flowed freely across national boundaries. In the southern colonies in North America, Spanish silver dollars circulated. In most colonies the money supply comprised coins. The coins were usually those issued by the country that established the colony. As banknotes came to be issued, the government would typically require that the banks place coin or bullion with the government as backing for the note issues. The agency of the government that oversaw the issue of notes and the safekeeping of the bullion was called a currency board. Under the currency-board system any colonial currency issued was treated as the equivalent of the currency of the home country. In this way the fortunes of the local economy were tied to those of the home economy. The local money supply rose whenever more goods were shipped and sold abroad than were imported, and vice versa. The money supply also rose whenever investment flowed in from outside the colony. A system of money control quite similar in concept was reintroduced in Hong Kong on 17 October 1983.

The Exchange Fund

The economic turbulence in the world economy in the 1930s precipitated many changes in the structure of financial institutions. In Hong Kong in 1935 the Government established the Exchange Fund.

The principal reason for the establishment of the Fund, as noted in Section 3 of the Exchange Fund Ordinance, was that it 'shall be used for the purpose of regulating the exchange value of the currency of Hong Kong'. The Fund is held in Hong Kong currency or any other currency or gold or silver and may be invested in securities. Through this Fund, the Financial Secretary can buy or sell Hong Kong dollars in the market for foreign exchange and, if the amounts traded are large enough, push up or down the market value or price of Hong Kong's currency *vis-à-vis* other currencies.

But a secondary function of the Exchange Fund may turn out to be more important than its original primary function. Section 4 of the Ordinance states that

The Financial Secretary is authorized to issue to any note-issuing bank, to be held as cover for bank notes lawfully issued in the Colony, certificates of indebtedness . . . and to require such bank to pay to him for the account of the Fund the face value of such/certificates to be held by the Fund exclusively for the redemption of such notes.

In Hong Kong, the Fund's Certificates of Indebtedness (CIs) are backed by gold, silver, foreign exchange, or foreign currency securities, and banknote issues are backed by CIs. For the most part, Hong Kong's currency can expand only if the Exchange Fund issues more CIs. In general, the Fund has been passive, issuing and redeeming CIs whenever the note-issuing banks approach it. Thus, money control in Hong Kong is in the hands of the Exchange Fund even though it is not a central bank.

The Operations of Typical Central Banks

Historical circumstances guide each central bank into its own unique methods of operation. But basically central banks have four means of controlling money, each of which depends upon private commercial banks maintaining deposit accounts with the central bank. A central bank is a banker for the government of the country and a banker for the country's banks and, when a bank needs currency or needs to make payments to the government or other banks, it can use its deposits with the central bank.

1. Changes in the Required Reserve Ratios.   Firstly, central banks can require banks to maintain a certain level of deposits with the central bank. Usually, the level of deposits required is some percentage of the individual bank's own deposit liabilities. Thus deposits with the central bank are viewed as reserves to 'back' the commercial bank's own outstanding liabilities. Since these required reserves are only a fraction of the outstanding deposit liabilities of the banks, the system is called a fractional reserve

system. And those in charge of the central bank can adjust the fraction, or legal reserve ratio, up or down in order to discourage bank lending, or to encourage it. By raising the reserve ratio, the central bank forces the banks to hold more reserves on deposit. Banks cannot lend as much money as they did before and the money supply is reduced. (The system works in the opposite direction as well.) By adjusting the reserve ratio, the central bank can influence the growth of the economy's money supply.

The liquidity ratios required for banks in Hong Kong, which are described in Chapter 1, do not act as a constraint on total lending in this fashion. The legal minimum liquidity ratio is 25 per cent, but the ratio typically held, as noted in Chapter 1, is nearly 50 per cent. In Hong Kong, the monetary base acts as the constraint on money creation. It is described in detail later in this chapter.

2. Changes in Loan Interest Rates.   A central bank can also lend to a bank that wishes to have more reserves temporarily. To make such a loan the central bank merely credits the individual bank's deposit account. The provision of these extra reserves allows more bank lending and allows the money supply to expand beyond what it otherwise would be. The central bank can encourage banks to borrow from it by setting a low interest rate on its loans. Banks borrowing from the central bank at low interest rates can lend more at higher interest rates on the market and earn profits for their shareholders. If a higher lending rate of interest is set by the central bank, then individual banks will want to cut back on their lending. Thus money growth is encouraged when low lending rates are set by the central bank, and vice versa. In England the central bank's lending rate is called the bank rate and in the United States it is called the discount rate.

3. Changes in the Volume of Bank Reserves.   A third means of control over money growth exercised by central banks is often called open-market operations. A central bank can buy an item, usually a financial security of some type, in the market-place. The seller of the security is given a cheque on the central bank. To collect the cheque, he must deposit it in a bank. The bank then sends the cheque to the central bank, where the individual bank's reserve account is increased by the amount of the cheque. The result is that bank reserves with the central bank are increased and banks can lend more and create more money in the process. Open-market purchases by a central bank cause the money supply to expand, and sales cause it to contract.

4. Moral Suasion.   A fourth means of money control is moral suasion. A government, through its agent the central bank, simply requests that banks limit the extent of their lending and deposit creation. The banks must respond if they wish to remain in the good graces of the government, and it must be assumed that the government is acting in the general interest of the people and the economy.

In summary, the four major tools of control of a typical central bank are:
(a) Changes in the required reserve ratios.
(b) Changes in the interest rates on loans to banks.
(c) Changes in the volume of bank reserves by purchases and sales on the open market.
(d) Moral suasion.

Other types of control are used from time to time, but these four are usually the major ones.

The third tool—changes in the volume of bank reserves by purchases and sales on the open market—is used mostly in countries that have large, active, and deep financial markets. Central bank operations disturb small markets, so smaller countries tend not to rely upon this tool as much as on the other three. In Hong Kong, the Government does not engage in open-market operations, nor is there a mechanism for government-backed loans to banks. The legal liquidity ratios are for prudential purposes for the protection of depositors and are not binding on banks. In Hong Kong the size of the monetary base acts as the ultimate constraint on money creation by the banks.

The Monetary Base

Governments usually provide currency through the minting and issue of coin, and the printing and issue of notes. With currency issue as a base, banks can lend and create cheque account deposits. These deposits are part of the money supply. Because banks hold only a fraction of their deposits in the form of vault cash, banks create additional money on the basis of this currency base.

Since banks in countries with central banks have deposits in the central bank, these deposits are, to the banks, as good as cash. The central bank will provide currency, dollar for dollar, for each dollar a bank has on deposit with it. Thus the monetary base includes bank deposits in the central bank because such deposits provide part of the basis for money expansion.

The monetary base of any country consists of those things issued and controllable by the government that provide the basis for money creation. If a government can control what it issues, then it can control the growth of the money supply. Since Hong Kong has no central bank, its monetary base consists of the Exchange Fund's issues of CIs that back the note issues of the banks, plus the Government issues of notes and coin.

Measures of Money and the Monetary Base

The Monetary Affairs Branch of the Hong Kong Government publishes monthly data on the money supply, with a one-month time lag. Forms are sent to all banks and Deposit-taking Companies (DTCs) and must be filed according to the Ordinance governing monetary statistics.

Tables 3.1 and 3.2 show the compilation of money supply data in the format in which they are published.

The Monetary Base

Table 3.1 shows data for the end of June 1984. The total value of the currency issued by the Government and the notes issued by the banks comprise Hong Kong's monetary base. One would normally think that

Table 3.1 Currency Circulation and the Money Supply as at the End of June 1984 (HK$ million)

	HK$	Foreign Currencies	Total
Legal tender notes and coins in circulation			
Commercial bank issues	13,846	–	13,846
Government issues	1,356	–	1,356
Total	15,202	–	15,202
Banks' and DTCs' holdings of legal tender notes and coins	2,450	–	2,450
Legal tender notes and coins in the hands of the public	12,752	–	12,752
Money supply (definition 1)	29,900	2,861	32,761
Money supply (definition 2)*	147,994	136,129	284,124
Money supply (definition 3)**	183,696	170,053	343,749

Notes: * M1 plus savings and time deposits with licensed banks, plus negotiable certificates of deposit issued by licensed banks and held outside the monetary sector.
** M2 plus deposits in DTCs.

Source: Monetary Affairs Branch, Hong Kong Government.

banknote issues are the responsibility of the banks and are not under Government control. But, as noted above, the law requires the two note-issuing banks to obtain CIs from the Exchange Fund to back their issues of notes. Thus the outstanding CIs will equal the outstanding banknotes. And the sum of the currency issued by the Government and the notes issued the the banks will be the same as the sum of the currency issued by the Government and the CIs issued by the Government. This sum makes up Hong Kong's monetary base.

The monetary base of a country consists of those liabilities issued by the government or by its agencies, such as a central bank, or in the case of Hong Kong the Exchange Fund, that provide for the country's money supply.

Table: 3.2 Deposits from Customers as at the End of June 1984 (HK$ million)

	HK$	Foreign Currencies	Total
Demand deposits with licensed banks	17,148	2,861	20,009
Savings deposits with licensed banks	60,973	13,144	74,117
Time deposits with licensed banks	55,619	116,740	172,359
Total deposits with licensed banks	133,739	132,745	266,484
Deposits with licensed DTCs	7,201	13,285	20,486
Deposits with registered DTCs	28,028	19,294	47,322
Deposits with all DTCs	35,229	32,579	67,808
Deposits with all deposit-taking institutions	168,968	165,323	334,292

Note: Totals may not add up, due to rounding.
Source: Monetary Affairs Branch, Hong Kong Government.

The Money Supply

By defining money carefully, those who are assigned the task of measuring it know what to look for. Unfortunately, definitions and measures of money are sometimes confused. As shown in Table 3.1, the Monetary Affairs Branch reports on 'definitions' of money when, in fact, what it provides is a set of measures of money. If there is one definition of money that is precise it will be exclusive. Money is defined in terms of its function. Money is what money does. It is what people use to discharge debt in an exchange economy. If you look around you to see what you have that will routinely discharge debts it is money and it consists of currency in public circulation and demand deposits owned by the public.

Some of the currency issued by the Hong Kong Government is held in bank vaults and some notes issued by the two note-issuing banks are held in the vaults of other non-note-issuing banks. Thus, bank vault cash is subtracted from the total value of currency issued in order to arrive at the measure of currency in the hands of the spending public, as indicated in Table 3.1. Individuals can spend this currency and they can also spend the deposits that they hold in current or cheque accounts. These two items make up Hong Kong's money—if money is defined to consist of anything people routinely use to discharge debt.

The first definition listed in Table 3.1 is the closest measure of money and is called M1. The other measures presented, although called definitions, are, in fact, measures. They represent a combination of money and other very liquid assets—savings accounts and time deposits. Money is a perfectly liquid asset and these other liquid assets are called liquid because they can be exchanged for money very easily. An imperfectly liquid asset is not money. Any asset can be sold for money. But most assets are difficult to sell. Liquid assets are easy to sell and easy to sell without loss of face value. But they are not money.

So measures of money plus other liquid assets are sometimes called broader measures of money. In the table, M2 consists of money plus savings and time deposits while M3 consists of M2 plus deposits in DTCs. Deposit levels in banks and DTCs are recorded in Table 3.2.

The Technical Treatment of DTC Vault Cash and Deposits

Vault cash in a bank is also represented by deposits. To include both would allow for some double counting of money. For example, if an individual deposits a dollar in a bank he now has a deposit instead of a coin, and the spendable money supply is unchanged. But if the bank vaults' money were counted as money too, then the money supply would rise with the deposit. It clearly does not rise, so measures of money should not include bank vault cash; vault cash is therefore subtracted, as shown in Table 3.1.

But DTC vault cash is also subtracted in Hong Kong's money data, as noted in Table 3.1. If deposits in DTCs cannot be spent, as is the case under the present institutional arrangements, then DTC deposits are not money. But if they are not money then DTC vault cash is money just like cash in any shopkeeper's cash register. Thus DTC cash should not have been subtracted from the measure of Hong Kong's money, M1.

On the other hand, if M3 is the measure of money one wishes to use, it is appropriate to add DTC deposits but to subtract DTC vault cash from these deposits to arrive at the figure to be added to M2.

This flaw in Hong Kong's money data is not substantial. As long as measures of money are carried out consistently, measurement data can reveal trends in money growth. But it is important that analysts are aware of the technical issues. Changes in the broader measures of money are often described, and are wrongly reported to be the more meaningful measures. The most useful measures are of the monetary base, or the M1 money supply if one is concerned with money supply control.

The Technical Treatment of Government Deposits

The Government may hold newly minted coins in its vaults. This not-yet-issued money is not part of the community's supply of things that can discharge debt. But such coins become money when the Government spends them, because then they are owned by an individual and provide that person with spending power.

The Government also holds deposits in commercial banks. These deposits should not be counted as part of the money supply. For example, if the Exchange Fund holds some foreign money or deposits in foreign banks, these monetary units are not part of Hong Kong's circulating medium. The Monetary Affairs Branch does not include short-term Government deposits with seven days or less to maturity in its measure of demand deposits in banks. It does, however, include Government deposits with maturity of more than seven days in its measures of time deposits with banks. To be consistent, it should also remove these Government time deposits from its money measures.

Foreign Currency Deposits

Prominently displayed in Tables 3.1 and 3.2 are figures on foreign currency holdings. These are added to Hong Kong's money supply to arrive at a figure labelled total money. This is like adding apples and oranges. Start with five baskets of apples and five baskets of oranges and declare that you now have ten baskets of apples. You could just as easily declare that you have ten baskets of oranges.

Foreign currencies and foreign currency deposits are not part of Hong Kong's money supply. It would be possible for foreign currency to be part, or all, of Hong Kong's money. The independent country of Panama, one of the world's emerging financial centres, has long used the United States dollar as its medium of exchange. Because of this, Panama should simply use United States dollar money supply data as its guideline. Just as it would make little sense for the State of Colorado in the United States to try to measure its money supply, so it makes little sense for Panama to worry about its money supply. And if Hong Kong were to legalize the United States dollar for circulation as its money, measuring the local money supply would be not only impossible but also largely meaningless.

It is useful to keep track of the foreign currency asset holdings in the form of deposits in local banks, just as it is useful to know about other assets such as gold. But pricing foreign currencies in terms of Hong Kong dollars and adding this figure to Hong Kong's money supply is both wrong and misleading. For example, assume that the prices of foreign exchange have risen by 10 per cent. A translation of this into Hong Kong dollars makes one believe that Hong Kong's money supply has risen by perhaps 5 per cent, even though no change has occurred in the volume of Hong Kong dollars and no change has occurred in the number of units of foreign currency owned by local people.

An entirely separate series of data showing holdings of foreign currency would be more appropriate. Indeed, it would be better to list the amount of United States dollars, in terms of United States dollars. This would give the most realistic measure of the amount of foreign money held in Hong Kong.

Until the Government amends its reporting procedures one must allow for the technicalities of money measurement in interpreting data on Hong Kong's money supply.[1]

The Exchange Fund: Currency Issue and Government Deposits

Government Deposits

In collecting taxes and borrowing money, governments find the services of banks useful. With a bank account, a government can pay its bills with cheques. In a country with a central bank the government uses the facilities of the central bank to provide most of these services.

In the United States, when the Government collects taxes, usually the taxpayer's cheque is deposited in a Government account in the same bank as that on which the cheque was written. The taxpayer's account is reduced and the Government's account, called a Treasury Tax and Loan (TT and L) account, is increased. Many banks hold the account for one day, and the following day they send the money to the Federal Reserve ('the Fed.') where the bank's reserve account is reduced and the Treasury's deposit account at the Federal Reserve is increased.[2]

In the initial phase of tax collection in the United States, the Government's bank deposits are increased and private demand deposits are reduced. Banks must hold reserves against all deposits, and so the required reserves are unchanged. But the money supply is reduced because there is less money available for private spending than there was before taxes were collected. If the Treasury were to hold these deposits idle and let them accumulate, the Treasury would literally be taxing and taking money from the hands of the public. A general rise in the level of Treasury bank deposits implies a general reduction in the outstanding money supply, dollar for dollar.

The next step is for banks to send the funds to the Treasury's account at the Federal Reserve. This action reduces bank reserve balances. In the absence of other events, a reduction in their reserve position requires banks to call in loans and reduce deposits, so that the money supply will fall even further than it did when the deposits remained in the banks. Thus higher levels of Treasury deposits maintained at the Federal Reserve imply reduced bank reserves and reduced money creation by banks.

The references above to levels of deposits and levels of reserves are necessary because the United States Treasury's function is not only to tax but also to pay the Government's bills. Thus the process described is routinely reversed when an individual is given a cheque for services by the Government. The individual deposits the cheque in the bank and his account increases. The bank sends the cheque to the Federal Reserve where its reserve account is increased and the Treasury's account is reduced. Thus bank reserves are replenished when the Treasury spends. Since the process of collection and spending is continuous, effects on the money supply occur only when the level of Treasury balances in the banks or at the Federal Reserve changes.

In the United States, the Treasury attempts to stabilize its level of deposits at the Federal Reserve in order not to disturb the control of the Federal Reserve over the outstanding volume of bank reserves and, therefore, over the money supply.

Since Hong Kong does not have a central bank as such, the Hong Kong Government could change the money supply in Hong Kong on a dollar-for-dollar basis by raising or lowering the level of deposits that it holds in banks. When a government's deposits rise, private deposits fall, and there is less spending money in the hands of the public. If a government does not have a surplus of tax collection over spending to do this, it can issue a debt. This absorbs the money supply, dollar for dollar. To expand the money supply it can redeem a debt.

This description of the role of government deposits is not necessarily intended to be a recommendation for the active implementation of a counter-cyclical monetary policy through a variation in government deposit levels. The purpose is to emphasize the necessity of monitoring government deposit levels, because changes in these levels have an important effect on the money supply.

Unfortunately, the Hong Kong Government chooses not to publish the level of its deposits in banks. Analysts are told only that Government deposits with seven days or less to maturity are subtracted from demand deposits in calculating M1, so that the M1 figure is accurate in this respect. That is, M1 will fall when Government deposit levels rise, and vice versa. But the other money measures are faulty at present because Government time deposits are not excluded from the totals.

The Exchange Fund's Deposits in Banks

The Exchange Fund holds deposits in banks in Hong Kong. These deposits are of course Government deposits. Therefore all of the above analysis applies to the deposits of the Exchange Fund.

If the Exchange Fund spends its deposits by buying an asset, it gives the seller a cheque on its account at the bank. The seller's deposit account will rise and so will the money supply. The purchase of assets will tend to push up asset prices, and interest rates will tend to decline. The increased money supply will also tend to push interest rates down. Overall, with lower interest rates the economy should be more expansionary than otherwise. Thus, by running down its balances, the Fund can stimulate money growth and economic expansion.

If the Fund chooses to buy United States dollars with its Hong Kong dollars, this will also tend to push up the price of United States dollars. The higher value of United States dollars will encourage exports and discourage imports. Both increased exports and decreased imports tend to exert expansionary influences on the economy. Thus the Exchange Fund's ability to manipulate the level of its accounts in local banks gives it a degree of control over the growth of Hong Kong's money supply and the level of economic activity.

The Lack of Control over Currency Issues

The mechanism of controlling Hong Kong's money by variations in the Exchange Fund's deposit levels in local banks would be a powerful tool of control over marginal money growth if there were not a gap in the system that allows money control to escape. This gap is the absence of control over the issue of CIs.

The balance-sheet changes that occur at a note-issuing bank when notes are issued are shown in Fig. 3.1.

Entry 1 in Fig. 3.1 shows the reduction of demand deposits that occurs when an individual withdraws cash from the bank in the form of banknotes. Entry 2 shows that the volume of outstanding notes has increased by the same amount. As noted earlier, the Exchange Fund Ordinance requires the banks to acquire CIs from the Fund to cover fully the value of the new notes issued. Until 1974, banks were required to give the Fund assets such as gold or pounds sterling for the CIs. Later, from 1974 to 1983, the Exchange Fund accepted a Hong Kong dollar deposit account in the note-issuing bank. However, as from 17 October 1983, the Fund began to require that it be

Fig. 3.1 A Sample Balance Sheet of a Note-issuing Bank when Notes are Issued

Assets		Liabilities	
4. Certificates of Indebtedness	+ 100	1. Demand deposits	– 100
		2. Notes payable	+ 100
		3. Exchange Fund demand deposits in US dollars	+ 100

given United States dollars rather than Hong Kong dollars. Thus entry 3 is a United States dollar account.

Furthermore the ' + 100' figure means HK$100 worth of United States dollars at HK$7.80 for each United States dollar. That is, the Exchange Fund pegged the value of Hong Kong's dollar to the United States dollar at HK$7.80 for every United States dollar.

On the balance sheet of the Exchange Fund the entries appear as shown in Fig. 3.2.

Entries 3^1 and 4^1 in Fig. 3.2 correspond to entries 3 and 4 on the balance sheet of the note-issuing banks (shown in Fig. 3.1). The Fund has HK$100 liability outstanding in the form of a CI, and it has HK$100 worth of United States dollars at a fixed price as backing for the CI.

It is important to observe that Hong Kong's money supply, currency plus demand deposits, is unchanged by the withdrawal of banknotes. A second observation is that the United States dollar deposit has simply been created by the note-issuing bank. Nothing that has happened in this process implies that the banks have acquired additional United States dollar assets, to give to the Exchange Fund in order to acquire CIs which would allow them to issue more money in the form of notes. If the note-issuing banks need to issue notes they simply create a United States dollar deposit and give it to the Government.

Little else occurs after this, unless the Exchange Fund should decide to use its United States dollar deposit to make a purchase. If it sells United States dollar deposits and buys Hong Kong dollar deposits, Hong Kong's money supply will fall, United States dollar prices will weaken, and interest rates in Hong Kong will tend to rise along with the tighter money supply. Some restraint will be exercised on economic expansion. This is precisely the opposite of the case cited above in which the Exchange Fund used its Hong Kong dollar deposit to buy United States dollars to stimulate the economy. Here, starting out with United States dollars, the Fund can sell these for Hong Kong dollars to dampen economic activity.

To recapitulate: if the Exchange Fund were to accept Hong Kong dollar deposits to back CIs as it did before October 1973, it could then expand money by buying something with these Hong Kong dollars. If, on the other hand, it accepted United States dollar deposits initially, as it currently does, then it would contract money if it sold them for Hong Kong dollar deposits. The result is that the impact on Hong Kong's money supply from the

Fig. 3.2 A Sample Balance Sheet of the Exchange Fund when Notes are Issued

Assets		Liabilities	
3^1. US dollar deposits	+ 100	4^1. Certificates of Indebtedness	+ 100

procedure for backing CIs, either with United States dollars or Hong Kong dollars, depends to a large extent upon what the Fund does with the deposits it receives.[3]

The gap in control over Hong Kong's money, therefore, is not found in the acceptance of Hong Kong dollar deposits in place of United States dollar deposits. It matters very little which type of deposit is accepted by the Exchange Fund, for it can always switch from one type to the other of its own volition. But what does matter is that the Fund exercises no limit on its willingness to issue CIs.

In other words, if a bank wishes to make a loan, it simply does so; it creates a deposit account for the borrower and the money supply expands. If the borrower withdraws currency, the bank simply issues banknotes and creates United States dollar deposits with the Exchange Fund to obtain the CIs needed to back the note issue. Thus Hong Kong's money supply expands whenever a bank manager considers that the extra value of a loan to the bank's profit position exceeds the extra cost of the liabilities created by the lending activity. CIs are issued by the Exchange Fund on the initiative of the banks rather than on the initiative of the Fund. This is the loose link in the money creation process under current institutional arrangements. There is no direct control over the extent of the currency issue.

A Proposal for a Fixed Rate of Growth of CIs

The label 'monetarism' is now widely attached to a policy of constant money growth. In years past many economists believed that money growth should be adjusted to counteract cycles or fluctuations in business activity. Thus, if business was depressed, money should be made to grow so that interest rates would fall and investment spending and consumer spending would create employment opportunities. And if the economy suffered from inflation, the money supply should contract, to inhibit borrowing and spending through high interest rates, and to bring economic activity under control. But many monetarists have argued that, although a contra-cyclical monetary policy may be desirable in theory, in practice it would be better to follow a monetary growth rule.[4] If one can expect real growth of 5 per cent per year, on the basis of experience of saving behaviour and productivity generally, then a 5 per cent growth in money would accommodate the 5 per cent real growth without inflation. A better approximation to economic stability may be realized under a growth rule than is likely to be realized under a system in which monetary authorities attempt to move money in a contra-cyclical way.

Large economies with a large government sector and a considerable portion of the economy subject to regulation of one sort or another may not benefit from a monetary growth rule. But a small economy characterized by the general absence of regulations and a small government sector is precisely the sort of economy that could achieve a large measure of economic stability through the imposition of such a rule. Market forces adjust rapidly in an economy that is unencumbered by trade restraints. Such an economy needs stable growth in money, but it does not need contra-cyclical monetary policies, because the pricing system absorbs any shocks that are likely to cause depression or inflation. Money growth rules may be more relevant to many smaller, open, and less developed economies than to major world economies.

Such a rule seems appropriate for Hong Kong. It would be simple for the Exchange Fund to announce a policy of allowing the issue of CIs to grow at the rate of 0.5 per cent per month, or at 6 per cent per year compounded monthly. This would hold Hong Kong's money growth in the same range. The mechanics of this process are more easily understood through a close look at Hong Kong's monetary base.

Hong Kong's Monetary Base

A very small change in the wording of the Exchange Fund Ordinance would give it discretion in the issue of CIs. With such authority, the Exchange Fund could announce a policy of allowing Hong Kong's currency supply to grow at a given rate each month. The volume of CIs issued by the Exchange Fund, along with the volume of coins issued by the Government, comprise Hong Kong's monetary base.[5] The terms to be used in the following discussion are listed in Table 3.3.

Money consists of currency in circulation in the hands of the public plus demand deposits, that is, $M = C + D$. The monetary base consists of currency in public circulation plus bank vault cash reserves, that is, $B = C + R$. In countries with central banks, commercial banks are required to hold reserves in the form of vault cash plus deposits maintained with the central banks. But since Hong Kong has no central bank, no bank reserves are held in such deposits. In Hong Kong, banks must have cash to issue to meet deposit withdrawals. Therefore in Hong Kong reserves are vault cash (that is, $R = V$), for all banks other than the two note-issuing banks whose reserves consist of their right to obtain CIs whenever they choose to issue notes against deposit withdrawals. It follows that $B = C + V = CI + GI$.

Table 3.3 A List of Monetary Terms

Abbreviation	Meaning
M	Money
C	Currency in circulation in public hands
D	Demand deposits of all licensed banks
S	Savings deposits
T	Time deposits
B	Monetary base
R	Bank reserves
V	Vault cash
CI	Certificates of indebtedness
GI	Government issue of coin

The total money supply is some multiple of the base, that is:

$$M = mB, \text{ or } m = \frac{M}{B} = \frac{C + D}{C + V}.$$

Let $k = C/D$. This ratio reflects the preference of the public for holding cash.

Let $r = V/(D + S + T)$. This ratio reflects the preference of the banks for holding vault cash reserves against all their deposits.

Let $s = S/D$. This ratio reflects the preference of the public for holding savings deposits.

Let $t = T/D$. This ratio reflects the preference of the public for holding time deposits.

By substitution of these ratios into the equation for m we have:

$$m = \frac{kD + D}{kD + r(D + S + T)}.$$

Dividing all terms in both numerator and denominator by D gives:

$$m = \frac{k + 1}{k + r(1 + s + t)}.$$

The ratio of currency in circulation in public hands to demand deposits was 0.74 at the end of June 1984. That is, out of every HK$100, about HK$43 was in the form of currency and HK$57 was in the form of cheque accounts.

The ratio of bank vault cash to total deposits in licensed banks was much less. It was only 0.018. Thus banks held only about HK$1.80 in cash in their vaults as reserves against the possibility of a withdrawal of a deposit of HK$100. The reserve ratio is quite low in comparison with that in other countries. It reflects the absence of legal reserve requirements and the absence of a need for cash reserves on the part of the note-issuing banks since they rely on the Exchange Fund.

The end of June 1984 data from Tables 3.1 and 3.2 give the following figures:

M = 29,900
C = 12,752
D = 17,148
S = 60,973
T = 55,619
V = 2,450
D + S + T = total deposits = 133,739.

Let $k = C/D = 0.74$
$s = S/D = 3.55$
$r = V/(D + S + T) = 0.018$
$t = T/D = 3.24$.

Substitution of these ratios into the formula for m gives:

$$m = \frac{0.74 + 1.00}{0.74 + 0.018(1.00 + 3.55 + 3.24)}$$

$$m = \frac{1.74}{0.74 + 0.018(7.79)}$$

$$m = \frac{1.74}{0.88} = 1.98.$$

Therefore M = 1.98B, where B is the sum of vault cash and currency in public hands, and is the equivalent of CIs plus the Government issues of notes and coin. If the base multiplier, m, stays steady at about 1.98, a steady rate of growth in B will be accompanied by a steady rate of growth in M.

The ratio m will, of course, be subject to change whenever the other ratios change. If banks become more restrictive they may increase r. This will reduce m and lead to a reduction in M. The ratios are such that an increase in k will cause m to decline, and therefore cause M to decline as well.

There is also an implicit assumption that there is a stable relation between the volume of notes that banks issue and the amount of coin that the Government issues. Thus, if notes grow by 6 per cent, the coin issue will grow by 6 per cent, so that the monetary base will also grow by 6 per cent.

The Control of Money Growth
Under the Pegged Exchange Rate System

The direct control of money growth through a control over the growth of Hong Kong's monetary base is but one of many methods of money control. Architects of the system of pegged exchange rates imposed in October 1983 argue that the supply of money can be controlled just as readily by fixing its price as by fixing its quantity. But by fixing the price rather than the quantity of money, the control over the growth of money is less direct and much looser. Setting the price of money is like setting a thermostat that is not very sensitive: the room becomes too cold, then it turns on, and the room becomes too warm and so on. Sometimes thermostats work well and sometimes they do not.

Under the fixed exchange rate system set by the Government on 17 October 1983, the Exchange Fund fixed the United States dollar price of CIs. A bank must pay US$100 for every HK$780 it receives in CIs from the Exchange Fund. In this sense the 'price' of HK$780 is whatever it takes to produce US$100 by selling things for United States dollars in the export market, or by selling Hong Kong assets to investors willing to supply US$100 or its equivalent. Money will only grow in Hong Kong, therefore, if exports rise or if foreign investment flowing into Hong Kong rises. In understanding this process, the gold standard provides an analogy.

The Gold Standard as an Example

In important respects the anchoring of the Hong Kong dollar price of the United States dollar at HK$7.80 is intended to control Hong Kong's money supply in a manner similar to the way in which the former gold standard regulated the money supply of a country that pegged the value of its currency to a fixed amount of gold. Therefore a very brief review of the working of the gold standard is in order.

Under the gold standard a unit of currency is defined in terms of an amount of gold, and gold either circulates in the form of coin or is used to back the government's issues of notes and/or the reserves of the banks that issue notes. Institutional arrangements varied greatly in the past, but the basic economic forces that propelled the gold standard as a device to regulate the money supply, in its many forms, worked as follows. When, for whatever reason, goods are cheap at home, more goods will be exported. Exports will exceed imports, and exporters will accept gold in exchange for their exported goods. Since gold either is money, or backs money in the form of bank reserves, the supply of money increases as gold flows into the economy. Banks will have more reserves and more lending ability. As they compete for loans they will lower interest rates. With more money and more loans, people will increase spending. This will only lead to inflation if the economy is at, or near, full employment.

But inflation means that foreigners who earlier bought goods from exporters will now find the prices too high. They will buy less. Inflation also means that foreign goods are cheaper. Importers buy more goods and use gold to pay for them. The gold flow is reversed. Gold flows out of the country. Since gold is money, the outflow of gold pushes interest rates up and, eventually, prices are pushed back down.

This mechanism was abandoned for many reasons, one of which is that the value of gold itself is very unstable over time. Thus, a country is not likely to have a currency with a stable value if it ties its currency to gold.

This review of the operation of the gold standard mechanism shows, by analogy, how Hong Kong's pegged system is intended to work.

Hong Kong's exporters sell goods to the United States and earn United States dollars. But in order to pay their workers, exporters must sell United States dollars to banks to obtain Hong Kong dollars. Banks in Hong Kong turn in United States dollars to the Exchange Fund for CIs and issue Hong Kong dollars. Hong Kong's money supply increases. Interest rates fall, spending increases, and prices rise. If prices rise so much that exporters sell less to the United States, but importers continue importing, the United States dollar earnings will fall. Importers will turn in Hong Kong dollars to buy United States dollars from the banks, and the banks will turn in Hong Kong dollars to the Exchange Fund. The supply of Hong Kong currency will fall as the Fund redeems CIs.

In this fashion, Hong Kong's money supply is controlled by the balance of trade. But it is clear that the adjustment process involves lags over time, and the mechanism itself produces upswings and downswings in economic activity in the local economy. Only through such swings does the mechanism produce the forces that lead to adjustments in the money supply. Because such swings are unacceptable to governments, governments around the world have rejected the gold standard.

The process described above depends upon changes in trade flows acting as the balancing factor. But capital flows are just as important and may be destabilizing. For example, when interest rates fall as a result of money expansion, the lower interest rates will reduce the value of Hong Kong's dollar, as investors from abroad will find Hong Kong investments unattractive. Thus, in spite of large exports, Hong Kong's money supply may expand only slowly when local interest rates are low.

Moreover, because the entire economy must swing around the fixed price of Hong Kong's dollar, the growth in money may be very erratic since it is controlled indirectly by setting the price of a foreign currency. Economic fluctuations may therefore be more pronounced than they would be if money growth were controlled directly by control over quantity.

Furthermore, in so far as the currency to which Hong Kong's dollar is pegged varies on world markets generally, so will Hong Kong's dollar vary in value. That is, setting the United States dollar price of a Hong Kong dollar does not establish a value for the United States dollar. In the 1960s Hong Kong suffered the same inflationary pressures as Great Britain, because at that time Hong Kong's dollar was tied to the pound sterling. Had Hong Kong pegged its dollar to the United States dollar in 1979, its depression would have been worse than the United States depression of 1980–3. The United States dollar dropped 14 per cent in value in March 1985. Because of the pegged system, so did Hong Kong's dollar. Thus, under a pegged system, the local dollar's fortune is tied to the fortune of the currency unit to which it is pegged.

But over a longer period under the current pegged system, money growth will be restrained by its price in terms of the United States dollars that must be earned and paid to the Exchange Fund as note issues expand. As long as the growth of United States dollars is stable, this system of money growth control may work reasonably well. It is difficult to know just how sensitive the thermostat over money growth is and how efficiently it will operate.

Long-term Savings and Investment

The foregoing analysis of the indirect control of money growth under a pegged exchange rate system assumes a growing and continuing free economy. Indeed, there is little or nothing in economics as a discipline to provide guidance in directing an economy towards a situation such as Hong Kong faces. In spite of the agreement between China and Great Britain, no one can predict what will happen when a group of six million people and their property are turned over to a socialist regime in 1997. The situation is unique in the annals of economic history. But it is clear that property owners in Hong Kong will wish to put their wealth into a form that will enable them to keep it. The only way to do this will be to export their wealth but even this action may not benefit them as they may be denied access to their wealth.

Nevertheless, one can reasonably expect the people of Hong Kong to do their best to earn United States dollars and then to store them in accounts abroad, rather than selling them for Hong Kong dollars. If they were to sell them for Hong Kong dollars, Hong Kong's money supply would expand. But if they did not, then Hong Kong's money supply would grow slowly, interest rates in Hong Kong would, on average, remain above those in the United States, and Hong Kong property owners would export the value of their investments by allowing their machinery to depreciate. This is the only practical way to export wealth in some aggregate sense. The pegged dollar will assist the transfer of wealth out of Hong Kong.

An oversimplified description of the pegging mechanism in graphic form may be of some interest. Fig. 3.3 shows the demand for and supply of United States dollars in Hong Kong with the price on the vertical axis and the quantity on the horizontal axis. The pegged price is HK$7.80, and a horizontal line is drawn at that level. Straight-line curves labelled D_0 and S_0 intersect at point a, indicating the initial state of equilibrium at the pegged price.

Now assume that the demand for United States dollars increases to D_1. There would be a tendency for their price to rise to the level indicated by point b. A larger quantity of United States dollars would be supplied at that price as indicated by point b. Thus the higher price would tend to encourage suppliers to bring forth additional quantities and the market would clear. The scarce supply would go to those willing to pay the market price. But the price of United States dollars is pegged or linked to Hong Kong's dollar. People in Hong Kong can turn in Hong Kong notes and receive United States dollars by paying only HK$7.80. They do not need to pay HK$7.90. Indeed, by paying HK$7.80 they can obtain United States dollars and sell them for HK$7.90 and make a profit of 10 cents (Hong Kong) on each Hong Kong dollar turned in.

Fig. 3.3 The Demand for and Supply of United States Dollars in Hong Kong

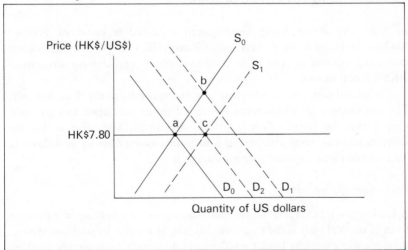

When individuals turn in Hong Kong dollar notes, the Exchange Fund retires CIs. These CIs represent a significant component of Hong Kong's monetary base. When the base goes down, as noted earlier, the money supply in Hong Kong drops and interest rates rise. Higher rates restrict spending, and cause recession and lower prices in Hong Kong.

Two forces tend to push the demand curve back to the left. First, imports fall with the recession and this means a reduced demand for United States dollars. Second, higher interest rates on Hong Kong dollar assets than on United States dollar assets encourage some investors to shift out of United States dollars. Thus the demand curve shifts to D_2 because of these forces.

The supply curve tends to shift to the right because lower prices in Hong Kong encourage a greater volume of exports and increased earnings of United States dollars. Thus the supply curve shifts to S_1 and the new long-term equilibrium level is represented by point c. And of course the entire system can work in reverse if there should be a decline in demand for United States dollars.

Just how long this process takes is impossible to predict. First, both demand and supply conditions are constantly changing. So it is quite unrealistic to depict a single shift and a gradual adjustment through money and exports, although the graph illustrates the basic forces at work. In reality the shifting of interest rates on a week-to-week basis probably dominates the shifts in demand for United States dollars, and brings the price of HK$7.80 back into line without great changes in the money supply.

Control over the money supply under this system is very indirect and loose. But nevertheless one could say that in this system the supply of money is controlled in the long run through setting its price. The pegging of Hong Kong's dollar thus constitutes a type of monetary policy which has been adopted, at least temporarily, by the Hong Kong Government.

The Hong Kong Association of Banks

In 1981 the Hong Kong Government legalized a cartel of licensed banks—the Hong Kong Association of Banks (HKAB). The HKAB now sets maximum rates of interest to be paid to depositors on deposit accounts of HK$500,000 or less.

A legalized cartel in an otherwise free-enterprise economy is an anomaly. The justification for its existence has rested principally upon two grounds. One is that the cartel will help protect depositors. The other is that the Government can exert pressure on it to push interest rates up and down to restrain economic expansion or encourage it.

Protection of Depositors

A banking cartel that sets interest rates on deposits is engaging in a perverse form of usury. Usury is the excessive charging of interest by someone who is, presumably, a wealthy lender who charges immorally high interest to those who are, presumably, poor borrowers. In this case, the lenders are the depositors who are lending their meagre funds to the banks. The banks are borrowers, and the law permits them to tell the small depositing lenders that they are asking too much interest of the big banks—illegal usurious interest.

Two results are possible. Either banks profit from this or they forego profits, by competing with one another in such ways as charging less for loans or providing extra services to depositors at below cost.[6] On either ground the cartel is unjustified. There is no economic justification for government-sponsored regulations that give profits to banks, or that give benefits to users of banking services.

But, one may ask, does not the interest ceiling on deposits ensure bank profits and thereby ensure that a depositor's money is safe? That is, if the ceiling were removed would not banks fail and would not depositors then lose their savings? Surely, the argument goes, the ceiling is there to protect depositors. This argument is, perhaps, the most insidious of all. It is designed to reassure the depositor that, although he is losing, he should be glad. After all, it implies, the loss is in the depositor's best interest: otherwise he might lose all his money.

Banks do not fail because they pay too much interest to depositors. Any contrary assertion is false. With the interest rate cartel in control, banks are more likely to make more bad loans than otherwise. Without it, they must be even more careful. If anything, the cartel encourages banks to be less careful in managing their depositors' assets.

But again, one may ask, would not the removal of the cartel lead to the failure of some banks which, because of excessively risky lending in the past, cannot afford to pay the higher market rate of interest on deposits? If one bank were to fail, it would not be too disruptive to the economy. But if four or five failed, would this precipitate a wholesale collapse of the banking system?

It is true that widespread bank failure would impose adjustment costs on the system as a whole. But if one believes such adjustment costs would be incurred, then one admits that, under present arrangements, banks employ inefficient management. If these institutions cannot meet the market test, then their management should go into some other line of work.

One must conclude that a phased or staged process of movement toward the repeal of the cartel should begin soon, to eliminate this inefficiency in the structure of financial institutions.

Interest Rate Controls as Monetary Policy Tools

This chapter is on monetary policy and it is appropriate here to examine the feasibility of controlling interest rate levels in order to control money growth indirectly. By setting rates high, borrowers are discouraged, the economy is restrained and inflation is held down. By lowering rates, borrowing is encouraged, money is created, and the economy is stimulated.

First, it is useful to note that setting rates that banks pay to depositors is not the same as setting rates on loans; banks charge customers for loans. Although lending rates to industry in Hong Kong tend to vary with the rates set on deposits, the relation can be quite loose. But even if the relation were very close, there is a flaw in the system because it can only work through a lagged reaction mechanism.

For example, if prices of property begin to rise, banks will be encouraged to make loans. Interest rate levels will rise and the money supply will expand simultaneously. Finally, the banks will follow the rise by raising deposit rates. This is viewed as a restrictive monetary measure when, in fact, it merely follows the excessive monetary expansion that preceded it. Only if the cartel had raised rates in anticipation of the explosion of property values could it have engineered a slower rate of money growth by this process. Thus an interest rate policy is almost always going to work in the same way that 'closing the stable door after the horse has bolted' works.

An interest rate control policy could, in theory, work to influence money growth. But in practice it may be less effective than a policy of direct control over money growth. After all, the objective of monetary policy is to control the money supply. The cartel is not justified on monetary policy grounds if alternative methods of money control exist.

Government spokesmen sometimes justify the cartel on the grounds that, even if it did not exist, the large banks would set interest rates on deposits. That is, there is a concentration of banking power in Hong Kong, and if the HKAB is legalized the Government can directly influence the cartel's decisions. Otherwise, the Government would have less influence and the potential for abuse by a concentration of power would be larger. Evidently, the Government's attitude is 'if you can't beat 'em, join 'em'.

No economic analysis justifies the continuation of the interest rate cartel. All paths of logic lead to the same conclusion. In the interest of economic efficiency, steps to disassemble it should begin.

Issues in Monetary Policy

This chapter has said little about reserve requirements in Hong Kong. As noted earlier, the system of specified liquid assets described in Chapter 1 does not limit money expansion. A legally imposed vault cash reserve as a proportion of deposit liabilities would act as a money control tool, but only if the Government limits the amount of vault cash that it and the note-issuing banks create. If the amount the Government creates is limited, there is no great need to supplement this limit with a rule for banks regarding their cash holdings. They want to stay in business and will manage their cash holdings to that end without Government regulation.

Reserves have also played a role in another Government activity involving Government deposits. If the Government's deposits have seven days or less to maturity, the banks are required to hold 100 per cent liquid asset reserves behind them. However, if the Government's deposit is for a period greater than seven days, only the usual 25 per cent liquid asset reserve is required. Thus, by reducing the term to maturity of its deposits, the Government can place the banks in a position of having to increase their liquidity reserves.

But since liquid reserves willingly held average about 50 per cent when the legal requirement is only 25 per cent, the liquid asset reserve ratio is not binding. It would take a wholesale shift in the maturity of deposits to have any significant effect on bank lending. Of course if required reserve ratios were binding, then, in theory, such shifting in the maturity composition of Government deposits could impose restraints on bank lending. But in view of the size of the task to be accomplished, it is safe to say that additional measures are required for an effective monetary policy.

The Lack of a Policy-making Process

Perhaps the greatest problem facing the Hong Kong Government with regard to monetary policy is that there seems to be no part of the Government that is explicitly given authority and responsibility for the implementation of a monetary policy. The Financial Secretary and the Monetary Affairs Branch have considerable authority in all the relevant and related matters. But the charge to manage the money supply is nowhere made explicit.

If the Exchange Fund Ordinance were amended very slightly, to instruct the Financial Secretary to control the growth of CIs issued by the Exchange Fund in the interest of economic stability, the setting of a rate of growth for Hong Kong's monetary base would be part of the Fund's responsibilities. If the rate of growth were to be changed from time to time on the basis of economic criteria, the change, and the explanation for it, would be in the Financial Secretary's hands. But, until someone is given some measure of authority and responsibility for the formulation and implementation of a monetary policy for Hong Kong, its money supply is likely to continue its random walk with loose constraints.

Notes

1. A Monetary Statistics Ordinance was implemented in 1980. See the reviews of it in *Asian Monetary Monitor,* September–October 1981 and November–December 1982, pp. 9–10.
2. Most large banks make special arrangements with the Treasury to put its funds into a TT and L note account where they earn interest for a few days until the Treasury asks the bank to forward the funds to the Federal Reserve. For more details see Richard Lang, 'TT & L Note Accounts', *Review,* Federal Reserve Bank of St. Louis, October 1979, pp. 3–14.
3. This view differs from the position taken by some economists who argued that by accepting Hong Kong dollar deposits in exchange for CIs, the Exchange Fund lost control over Hong Kong's money supply. See *Asian Monetary Monitor,* November–December 1982, p. 49.
4. See Milton Friedman, *A Program for Monetary Stability* (New York, Fordham University Press, 1959), p. 98.
5. This section on the monetary base is largely taken from R.H. Scott (1984), pp. 65–9.
6. A study by Y.K. Ho indicated that banks may profit, but not by an amount that is statistically significant.

References

The author has published a small book that covers several aspects of Hong Kong's monetary system: *Saving Hong Kong's Dollar* (Hong Kong, University Publisher and Printer, 1984). An excellent book that has several chapters related to Hong Kong's financial system is David Lethbridge (ed.), *The Business Environment in Hong Kong* (Hong Kong, Oxford University Press, second edition, 1984).

The Hongkong and Shanghai Banking Corporation produces a monthly publication, *Hong Kong Economic Report*, with financial data and brief commentaries on economic and financial issues.

A bimonthly publication, the *Asian Monetary Monitor* (P. O. Box 30724, Causeway Bay, Hong Kong), carries many articles about Hong Kong's financial system. See especially the articles by John Greenwood, 'The Operation of the New Exchange Rate Mechanism', January–February 1984, pp. 2–12, and 'Why the HK$/US$ Linked Rate System Should Not be Changed', November–December 1984, pp. 2–17. The second of these articles contains a brief appendix with graphs similar to the one in the text above (Fig. 3.3), and other graphs showing the operation of a system under which the monetary base is controlled.

Also see Tai Ming Kee, Wong Kwong Ling, Leung Chiu Fan, 'Fixed Versus Flexible Exchange Rate', *Business Administration Academic Bulletin* (New Asia College, Chinese University of Hong Kong, 1984), pp. 57–65, and Lee Chin Leung, 'Economic Factors Contributing to Hong Kong Dollar's Depreciation', in the same issue, pp. 67–72.

A useful recent discussion is contained in John G. Greenwood, A.R. Latter, and Victor Menezes, 'Forum on the Hong Kong Currency', *Hong Kong Economic Papers*, No. 15, 1984, pp. 119–31.

4. The Hong Kong Stock-market: its Development and Control

K. A. WONG

WE have so far described the operations of commercial and merchant banking in Hong Kong, and Hong Kong's monetary policy. We now turn to the operations of financial markets. This chapter will describe how stock-markets operate and will examine the development and control of the stock-market in Hong Kong.

The Role of a Stock-market

A stock-market is an elaborate structure geared to bringing together buyers and sellers of securities. It consists of a new issue market and a secondary market. The former is essentially a group of financial institutions which facilitate the distribution of new securities, while the latter consists of stock exchanges and brokerage firms which facilitate the trading of existing securities.

The performance of a stock-market influences the financial affairs of a considerable proportion of the population. Many people are engaged directly in buying and selling securities, while many more people are affected since their retirement funds and insurance schemes are largely invested in corporate securities. The performance of a stock-market also affects the national economy, since this market provides information to facilitate effective decisions in production activities. The economic characteristics of this market have a profound influence on the allocation of capital resources.

First, the secondary market of a stock-market is a primary source of information for corporate managers on the cost and availability of capital funds. Managers need this information in order to determine the appropriate amount of investment that their companies should undertake. Companies whose share prices are high in relation to their expected earnings are encouraged to obtain more equity capital for expansion. Moreover, the market promotes the demand for new securities, since it provides a means through which subscribers can dispose of their holdings in future if they so desire.

Second, a secondary market permits long-term investment to be financed by short-term funds. Many savers wish to make their funds available for a short period only, or to be able to withdraw them at will. Without a secondary market, the funds available for subscription to new shares would be very limited, since any subscription would mean a long-term 'lock in'.

Thus a secondary market that functions well enables companies to raise capital funds at a lower cost than would otherwise be possible.

Thirdly, through the trading activities of its stock exchanges, the secondary market offers a simple mechanism for the transfer of security ownership and hence of funds. The transfer needs only a minimum amount of administrative effort by buyers and sellers of securities. Prices are determined by matching buying orders and selling orders, and the actual transactions and quotations are continuously reported by the stock exchanges. Moreover, the exchanges require the release of financial information by listed companies, so that investors are able to evaluate the performance of a company before making an investment decision.

Finally, the stock-market as a whole encourages the growth of enterprises, since it offers numerous entrepreneurs access to funds. Many of them possess only relatively limited capital and yet, by selling securities through the market, they can obtain funds to carry out large investment projects and mass production plans to achieve economies of scale.

Corporations are important economic institutions in a free enterprise economy and they require large amounts of capital to finance their activities. An effective stock-market makes funds more readily available to those companies which can make the best use of them. Because of this, we say that such a market is efficient.

Although a large stock-market is not necessarily effective, the breadth and absorptive capacity of a market are the principal facets of efficiency. If a stock-market is narrow and shallow, its efficiency in allocating capital funds will consequently be reduced. This is because activity in the secondary market cannot provide reliable guidelines for investment decisions in production activities. In recent years, the Hong Kong stock-market has developed rapidly in terms of trading volume and absorptive capacity. However it is, of course, still relatively small by comparison with the New York and London markets.

Stock-market Activity in Hong Kong prior to 1969

Although formal stock-trading activities began in Hong Kong as early as 1891, the stock-market has only been an important source of capital funds for business enterprises since about 1969. During Hong Kong's industrialization in the early 1950s, most firms started as modest sole-proprietor ventures, which gradually changed into partnerships or private companies. Firms which were incorporated or controlled from abroad also formed an important part of the business community. Public corporations were not common until the late 1960s.

The Hong Kong Stock Exchange was founded in 1891 and the Hong Kong Sharebrokers' Association was formed in 1921 by dealers who could not join the Exchange as members. These two organizations merged to become the present Hong Kong Stock Exchange Ltd. in 1947.[1]

There was a minor boom in the stock-market during the years 1946–8 as political changes in China drove many Shanghai businessmen to look for a foothold in Hong Kong. However, the Communist seizure of control in China created uncertainty in Hong Kong and thus caused the prices of all shares to fall rapidly until mid-1950, when the outbreak of the Korean War brought new trade opportunities to Hong Kong.

As shown in Table 4.1, the end of the Korean War in 1953 helped to restore confidence in Hong Kong's stability, and the value of stock turnover increased in that year. Furthermore, a trade recession and low activity in the property market caused the investment of some local idle funds in the stock-market. However, as a result of an increase in interest rates, credit restrictions imposed by banks to discourage share speculation, and a recovery in the property market, the share market was relatively depressed from 1955 until 1958.

Rapid industrial development during the late 1950s brought a massive influx of foreign capital to Hong Kong, part of which flowed to the stock-market for temporary investment. This temporary investment stimulated the participation of local investors and led to a major boom in the market during the years 1959–61. The value of stock turnover reached its highest post-war peak during this period, and share prices, on the average, doubled between 1959 and mid-1961, bringing dividend yields to levels similar to

Table 4.1 The Value of Stock Turnover 1948–84 (HK$ million)

Year	Turnover	Year	Turnover
1948	159	1967	305
1949	88	1968	944
1950	60	1969	2,546
1951	141	1970	5,989
1952	142	1971	14,793
1953	151	1972	43,758
1954	252	1973	48,217
1955	333	1974	11,246
1956	211	1975	10,335
1957	148	1976	13,156
1958	150	1977	6,127
1959	360	1978	27,419
1960	876	1979	25,633
1961	1,414	1980	95,684
1962	701	1981	105,987
1963	521	1982	46,230
1964	748	1983	37,165
1965	389	1984	48,790
1966	350		

Source: Hong Kong Statistics 1947–67 (Hong Kong, Census and Statistics Department); *Hong Kong Monthly Digest of Statistics* (Hong Kong, Census and Statistics Department), various issues.

those of the United States and the United Kingdom. This situation was checked soon after a local bank went into difficulties in June 1961.

During the 1960s the market was further affected by several distinct events. There was a minor boom in 1964 following the Government's announcement of a new scheme of partial control over the electricity supply companies. But over-speculation by some banks led to a banking crisis in 1965, in which share prices fell. During the crisis the fall was sudden and severe since some banks called in loans secured by quoted shares while others disposed of their own shareholdings. Although, in most cases, increased company profits were reported in early 1966, the unstable political situation in China (specifically the activities of the Red Guards) held share prices at a low level. In 1967, share prices and turnover fell to the lowest point since 1961 as a result of the political disturbances which occurred in Hong Kong in that year. During the disturbances, the Hong Kong Stock Exchange twice suspended operations for periods of about 10 days to prevent panic selling.

Although the sustained growth of the Hong Kong economy, as measured by stock turnover, began in 1959, following the heavy industrialization of the previous few years, few companies were added to the stock exchange list in the period 1957–67. During these years, the number of companies listed on the Hong Kong Stock Exchange fluctuated between 50 and 70, but active dealings were confined to the shares of fewer than 25 of these companies. Of the most active stocks, 8 were the stocks of utility companies. Table 4.2 presents the distribution of listed companies by industry group in five selected years from 1957 to 1984. The table shows that, in the years 1957–67, the public utilities were the largest group of companies. Few industrial companies came to the market to raise capital funds for expansion during this decade.

Several factors were responsible for the narrowness of the stock-market in

Table 4.2 The Number of Listed Companies by Industry Group

Industry Group	1957	1967	1977	1984
Banking and finance	5	4	16	25
Utilities	9	12	8	9
Land and construction	3	4	113	102
Commercial and industrial	5	9	44	41
Docks, wharves, and godowns	4	6	4	3
Hotels	2	4	9	13
Investments	3	4	10	11
Shipping	4	5	18	16
Textiles	2	4	20	17
Miscellaneous	14	17	16	11
Total	51	69	258	248

Sources: Compiled from Hong Kong Stock Exchange Yearbook (Hong Kong, Hong Kong Stock Exchange Ltd.), various issues; Far East Exchange Yearbook (Hong Kong, Far East Exchange Ltd.), various issues; Hong Kong Economic Journal Monthly, various issues.

Hong Kong before 1969. Undoubtedly, the uncertainty over Hong Kong's future, which was due to the special political relationship with China, restricted the development of the stock-market by discouraging equity investment. The dominance of Chinese family firms in the Hong Kong economy also contributed to the short list of quoted companies. There was a considerable reluctance to release the tight family control to a board of directors elected by shareholders. Another factor affecting the development of the stock-market was the ready availability of facilities for Hong Kong investors to invest in foreign securities. Furthermore, the stability of prices and the increase in bank deposit interest rates after 1961 (due to keen competition between the banks) also made investment in local shares a relatively unattractive proposition.

Development of the Stock-market in Hong Kong since 1969

Tables 4.1 and 4.3 show that turnover volume and share prices increased rapidly during the major boom in the stock-market which occurred in the period 1969–73. From December 1971 to March 1973, the Hang Seng Index

Table 4.3 The Performance of the Hang Seng Index of Share Prices

Year	High	Low	Closing
1965	103.5	78.0	82.1
1966	85.1	79.1	79.7
1967	79.8	60.2	66.9
1968	107.6	63.1	107.6
1969	160.1	112.5	155.5
1970	211.9	154.8	211.6
1971	405.3	201.1	341.4
1972	843.4	324.0	843.4
1973	1,775.0	400.0	433.7
1974	481.9	150.1	171.1
1975	352.9	160.4	350.0
1976	465.3	354.5	447.7
1977	452.2	404.0	404.0
1978	707.8	383.4	495.5
1979	879.4	493.8	879.4
1980	1,654.6	738.9	1,473.6
1981	1,810.2	1,113.8	1,405.8
1982	1,445.3	676.3	783.8
1983	1,102.6	690.1	874.9
1984	1,206.8	746.0	1,200.4

Note: 31 July 1964 = 100.

Source: Hang Seng Bank Ltd.

rose by 5.3 times or at a compound rate of over 13 per cent per month.[2] Stock prices then fell sharply by 91.5 per cent toward the end of 1974, reaching the lowest level since 1969. The Index began to recover gradually and rose by 3.1 times by March 1976, but it was still only about one-quarter of the 1973 peak level. By November 1978, the Index was at about the same level as that of March 1976. However a new boom started which pushed the Index up by 3.5 times to 1,654.6 by November 1980. After some adjustments, the Index went up to 1,810.2 on 17 July 1981. This was the highest level recorded for the Hong Kong stock-market. Turnover volumes showed a similar movement with the year 1981 achieving the highest record.

A number of favourable factors were responsible for the major boom in the stock-market during the period 1969 to 1973: the restoration of business confidence after the political disturbances of 1967; the remarkably consistent performance of the Hong Kong economy; the impressive growth of profits in most listed companies; the uninspiring performance of the New York stock-market; the extreme liquidity of the banking sector, which was caused by an inflow of overseas funds due to the international currency crisis; the opening of three new stock exchanges; and, most important of all, the repeated indications by China that Hong Kong was not regarded as a priority issue, but as an issue to be dealt with when the time was ripe. These indications enabled Hong Kong to measure its future in decades rather than years. This change in thinking was discernible in the planning and investment undertaken by corporations, and led to a big boom in the property market.

It is believed that, before 1969, the volume of capital outflow for investment in foreign securities was very high, though there is no way of estimating the volume of this outflow.[3] Hong Kong investors had for a long time been able to invest in foreign securities as, since the 1950s, foreign security firms had established branches in Hong Kong. They had done so because there were few restrictions on the operations of such branches, and because foreign exchange was readily available from the free market to finance overseas transfers. Foreign brokerage firms, mutual funds, and unit trusts have continued to be represented in Hong Kong, and offer Hong Kong investors a wider selection of titles and services than is available on the local market. American firms, moreover, have a continuous telex link with the New York market. However, the sharp fall of share prices on the New York stock-market, which began early in 1969, encouraged local and Southeast Asian funds to turn to the Hong Kong stock-market. In 1970, this trend was enhanced by the troubles of mutual funds, such as Investors Overseas Services, in which Hong Kong investors had invested substantially.

The establishment of three new stock exchanges (Far East, Kam Ngan, and Kowloon) during the years 1969–72 was partly stimulated by the sharp upsurge in stock-market activities. Their establishment also enhanced market development because they brought in several hundreds of new stockbrokers, thus stimulating interest among the public in share trading. Though these new stock exchanges quoted mainly the same stocks as those of the Hong Kong Stock Exchange, they were all recognized by the Government shortly after their formation. However, a bill was passed early in 1973 to stop the establishment of further stock exchanges. The boom also led to the establishment of the Securities Commission and the Office of The Commissioner for Securities, in order to 'curb questionable practices' on the stock-market.

Since the rising stock-market during the period 1969–73 was accompanied by a rush of new companies seeking a quotation on the stock exchanges, merchant banks were established to underwrite and handle the flotation of new issues. The first merchant bank, Schroders & Chartered Limited, formed by the Chartered Bank, Schroders Limited of London, and Sir Elly Kadoorie Continuation Limited, opened for business in early 1971. This was followed by, among others, Jardine Fleming & Company Limited, a joint operation between Jardine Matheson & Co. Limited and Robert Fleming Holdings Limited, and by Wardley Limited, a wholly owned subsidiary of the Hongkong and Shanghai Banking Corporation. Many larger commercial banks and finance companies also carried out certain merchant banking activities. Furthermore, the booming market attracted a number of large financial institutions from Europe to seek bases for expansion in Hong Kong.

In the buoyant stock-market between 1969 and 1973, a large number of new companies were listed (see Table 4.4). Although about half of these new companies were property firms, there was also a significant increase in the number of textile, shipping, banking and finance, and industrial and commercial companies, as shown in Table 4.2. The growth of the market seems to have been induced partly by the modern financial concepts introduced by the major financial institutions from Europe which began

Table 4.4 The Number and Volume of New Share Issues by New Companies (HK$ million)

Year	No.	Amount	Year	No.	Amount
1959	1	9.9	1972	98	1,930.0
1960	1	27.8	1973	110	1,360.0
1961	4	65.0	1974	3	176.2
1962	1	8.0	1975	0	0.0
1963	3	34.2	1976	0	0.0
1964	2	21.5	1977	1	151.3
1965	1	3.5	1978	0	0.0
1966	0	0.0	1979	1	34.5
1967	0	0.0	1980	6	1,035.5
1968	1	24.0	1981	13	2,986.1
1969	5	130.3	1982	2	76.1
1970	25	339.6	1983	4	419.5
1971	13	203.0	1984	8	1,049.4

Note: Excluding new companies seeking a quotation by introduction.

Source: Compiled from Hong Kong Economic Yearbook (Hong Kong, Economic Information Agency Ltd.), various issues; Hong Kong Yearbook (Hong Kong, Wah Kiu Yat Po), various issues; and press reports.

operating in Hong Kong, and partly by the extremely high share prices which lowered the cost of raising capital. Investors, on the other hand, were attracted by the handsome short-term capital gains as new issue prices were usually set significantly below the market price.

The Stock-market Slump of 1973–4

The great boom in the stock-market was followed by a slump during the years 1973–4. The slump was initially caused by the discovery of forged share certificates in certain companies and was intensified later with the introduction of a profit tax on stock-trading, rent control imposed by the Government (which undermined the profitability of real estate companies), and the tightening of credit conditions. The Hang Seng Index halved in six weeks before falling more gently to 433.7 by the end of 1973. The fall in stock prices was further aggravated by the international oil crisis and economic stagnation in 1974, in which both company profits and dividends fell, while output and total exports were contracting.

Economic Recovery and the Stock-market Boom

During the years 1975–9, the economic recovery and subsequent inflationary growth resulted in greater company profits and dividends. However, only a few new companies were added to the stock exchange list in the years 1974–9, as shown in Table 4.4. Stock prices rose gradually to the level of December 1972. This situation was further stimulated by the open-door policy of China, which led to an expansion of its Western contacts in trade and investment, and altered investors' perceptions of Hong Kong's political risk. This favourable factor, together with impressive economic growth—an average increase of 11.3 per cent in real Gross Domestic Product (GDP) for the five years 1976–80—led to a great property market boom, which in turn caused a stock-market boom in the years 1979–81. This was because a very large proportion of listed Hong Kong stocks were stocks of property and property-related companies. Moreover, the open-door policy of China encouraged many foreign companies to set up offices in Hong Kong, and this not only stimulated the demand for residential and office space but also caused an influx of capital from various countries, particularly from South-east Asia. Property prices in general more than trebled in about five years as a result of excessive speculation.

The Collapse of the Property Market and Political Uncertainties

The collapse of the property market in the second half of 1982 brought the Hang Seng Index down by about 40 per cent. The slump was enhanced by uncertainty about the political future of Hong Kong and the world-wide recession which depressed Hong Kong's key export sector. Several finance companies and property groups became insolvent. Moreover, the first visit of the British Prime Minister, Mrs Margaret Thatcher, to Beijing in September 1982 for talks about the future of Hong Kong after the expiry of the lease of the New Territories in 1997 did not cause confidence in Hong Kong. It became increasingly apparent at this time that the only solution was the return of Hong Kong to China. The Hang Seng Index crashed to 676.3 towards the end of 1982. It recovered by over 40 per cent before the value of the Hong Kong dollar plunged to its lowest figure in September 1983. This fall was largely caused by the slow progress of the negotiations between Britain and China on the settlement of the lease, so that Hong Kong people lost further confidence in the future of Hong Kong. The Index plummeted to about 700 again in October 1983. When the more concrete proposals which were put forward to maintain the stability and prosperity of Hong Kong after the expiry of the lease were accepted by the people of Hong Kong, stock prices began to recover again in January 1984. The settlement of the lease issue, which was announced in September 1984, was favourably received by the stock-market and, during 1984, the Index achieved a net gain of about 40 per cent, closing at 1,200.4. In early 1985, the market remained active but speculative.

The stock-market boom in 1980–1 also added a significant number of new companies to the list of companies quoted on the stock exchanges. Because of the great boom in the property market, a majority of them were again real estate companies. These companies were very much larger than those quoted in the 1972–3 market boom, but the total number of companies was much smaller.

The Boom of the New Issue Market in Hong Kong

The main and most direct impact of any stock-market on economic development comes from the facilities which enable the government and corporations to issue new securities. Through such new issues, they obtain capital funds for investment activities.

New share capital raised by companies from a stock-market can be divided into two categories: share issues made by new companies seeking a listing for the first time and rights issues by those that are already quoted on the stock exchange. In a rights issue, existing shareholders have the rights to subscribe to new shares in proportion to the number of shares which they already hold. Shareholders who decide not to take up the offer can sell their rights on the stock-market. Rights issues do not use all the facilities of the new issue market whereas share issues by new companies do. Therefore, in order to understand the workings of the new issue market, we are more interested in share issues by new companies seeking a listing.

The capital raised in Hong Kong by new companies and those which were already listed on the stock exchange in the period 1954–63 was about HK$542 million. The corresponding figure for the years 1945 to 1953 was estimated at less than HK$100 million.[4] The amount increased to HK$5,476.6 million in the period 1964–73, while the volume rose to HK$24,884.7 million in the years 1974 to 1983, with HK$9,773.8 million in the peak year 1981. As shown in Table 4.5, there were no debenture or convertible issues before 1971 but such issues were popular during the

Table 4.5 The Volume of New Issues (HK$ million)

Year	Equity issues*	Year	Equity issues*	Debentures and Convertibles	Total
1954	13.8	1971	837.4	87.0	924.4
1955	17.8	1972	1,989.8	0.0	1,989.8
1956	39.5	1973	1,416.0	0.0	1,416.0
1957	61.1	1974	205.6	253.5	459.1
1958	31.2	1975	366.4	870.0	1,236.4
1959	49.2	1976	366.9	520.0	886.9
1960	42.5	1977	461.0	895.0	1,356.0
1961	164.0	1978	362.8	300.4	663.2
1962	26.3	1979	442.1	617.9	1,060.0
1963	96.6	1980	4,544.3	1,317.5	5,861.8
1964	145.8	1981	9,173.0**	600.0	9,773.8
1965	36.5	1982	2,061.4**	0.0	2,061.4
1966	43.5	1983	1,526.1	0.0	1,526.1
1967	1.5	1984	2,542.8	1,000.0	3,542.8
1968	48.2				
1969	347.4				
1970	523.5				

Note: *Including new equity issues and rights issues.
** Including preference shares HK$794.6 million in 1981 and HK$450 million in 1982.

Sources: 1954–70: Compiled from *Hong Kong Stock Exchange Yearbook* (Hong Kong, Hong Kong Stock Exchange Ltd.), various issues; *Hong Kong Economic Yearbook* (Hong Kong, Economic Information Agency Ltd.), various issues; and *Hong Kong Yearbook* (Hong Kong, Wah Kiu Yat Po), various issues.

1971–81: From S.G. Roberts, 'The Capital Market in Hong Kong', presented at the Seminar on a Unified Stock Exchange and Capital Market in Hong Kong, 2 March 1983, Hong Kong.

1982–4: Press reports.

period 1974–81. There were almost no Government issues over the 30-year period 1954–83. In 1984, the Hong Kong Government raised HK$1,000 million by bearer bonds at an interest rate of 10 per cent.

By comparison, the number and volume of new share issues by new companies in Hong Kong since 1959 are shown in Table 4.4. As can be seen from the table, the number of new companies coming to the stock-market and the volume of capital funds raised from the stock-market were small prior to 1969. There have been two major booms in the new issue market since 1959, which correspond to the two great booms in the property market. The first boom was in 1970–3 and the second in 1980–1. Most of the newly listed companies in these two periods were property companies. The first period was notable for the number of new companies while, in the second period, the average market value of the newly listed companies and the funds raised by them were greater.

New Issue Methods

There are four methods by which new companies seeking a quotation for the first time can make share issues: an offer for sale, a stock exchange placing, an introduction, and a prospectus issue.

1. An Offer for Sale.   In an offer for sale, an issuing company gives a complete block of new shares to an issuing house, at an agreed price. The issuing house then offers the complete block of new shares for sale by public subscription at a stated price. In return for the backing of its reputation and its administrative and advisory services in the issue, the issuing house receives a fee from the issuing company. The issue will usually be underwritten to avoid the possibility that part of the issue may not be subscribed to by the investing public. The issuing house usually serves as an underwriter of the issue and receives an underwriting commission at the same time. In an offer for sale, the issue price is fixed by the issuing house and agreed to by the issuing company, and is stated in the prospectus. Other information required by a prospectus in Hong Kong is prescribed in the Hong Kong Companies Ordinance and the stock exchange regulations.

2. A Stock Exchange Placing.   In a stock exchange placing, the issuing company does not offer the shares directly to the public, but places them with brokers on the stock exchange. The brokers distribute a share prospectus to their clients, who then subscribe to the shares via the brokers. The shares are placed at a fixed price, which is stated in the prospectus. The contents of this prospectus are the same as those in the prospectus of an offer for sale. As there is no rule in Hong Kong that shares allocated to brokers must be passed on to their clients, many brokers in the buoyant market of 1972–3 retained most of these shares for themselves. They then sold them at substantial premium prices when dealing began, instead of passing them on to their clients and earning brokerage fees. An issuing house often also underwrites a stock exchange placing, thus earning a fee and an underwriting commission.

However, placing has not been encouraged in recent years and approval must be sought in advance from the exchange. It is normally allowed only in respect of issues which are small in market capitalization and when it is justified to save expense.

3. An Introduction.   An introduction is merely a method of creating a market in the existing shares of a company which is seeking a quotation for the first time. Stock exchanges normally require that a company applying for an introducton must have the requisite market capitalization, sufficient shareholders, and a satisfactory spread of shares for establishing an adequate market. In contrast to a placing, none of the shares in an introduction is committed for sale to the public through the market. However the sponsors of such an issue always know of a potential seller of a certain number of shares if this should be required for smoothing the beginning of dealings in the shares. Thus an introduction alone cannot raise new money for the company concerned. The information which must be included in the prospectus for an introduction is similar to that required in the prospectuses associated with other methods of issue. Introductions have largely been used in Hong Kong to introduce stocks which have already been quoted on a

recognized local or foreign stock exchange, or stocks issued by a newly formed holding company in exchange for those of one or more existing listed companies.

4. A Prospectus Issue.   In a prospectus issue, an issuing company offers new shares directly to the public for subscription at a stated price. The issuing house concerned is paid a fee only for its advisory services. The company itself receives the proceeds of the issue and is directly responsible for all the costs of the issue, including commissions to the underwriters. The underwriting of the shares in a prospectus issue is to some extent an endorsement of their worth. The basis of the issue is again a prospectus with strictly prescribed minimum contents. This method of issue is rarely used in Hong Kong.

The Organization of the New Issue Market in Hong Kong

As there were very few new issues before 1969, there was no clear framework for the organization of the new issue market in Hong Kong, and almost all the issues were handled by the leading commercial banks. Since the early 1970s, however, the major issuing houses have developed certain uniform patterns in handling new issues, and thus three stages in the process of issue can be identified.

During the first stage, when a company wishes to make an issue, it approaches an issuing house, which usually inquires into the reason for the issue and considers whether or not it deserves support. If the issuing house decides to support the issue, it advises the company on market conditions, the size of the issue, the price and the time at which the shares should be issued, the procedure for making the issue, and the details for acquiring a stock exchange quotation.

The issuing house and the issuing company must together decide upon the method of issue. A prospectus must be prepared and approved by the Government and the stock exchange authorities. The first stage is of special importance from an economic viewpoint, because the issuing house screens companies and new issues before they become available to the investing public. Since the issuing house acts as an intermediary between the issuing company and the investing public, its skill and judgement at this stage can influence the direction in which financial resources flow.

The second stage of making an issue entails the preparation of an underwriting agreement which ensures that the issuing company will receive a definite amount of funds on a certain date for the share issue. This sum is assured since, if the public fail to subscribe for all the shares, the balance will be taken up by the underwriter. For a few weeks after the finalization of the underwriting agreement, the underwriter frequently bears the full risk of a change in market conditions. This is a weakness of the arrangement. However, it does not seem to be a serious drawback to underwriters in Hong Kong since most of them are either the major banks themselves, or merchant banks, or finance companies affiliated to the leading banks.

The final stage in the process of making a new issue is to sell the shares to investors. The full prospectus must be published in at least two major daily newspapers, one English and one Chinese, in order to inform the public about the issue. In an offer for sale, an issuing house frequently allocates prospectuses and application forms to the offices of its related banks and to members of the stock exchange to which an application for a quotation has been made. This ensures a wide distribution of prospectuses to the clients of these bodies. In a placing, prospectuses are distributed only through members of the stock exchange for their own clients.

As the ability of an issuing house to handle large issues depends partly on its distributive capacity, large issues are usually handled by one of the issuing houses affiliated to the leading banks. Sometimes one issuing house joins with several others in handling a large issue in order to off-load its underwriting risk and to bring the issue to a wider range of investors.

Control over New Issues

It is clear that a company must comply with certain statutory regulations and stock exchange rules before it may make an issue. In Hong Kong, as in Britain, the emphasis of these regulations is on the disclosure of adequate information to the investing public. The main source of information to aid investors in making subscription decisions is the new issue prospectus. The issue of any form of application for securities must be accompanied by a prospectus. The main statutory regulations are therefore related to the issue of prospectuses. The Hong Kong Companies Ordinance defines a prospectus as 'any prospectus, notice, circular, advertisement, or other invitation, offering to the public for subscription or purchases any shares or debentures of a company'.[5] It is a legal requirement that a prospectus must be issued to accompany any form of application with all methods of issue other than rights issues and introductions since, with these methods, securities are not issued to the general public.

Until December 1972, the requirements regarding the information which a prospectus must disclose were incomplete. At that time, only Section 38 and the Third Schedule of the Hong Kong Companies Ordinance dealt with the information that must be disclosed. The stated requirements did not include disclosure of the authorized, issued and paid-up capital of the issuing company. Nor did they include disclosure of the nature of the business, the purpose of the issue, or the consolidated accounts of an issue made by a holding company. All these loopholes, however, were tightened in the Hong Kong Companies (Amendment) Ordinance of 1972. The amendments were in line with the recommendations made in 1971 by the Companies Law Revision Committee.[6] The amendments required the prospectus to include the business history and the management of the company, the record of its past five years' profits, the company's capital and asset structure, its commitments for capital expenditure, the probable prospects of the company, and its expected profits and dividends for the coming year. Moreover, the Ordinance also fixed responsibility for the accuracy and adequacy of the information on those making a new issue. The issuing company had to submit the prospectus to the Registrar of Companies for approval.

To obtain a stock exchange listing for the shares issued, an issue must also comply with the rules and regulations of the stock exchange. Although there are at present four stock exchanges in Hong Kong, they have very similar rules. Essentially, as with the statutory regulations, their rules concentrate upon the disclosure of information. The rules of each exchange require the information to be supplied in an approved form of prospectus, whatever the method of issue, and advertised in all cases. However, no advertisement is required for applications for a quotation from companies whose securities have already been quoted on another recognized local stock exchange, and who are making no further issue. Finally, further information may be required on any aspect of the company's activities.

To ensure that there will be an adequate future market for the shares on issue, stock exchanges always impose a minimum size limit on new issues. Before March 1973, a company wishing to apply for a listing on the Hong Kong Stock Exchange was required to have a minimum market value at issue price of HK$4 million and, for any one class of security, a value of HK$2 million. The issuing company had to offer to the public shares which represented at least 25 per cent of the capital issued and to be issued (in the current issue), and at a price approved by the stock exchange authorities.

The Securities Commission was established to set up certain administrative regulations to control the speculative activity which occurred in the 1972–3 stock-market boom. In March 1973 the Commission asked the stock exchanges to stipulate that new issues by placings must have a minimum paid-up capital of HK$20 million, and that the minimum proportion of share capital to be made available to the public would vary with the paid-up capital. (The recommended variation is shown in Table 4.6.)

The Securities Commission also asked the stock exchanges to stipulate that an issuing company making a public offer should have a minimum paid-up capital of HK$50 million. In addition, it required that the minimum proportion of share capital to be made available in a public offer should be 25 per cent, and that no part of the offer should be set aside as a placing. Therefore, companies with a paid-up capital of less than HK$20 million would not be able to apply for a listing. (In both a public offer and a placing, the paid-up capital had to include the amount of the issue to be offered in the public offer or the placing.)

Table 4.6 The Share Capital Available to the Public in Stock Exchange Placings

Paid-up Capital (HK$ million)	Minimum Proportion Available (per cent)
20	40
25	35
30	30
over 35	25

Furthermore no person who is an existing shareholder of an issuing company will be permitted to subscribe to the shares on issue either in his own name or in the names of nominees. However, on request, a maximum of 10 per cent of the shares on issue will be offered to the employees of the issuing company or its subsidiaries on special application forms. The issuing company must provide the Commissioner for Securities with a list giving details of each employee who has been allotted shares, shortly after the opening of dealing. A new unified stock exchange will come into existence in Hong Kong during 1986 (see below). It is stated that the new exchange will implement all these recommendations.[7]

As the stock exchanges provide an official market for the trading of shares after an issue has been made, their regulations also provide a measure of surveillance over listed companies. An issuing company has to sign a form of general undertaking to accompany a formal application for a listing. The company must undertake to inform the stock exchange on which it is listed, without delay, of any information which is necessary either to enable its shareholders to appraise its position, or to avoid the establishment of a false market in its shares. The specific events of which the stock exchanges have to be immediately notified include the announcement of dividends and changes in the capital structure, the directorate, the Memorandum and Articles of Association, the nature of the company's business, and the control of voting. Further, companies must supply the stock exchanges with copies of all circulars, reports, and financial statements issued to shareholders. The final sanction behind the rules is the power of the exchanges to remove from the official list the name of any company which does not comply with these rules.

The Operation and Control of Trading Markets in Hong Kong

The Operation of the Stock Exchanges

As it was considered that the services provided by the Hong Kong, Far East, Kam Ngan, and Kowloon stock exchanges were adequate, the Stock Exchange Control Ordinance of 1973 was passed to impose heavy penalties on anyone operating a stock exchange which was not recognized under the Ordinance. This Ordinance effectively prevented the establishment of any new stock exchanges after that date.

The existence of as many as four stock exchanges in a small place such as Hong Kong has been criticized. Therefore, in November 1977, the authorities of the stock exchanges, supported by the Securities Commission, formed a working party to draw up a plan to merge the four exchanges. The Stock Exchange Unification Ordinance was enacted in August 1980. The new unified stock exchange is expected to open in 1986.

At the time of writing, the four stock exchanges have about 1,000 local members and some overseas members. The Far East Exchange has the largest membership, totalling about 420, while the Hong Kong Stock Exchange has the smallest—only about 135. In terms of trading volume, the Far East and Kam Ngan exchanges account for about 80 per cent of the total turnover, while the Hong Kong Stock Exchange has about 20 per cent. The Kowloon Stock Exchange represented more than 10 per cent of the total trading in its first two years of existence, 1972 and 1973, but it swiftly declined and now its share is less than 1 per cent. For the last five years, the total trading volume of the four exchanges has been equal to, on average, 35 per cent of GDP. The Hong Kong Stock Exchange is the oldest exchange and has the most overseas members and the most foreign companies listed. Securities can be listed on more than one exchange and almost all of the 248 stocks traded are listed on all four exchanges.

The four stock exchanges are quite similar in structure. They are private, non-profit-making companies with limited liability and their member brokers are the shareholders, limited in number. Overseas members must also be members of their home countries' stock exchanges. Overseas members are permitted access to the floor for information but they must place their orders through local brokers. Each exchange is governed by a general committee, the members of which are elected by an annual general meeting of the exchange members. The committee has absolute power over the administration of the exchange. Bank employees are not allowed to be members of a stock exchange, although corporate members have been permitted since 1977. A member of a stock exchange may conduct business as an individual, a partnership, or a corporation. Corporate memberships were not allowed originally, because a corporate firm has only limited liability.

Stock-trading is conducted by auction at the quotation board in each stock exchange. Each member has authorized clerks to conclude sales, and runners to assist in the trading. Multiple closed-circuit televisions are installed on the floor and from his seat a member can monitor different parts of the board. Similar monitors are installed in stockbrokers' firms and other financial institutions. All round-lot trades, which normally comprise 500, 1,000, and 2,000 shares must be done on the board. Any quantity less than one round lot is generally sold at a modest discount from the round-lot price. Each unit of share price movement is set at a specified amount, known as a spread, which varies in accordance with the market price level of the stock. Settlement takes place with the delivery of the share certificates and the attached transfer deeds on the trading day following the day of the conclusion of the sale. There is no over-the-counter market; all stock transactions have to be completed within the exchange floors. Moreover, short selling is not legal in Hong Kong. In short selling, a person sells stock which he does not own. He borrows the stock for delivery from or through his stockbroker and hopes that its price will decline, at which time he will buy the stock at a lower price and realize gains.

The cost of stock-trading is generally composed of two principal items, brokerage commission and stamp duty. Both buyers and sellers of securities are charged commission and stamp duty. The commission rate is 0.5 per cent of the total value of a transaction, with a minimum of HK$25, while the stamp duty is 0.3 per cent. The commission rate may be reduced to 0.25

per cent for overseas members and members of other Hong Kong stock exchanges.

Many banks provide custodial and nominee services, with charges for transactions, safe custody, and the collection of dividends. There is no capital gains tax or dividend income tax. There is also no foreign exchange control; money flows freely in and out of Hong Kong.

Legislation

A brief outline of the legislation controlling stock-trading in Hong Kong is given in the following paragraphs. To improve the standards and to check the qualifications of the stockbroking profession, Part Four of the Securities Ordinance of 1974 and the Securities (Dealers, Investment Advisers and Representatives) Regulations of 1974 required all dealers, investment advisers, and their representatives to register with the Commissioner for Securities. The Ordinance regulated dealing in securities. It also required the four exchanges to become members of the Hong Kong Federation of Stock Exchanges which is responsible, among other things, for developing uniform procedures for securities dealing, for providing training facilities for brokers, and for encouraging research into investments in securities.

Moreover, the Ordinance has established a stock exchange compensation fund to compensate persons who suffer losses as a result of default by stockbrokers. The Commissioner has the power to inspect dealers' books and to appoint inspectors to conduct investigations whenever necessary.

The Protection of Investors Ordinance of 1974 was passed on the same day as the Securities Ordinance. The object of this Ordinance is to forbid trading in securities or other property through fraudulent or reckless means. It requires advertisements which invite the public to invest in any form of property to be authorized by the Securities Commission.

In 1976, the Securities Ordinance of 1974 was amended in order to institute control over insider trading and the creation of a false market, and to restrain dealers from speculation. The Commissioner for Securities has the power to investigate the directors of listed companies, stockbrokers, dealers, and investment advisers. Moreover, the Securities Commission has also tried to tighten control over short selling and delayed deliveries, in order to curb excessive speculation.

Control over Take-overs and Mergers

On 14 August 1975, the Securities Commission approved the Hong Kong Code on Takeovers and Mergers. The Code was drawn up after discussions with underwriters, merchant banks, the Hong Kong Federation of Stock Exchanges, and other professionally interested bodies. The Code is administered by a Committee on Takeovers and Mergers consisting of members from the Securities Commission and representatives from financial institutions. The purpose of the Code is to provide guidelines for companies and their advisers who contemplate, or who become involved in, take-overs and mergers. The Code is operated on a voluntary basis, but it has received the support of all those concerned professionally.

They considered that the best method of protecting investors in Hong Kong would be to use self-regulatory agencies under the surveillance of a single commission. Since all Government regulations would be channelled through this body, it could be more expert, cheaper, and faster than if there were a number of bodies.[8]

The Code does not have, nor does it seek to have, the force of law, rather it represents the consensus of opinion on business standards of those concerned professionally in the field of takeovers and mergers and of the Securities Commission. [It] sets out the general principles which constitute acceptable standards of commercial behaviour and which should govern takeovers and mergers in Hong Kong.[9]

The principle behind the Code is 'fair practice for shareholders, which is broadly based on a concept of equity between one shareholder and another'. It has been said that, in general, 'law lays down minimum requirements applicable to the whole range of companies covered by the legislation, whereas the code aims to secure in its context the standards we require but which are difficult to translate into precise legislation.'[10] The advantages of this system are that it operates through the practitioners, who have expertise in the matter under regulation, and it permits the flexibility needed to meet exceptional circumstances.

The Code and the Committee are concerned with the presentation and implementation of take-over and merger proposals. Shareholders should be presented fairly with relevant information and should have time in which to make up their minds. There should be no change in the normal price level of the shares until the relevant information has been made available. Partial offers should be submitted for the prior consent of the Committee.

Furthermore, the general body of shareholders should be informed at the appropriate time about transfers in the control of a company. The controlling shareholders are those who hold 30 per cent or more of the voting rights. They should extend to other shareholders, as soon as possible, an offer of shares on the same terms as those on which they have bought shares in the preceding six months. No action should be taken on an offer without the approval of a general meeting of the shareholders of the company. The company concerned can appoint independent financial consultants to protect the general interests of the shareholders. The processes and mechanics of all take-overs and mergers are in accordance with the principles, the rules, and the spirit of the Code.

The penalties for those who breach the Code include 'private reprimand or public censure or further action as appropriate'. Those who fail to comply with the Code would lose their reputation if their fellow professionals knew that they had fallen below the 'acceptable standards of commercial behaviour'. In the longer term, non-compliance with the Code may change the Government's attitude and thus affect the development of the stock-market.

It has been argued that 'the most important and immediate measures required are for some sensible Disclosure Laws. Without them the Code is virtually meaningless'.[11] Non-compliance with the Code usually leads to a situation in which small shareholders suffer most. It is argued that, to protect small shareholders, the take-over and merger business in Hong Kong requires more government supervision.

The Economic Efficiency of the Stock-market

In the first section of this chapter we stated that, in an efficient stock-market, a company's management uses the level of its share prices as a primary source of information about the cost and availability of capital funds. Companies whose earning power is high have high share prices (with due allowance for risk differences). These high prices encourage them to obtain more capital for expansion. Companies whose operations are not profitable have depressed share prices and funds are available to them only on unfavourable terms. In this way, funds tend to flow to companies that will use them most profitably.

In an efficient market, all relevant information is fully reflected in stock prices so that no investor may make excessive profits by exploiting any special information. Although any one investor would find it extremely difficult to obtain and study all the relevant information, there are enough informed investors to ensure that the current market price of a stock approximates the best estimate of its intrinsic value. Stock values reflect a company's earning power. As informed investors continue to search for under- and over-valued stocks, all stocks in the market are fairly priced in terms of risk and expected return.

Examination of the workings of the New York stock-market has led to the formulation of the efficient market theory. The efficient market theory has three forms, which relate to three different subsets of information, namely, the 'weak' form, the 'semi-strong' form, and the 'strong' form. The weak form holds that the history of share prices does not contain any information which investors can exploit to earn excessive profits because the market price already reflects the information that history provides. The semi-strong form focuses on whether all the publicly available information is reflected in the share prices, so that investors cannot make excessive returns by exploiting such information. The strong form considers the question of whether some investors have monopolistic access to information which is relevant in determining share prices. All three forms are supported by empirical evidence from the New York stock-market. The data have not shown that the New York market is inefficient. The support for the weak form of market efficiency is particularly compelling. Evidence for the strong form of market efficiency is mostly drawn from indirect tests based on the performance of professional investment managers.

The Hong Kong stock-market is much smaller than the New York stock-market. Most of the studies done on the Hong Kong market are tests of the weak form of the market efficiency theory, which is the most basic of the three forms. If the market is not efficient with respect to simple information, such as historical prices, it is unlikely that it would be efficient with respect to information which is more complex or less freely available. Thus, if the Hong Kong market cannot pass the weak-form tests, we may assume that the market is also not likely to be efficient in the stronger forms. A number of studies of the Hong Kong stock-market suggest that it is inefficient. The results of these studies are briefly summarized below.

Evidence reported by Ang and Pohlman reveals that there was a sequential correlation between bi-weekly share price changes in the Hong Kong market during the years 1967–74.[12] Law examined the daily prices of 56 stocks in which there was continuous trading during the period September to November 1979. He found that the daily price changes of 32 out of the 56 stocks were non-random.[13] Wong and Kwong analysed the daily closing prices of the Hang Seng Index constituent stocks during the years 1977–80. They concluded that the evidence failed to give clear support to the weak-form efficiency of the market.[14] They found that historical stock price changes could be useful for predicting future price movements.

Moreover, in a study analysing stock recommendations by the largest securities firm in Hong Kong, Dawson suggested that the Hong Kong market was inefficient in both the strong and the semi-strong form.[15] Investors were able to make excessive profits by following the stock recommendations produced by the securities firm.

The inefficiency of the Hong Kong market could be largely due to its speculative nature, the disclosure of insufficient information, and the weakness of the security analysis profession. To improve the efficiency of the market in the long term, we need to improve the standards and strengthen the position of the profession of security analysts. A strong group of security analysts would be able to develop, disclose, and disseminate more information that is useful to investors than at present. Such a group could also exert pressure upon the authorities concerned to disclose more information. The Securities Commission should, at the same time, continue to improve the relevant regulations in order to minimize the opportunities for speculation, which has such a destabilizing effect.

Conclusion

The forthcoming unified stock exchange will operate with one modern floor and a common market discipline. It is a result of the changes which have largely reshaped the Hong Kong market over the past 15 years. Although the unified exchange is not an entirely new body, it will bring a number of benefits which will further strengthen the development of the market. It will:

(a) establish professional standards for stockbrokers by means of competition and qualifications;
(b) exercise greater control over the type and quality of companies seeking a listing;

(c) enhance the scope and speed of dissemination of market and company information;

(d) improve the absorptive capacity of the market and thus achieve a less erratic market;

(e) allow the securities legislation to be more economically and forcibly implemented; and

(f) stimulate more market and securities research which will in the long run increase the overall efficiency of the market.

The favourable settlement of Hong Kong's political future will also enhance the further development of the stock-market. In fact, the Hong Kong stock-market regained the attention of international investors when its stock prices rose by about 50 per cent in the four months after China and Britain signed the agreement which settled the 1997 lease issue on 26 September 1984. China has pledged to leave Hong Kong's capitalist economy and way of life intact for 50 years after 1997. As a Special Administrative Region of China, Hong Kong will have its own locally elected government, civil service, police force and courts. Freedom of speech, of the press, and of movement are guaranteed. The Hong Kong dollar will remain a convertible currency and capital may continue to flow in and out of Hong Kong freely. This sound foundation has removed the uncertainty over Hong Kong's future. In this new environment, the unified stock exchange, with its strengthened regulatory and innovatory powers, will attract more overseas investors and will strengthen Hong Kong's position as an international financial centre.

Notes

1. Szczepanik, Edward, 'Financing the Post-war Economic Growth of Hong Kong', *Far Eastern Economic Review*, 20 December 1956, p. 781.

2. The Hang Seng Index of share prices consists of 33 blue-chip stocks of different industries, which represent about 60 per cent of the total market capitalization value. The base date is 31 July 1964. The Index is compiled on an arithmetic basis, weighted by the market capitalization of each constituent stock.

3. It has been suggested that HK$57 million per month was leaving Hong Kong for investment in the United States. Part of the funds represent transactions on behalf of residents of other South-east Asian countries. See *Far Eastern Economic Review*, 20 October 1966, p. 137.

4. Industrial Bank Committee, 'Report on the Establishment of the Industrial Bank', 1966, mimeo.

5. Companies Ordinance 1932, S.2(1).

6. Companies Law Revision Committee, First Report of the Committee, *The Protection of Investors* (Hong Kong, Government Printer, 1971), Chapter 8.

7. Yu, Kenneth, 'Listing Rules of the New Exchange', paper presented at the Seminar on a Unified Stock Exchange and Capital Market in Hong Kong, 2 March 1983, Hong Kong, p. 2.

8. Fell, Robert, 'The Basic Philosophy Behind the Take-over Code', speech at the Seminar on Take-overs and Mergers, 14 April 1980, Hong Kong, pp. 3–6.

9. Hong Kong Code on Takeovers and Mergers, 1975, paragraphs 1 and 2.

10. Fell (1980), p. 6.

11. Pearson, P.J., 'How Can the Takeovers and Mergers Industry be Improved? An Investor's View', paper presented at the Seminar on Take-overs and Mergers, 14 April 1980, Hong Kong, pp. 7–8.

12. Ang, J. S. and Pohlman, R. A., 'A Note on the Price Behavior of Far Eastern Stocks', *Journal of International Business Studies* (Spring–Summer 1978), pp. 103–7.

13. Law, C. K., 'A Test of the Efficient Market Hypothesis with Respect to the Recent Behavior of the Hong Kong Stock Market', *Developing Economies*, 1982, No. 20, pp. 61–72.

14. Wong, K. A. and Kwong, K. S., 'The Behaviour of Hong Kong Stock Prices', *Applied Economics*, December 1984, No. 16, pp. 905–17.

15. Dawson, S., 'Is the Hong Kong Market Efficient?', *Journal of Portfolio Management* (Spring 1982), pp. 17–20.

5. The Money Market and the Foreign Exchange Market

YAN KI HO

THE money market is an integral and significant part of the financial system. The financial instruments traded in the money market usually have an original maturity of less than one year. The minimum transaction is generally very large and is, therefore, wholesale in nature. It is a very dynamic and exciting market, in which banks, finance companies, brokers, and dealers carry out their day to day transactions. As the major participants in this market are institutions, most small investors are unaware of its existence. The significance of the market lies in the fact that it is predominantly a free and competitive market and can respond to forces of supply and demand in the most efficient way. In this chapter, we will cover in detail two of the major markets which make up the money market in Hong Kong: the inter-institutional market and the Negotiable Certificates of Deposit (NCD) market. Various money market instruments will also be mentioned. We will briefly examine the development and the future prospects of the foreign exchange market in Hong Kong. This market has a close relationship with the money market and its significance stems from Hong Kong's position as a centre for trade and international finance.

The Inter-institutional Market

The Development of the Inter-institutional Market

The Hong Kong inter-institutional market started in the 1960s but, until the 1970s, it operated on a small scale and was used by domestic banks to balance their liquidity position. Banks with surplus funds would lend to banks that were deficient in funds. In the late 1970s, many foreign banks started operating in Hong Kong. This was partly a response to the lifting of the moratorium on bank licences in 1978 and was partly due to the booming economy, especially in the property sector. Most of these foreign institutions were very large international banks. But they lacked a large deposit base because local deposit funds were (and still are) heavily concentrated in a small number of domestic and British banks (the Hongkong and Shanghai Banking Corporation, Hang Seng Bank and Standard Chartered Bank). These banks have been relatively successful in maintaining their share of deposits because they have a wide network of branches and because they can offer a greater variety of banking services than the foreign banks. Thus foreign banks can not depend on their deposit base to finance their earning assets, notably loans to local customers, and they have to resort to inter-bank liabilities to satisfy the demand for loans.

Transactions between borrowing banks and lending banks can be carried out directly or through brokers, who earn commissions from providing such a service. (Brokers do not take any position in the market themselves, in that they buy and sell for their clients but not for their own benefit.) Besides lending to other banks, banks with surplus funds can lend to DTCs or vice versa. There is also a market among the DTCs.

The Activities of the Inter-institutional Market

1. The Inter-bank Market.   The inter-bank market is a market for lending and borrowing between banks. Table 5.1 indicates that, in 1978, the size of this market was very modest, with inter-bank liabilities of about HK$7.7 billion, but inter-bank activities more than doubled to about HK$17.6 billion within one year, in response to the influx of foreign banks (an increase of 128 per cent). By the end of 1984, the total volume of inter-bank liabilities was HK$113.2 billion, with an average annual rate of growth of 56.4 per cent. However, this apparently rapid growth rate may be exaggerated by the depreciation in the value of the Hong Kong dollar. The Government has published data on the currency composition of banking statistics since 1980, so it is possible to compare the growth rate of the total inter-bank liabilities with the inter-bank liabilities in Hong Kong dollars from 1980. Table 5.2 shows the inter-bank liabilities denominated in Hong Kong dollars for the years 1980–4. From 1980 to 1984, the average annual growth rate of the Hong Kong dollar component was only 32.6 per cent compared with a growth rate of 43.4 per cent for the total inter-bank liabilities (Hong Kong dollars and foreign currencies) during the same period. There was, during these years, a consistent decline in the share of the Hong Kong dollar component. This decline was especially pronounced in

Table 5.1 Inter-bank Liabilities 1978–84 (HK$ million)

| End of Year | Demand and Short Notice | | Time Deposits | | Total |
	Value	Per cent of Total	Value	Per cent of Total	
1978	4,588	59.36	3,141	40.64	7,720
1979	8,699	49.34	8,930	50.66	17,629
1980	10,206	38.10	16,579	61.90	26,785
1981	15,303	33.49	30,394	66.51	45,698
1982	19,092	30.56	43,389	69.44	62,481
1983	26.620	31.38	58,213	68.62	84,833
1984	32,090	28.36	81,074	71.64	113,164
Average annual growth rate					
1978–84		38.29%		71.91%	56.44%

Source: Hong Kong Monthly Digest of Statistics (Hong Kong, Census and Statistics Department), various issues.

Table 5.2 The Hong Kong Dollar Component of Inter-bank Liabilities 1980–4 (HK$ million)

End of Year	Demand and Short Notice			Time Deposits			Total	
	Value	Per cent of Total HK$ Liabilities	HK$ Share as Per cent of Total Liabilities*	Value	Per cent of Total HK$ Liabilities	HK$ Share as Per cent of Total Liabilities*	Value	HK$ Share as Per cent of Total Liabilities*
1980	8,210	48.5	80.44	8,732	51.5	52.61	16,933	63.22
1981	10,739	40.2	70.18	15,982	59.8	52.58	26,721	58.47
1982	13,321	36.6	69.77	23,090	63.4	53.22	36,411	58.28
1983	13,889	33.4	52.18	27,654	66.6	47.50	41,543	48.97
1984	15,468	29.6	48.20	36,875	70.4	45.48	52,343	46.25
Average annual growth rate 1980–4	17.16%			43.39%			32.59%	

Note: *These figures represent the share of the Hong Kong dollar component in the corresponding item in Table 5.1.

Source: Hong Kong Monthly Digest of Statistics (Hong Kong, Census and Statistics Department), various issues.

the short-term transactions (the short end) of the market. This decline in the importance of the Hong Kong dollar may reflect the increasing importance of Hong Kong as one of the Asian dollar centres, in which the United States dollar is the principal currency traded. Hong Kong's prominence in this market increased after 1982, when the Hong Kong Government abolished the tax on the interest on foreign currency deposits. Banks making foreign currency loans may need to borrow from other banks which have excess foreign currency funds.

In 1978 and 1979, about half of the inter-bank activities were short term. However, from late 1979, the composition of the maturities of inter-bank liabilities changed. After 1982, short-term liabilities accounted for roughly one-third of the total volume, while long-term liabilities accounted for two-thirds. This may be an indication that from 1982, the banks used the inter-bank market to balance their short-term liquidity position, and also used funds from this market to finance longer-term assets, such as loans.

2. The Inter-DTC Market.   The inter-DTC market is a market for lending and borrowing between DTCs. Table 5.3 shows that the size of this market increased from HK$4.5 billion in 1978 to HK$23.1 billion in 1984, an average annual growth rate of 31.2 per cent. The most rapid growth in the DTC market, as in the inter-bank market, occurred in 1979. In the inter-DTC market, however, unlike the inter-bank market, short-term loans between DTCs gained greater importance until 1982. Short-term liabilities comprised 10.4 per cent of the inter-DTC market in 1978 and reached a peak of 30.1 per cent in 1982. An examination of the Hong Kong dollar component of the inter-DTC market confirms this trend (see Table 5.4). Short-term loans between DTCs in Hong Kong dollars comprised around 40 per cent of the inter-DTC market from 1980 to 1983 but suffered a tremendously rapid fall to 7.58 per cent in 1984.

The large share of the market held by short-term loans in Hong Kong

Table 5.3 Inter-DTC Liabilities 1978–84 (HK$ million)

| End of Year | Demand and Short Notice | | Time Deposits | | |
	Value	Per cent of Total	Value	Per cent of Total	Total
1978	468	10.36	4,051	89.64	4,519
1979	1,045	14.96	5,942	85.04	6,987
1980	2,286	22.61	7,823	77.39	10,109
1981	3,937	26.35	11,005	73.65	14,941
1982	4,904	30.12	11,379	69.88	16,283
1983	2,995	22.74	10,178	77.26	13,173
1984	3,654	15.83	19,436	84.17	23,090
Average annual growth rate					
1978–84	40.85%		29.87%		31.24%

Source: *Hong Kong Monthly Digest of Statistics* (Hong Kong, Census and Statistics Department), various issues.

Table 5.4 The Hong Kong Dollar Component of Inter-DTC Liabilities 1980–4 (HK$ million)

End of Year	Demand and Short Notice			Time Deposits			Total	
	Value	Per cent of Total HK$ Liabilities	HK$ Share as Per cent of Total Liabilities*	Value	Per cent of Total HK$ Liabilities	HK$ Share as Per cent of Total Liabilities*	Value	HK$ Share as Per cent of Total Liabilities*
1980	1,190	36.13	52.06	2,104	63.87	26.90	3,294	32.58
1981	1,992	42.20	50.60	2,728	57.80	24.79	4,720	31.59
1982	1,800	42.43	36.70	2,442	57.57	21.46	4,242	26.05
1983	1,003	37.20	33.49	1,693	62.80	16.63	2,696	20.47
1984	926	7.58	25.34	11,292	92.40	58.10	12,218	52.91
Average annual growth rate 1980–4		– 6.08%			52.21%			38.78%

Note: *These figures represent the share of the Hong Kong dollar component in the corresponding item in Table 5.3.

Source: Hong Kong Monthly Digest of Statistics (Hong Kong, Census and Statistics Department), various issues.

dollars between DTCs may have been due to the three-tier banking system which came into effect in July 1981. The new system required registered DTCs to accept short-term deposits with a maturity of at least three months. It allowed registered DTCs a transition period of two years to meet the new requirement. The new system did not impose any maturity requirement on licensed DTCs (please see Chapter 2 for details). Thus the effect of the new system was that registered DTCs had to meet their liquidity needs during the transition period by borrowing heavily in the money market. This was particularly true for the smaller registered DTCs which did not have a close affiliation with any banks and therefore had to borrow from other DTCs (including the licensed DTCs and DTCs which were subsidiaries of banks). The rapid fall in the total number of short-term transactions which occurred in 1984 may indicate that the DTCs had successfully survived adjustment in their asset portfolios.

Another feature in Table 5.4 worthy of mention is the fall of the Hong Kong dollar component in all inter-DTC transactions (both short- and long-term) until 1983. At the end of 1983, the Hong Kong dollar component accounted for only 20.47 per cent of the total transactions. This indicates that foreign currency was being more actively traded as Hong Kong's role in the Asian dollar market grew. However, there was a decisive reversal of this trend in 1984 when the share of time deposit transactions in Hong Kong dollars increased to 58.10 per cent. There are two possible reasons for this growth. First, the restoration of confidence in the political future of Hong Kong as the Sino-British talks progressed during 1984 strengthened the value of the Hong Kong dollar, and investors switched their deposits from foreign currencies to Hong Kong dollars. Second, political uncertainty and slow economic growth in countries like Indonesia and the Philippines caused a flow of funds from these countries to Hong Kong for short-term gain. (Such funds are known as 'hot' money.)

3. The Bank–DTC Market.   The bank–DTC market is the market for lending and borrowing between banks and DTCs. Table 5.5 shows that the banks' liabilities to the DTCs increased from HK$6.9 billion in 1978 to HK$48.3 billion in 1984, with an average annual growth rate of 38.2 per cent. The DTCs' liabilities to the banks experienced a much larger average annual growth of 53.7 per cent during the same period.

The Hong Kong currency component of the banks' liabilities to the DTCs fell from 85.12 per cent in 1980 to 56.46 per cent in 1984. This fall indicates that a more mature short-term foreign currency market was developing in Hong Kong. However, although the DTCs' liabilities to the banks grew rapidly, the local currency component of this item remained at around 30 per cent, reflecting the DTCs' heavy dependence on banks for their local currency requirements.

From 1978 to 1981, the banks were net debtors to the DTCs, and this reflects the banks' use of their subsidiary DTCs to attract deposits. However the trend started to reverse in 1982. The DTCs owed the banks a net amount of HK$21.3 billion in 1982 and that amount increased to HK$35.8 billion in 1984. This increase was due to the establishment of the three-tier banking system which made the DTCs more dependent on the banks for funds.

Table 5.5 The Bank–DTC Market 1978–84 (HK$ million)

End of Year	Banks' Liabilities to DTCs		DTC's Liabilities to Banks		Value of Banks' Net Liabilities to DTCs
	Value	Per cent Share of HK$ Component	Value	Per cent Share of HK$ Component	
1978	6,929	n/a	6,386	n/a	543
1979	20,029	n/a	11,463	n/a	8,566
1980	28,975	85.12	21,288	29.83	7,687
1981	42,550	81.79	31,120	32.52	11,930
1982	35,231	63.82	56,494	35.61	−21,263
1983	46,904	58.79	81,751	30.79	−34,847
1984	48,318	56.46	84,120	26.68	−35,784
Average annual growth rate 1978–84		38.22%		53.67%	

Note: n/a = not available.

Source: Hong Kong Monthly Digest of Statistics (Hong Kong, Census and Statistics Department), various issues.

Certificates of Deposit

A Certificate of Deposit (CD) is a form of time deposit. A time deposit may be in the form of a certificate issued by a financial institution. Such a certificate states that deposits of a specified value are accepted, and that the issuer promises to pay to the holder of the certificate the amount of the principal and the interest on the maturity date of the certificate. A CD differs from a time deposit in that it can be negotiable or sold to another party before the maturity date. Thus the funds invested are not 'locked in' until maturity. CDs are therefore often called Negotiable Certificates of Deposit (NCDs).

The Development of the NCD Market

The first CDs in the world financial markets were issued in the 1960s. In the United States, the first domestic NCDs, which were backed by a dealer commitment to develop a secondary market, were introduced in 1961. Since then, the sale of CDs has become a major source of funds for banks in the leading money centres. In the United Kingdom, the first NCD was issued in 1968. The first NCD issued in Hong Kong was offered by a merchant bank, Slater Walker Hutchison, in February 1973. The NCD was in units of between HK$0.25 million and HK$2.0 million, and was for periods of 93 days and over. This issue was made available to banks, financial institutions, and corporations. Although other merchant banks intended to follow suit during the same year, an active NCD market was not established until 1977. In that year Wardley Ltd. introduced a fixed-rate NCD worth HK$50 million in denominations of between HK$100,000 and HK$1 million, and for terms of between three months and five years. Wardley Ltd. also undertook to develop a secondary market.

The first floating-rate NCD was launched in September 1977 by Chase Manhattan Bank. The amount of the issue was HK$100 million for a duration of five years, in denominations of between HK$50,000 and HK$1 million. The interest rate was adjustable every six months to correspond to the average best lending rate (set by the Hongkong and Shanghai Banking Corporation). Chase Manhattan Bank N.A. promised to pay an interest rate of not less than 5.25 per cent. After 1977, other large multinational banks such as Citibank N.A., Bank of America N.T. & S.A., Banque Nationale de Paris, and Bank of Tokyo Ltd. have issued NCDs. Foreign banks and local financial institutions, including Wardley Ltd., Jardine Fleming & Company Ltd., Sun Hung Kai Bank Ltd., Sumitomo Bank Ltd., BNP Finance (Hong Kong) Ltd., BA Asia Ltd., and Manufacturers Hanover Trust Co., agreed to develop a secondary market.

All the CDs issued after 1977 were on a negotiable basis and were issued through public channels. The total volume of Hong Kong dollar NCDs issued since 1977 is about HK$7,000 million. Official statistics on outstanding NCD issues have been available since the end of 1980. In that year, it was reported that the total outstanding Hong Kong dollar NCDs issued by both banks and DTCs amounted to HK$1,881 million, with an average annual growth rate of 33.4 per cent.

Table 5.6 indicates that the outstanding Hong Kong dollar NCDs experienced a rapid growth in 1981 with a growth rate of 88 per cent. The growth rate slowed a little in 1982, to 50 per cent growth. The rapid increase in Hong Kong dollar NCDs issued indicated that the banks, especially the foreign banks, were actively seeking funds through this channel. During 1983, fewer NCDs were issued, for three reasons. First, the cost of attracting funds was rising, secondly the demand was weak and, finally, the rapid depreciation of the Hong Kong dollar (as a result of the political uncertainty about the future of Hong Kong) made investing in NCDs unattractive, because of the currency risk.

Although the value of the Hong Kong dollar stabilized in 1984, the environment was still not particularly favourable for the NCD market. This was because there was a weak demand for loans in Hong Kong at that time, so that the banks were highly liquid and therefore did not have a strong incentive to attract funds by issuing NCDs (which is a more costly method of attracting deposits than regular time deposits).

The interest rate agreement between the banks (described in Chapter 1) does not apply to bank deposits with maturities over 15 months. The maturity of the NCDs issued by banks is usually longer than 15 months. Thus the issuing banks need not comply with the interest rate agreement. Instruments paying market interest rates were increasingly attractive in the late 1970s and early 1980s when the inflation rate was usually greater than 10 per cent. This rate was usually higher than the bank deposit rates offered under the interest rate agreement.

There is also an NCD market denominated in United States dollars in Hong Kong. The first United States dollar NCDs were issued in May 1980 when European Asian Bank and Fuji Bank Ltd. each issued an NCD of US$20 million, for four years and three years respectively. Since then, several large banks, notably the Japanese banks, have issued United States dollar NCDs. Table 5.6 shows that the average annual growth rate of the United States dollar NCDs which were outstanding from 1980 to 1984 was about 77.5 per cent. The growth in the first three years was especially rapid, with an average annual growth rate of 163 per cent. During 1983 and 1984

Table 5.6 The Hong Kong Dollar and Foreign Currency NCDs Outstanding 1980–4 (HK$ million)

End of Year	Hong Kong Dollar			Foreign Currency		
	Bank	DTC	Total	Bank	DTC	Total
1980	1,252	629	1,881	789	102	891
1981	2,568	975	3,543	2,237	455	2,692
1982	4,177	1,141	5,318	5,752	413	6,165
1983	4,549	868	5,417	6,817	1,060	7,877
1984	4,838	1,124	5,962	6,765	2,074	8,839
Average annual growth rate						
1980–4	40.2%	15.6%	33.4%	71.1%	112%	77.5%

Source: Hong Kong Monthly Digest of Statistics (Hong Kong, Census and Statistics Department), various issues.

this growth rate slowed down because the syndication loan market declined during that period and the banks were therefore less eager to issue NCDs to attract funds.

Hong Kong formerly issued fewer NCDs than Singapore, in terms of the total number and the value. However, this situation was reversed in 1984 when the financial institutions in Hong Kong made 13 issues of United States dollar NCDs with a total value of US$350 million, compared with 11 issues with a total value of US$300 million in Singapore.

Maturity and the Interest Rate Structure

Most of the Hong Kong dollar NCDs issued over the past four years had a maturity period of three years. Only a few issues had maturity periods of four to five years, for example, the five-year HK$50 million NCD issued by Bank of Tokyo Ltd. in December 1979, the five-year HK$200 million NCD issued by Citibank N.A. in November 1981, and the four-year HK$150 million NCD issued by Barclays Bank International Ltd. in November 1982. One relatively long-term NCD (of seven years) was issued in early 1983 by Banque Nationale de Paris. Some NCDs were also issued with much shorter maturities, and in smaller denominations, to attract small investors. For example, in June 1982 Chase Manhattan Bank N.A. issued an NCD with a maturity of 15 months plus 3 days and with a denomination of HK$5,000 to HK$50,000. The United States dollar NCDs also generally had a maturity of three to four years.

The widely fluctuating interest rates in the 1970s caused floating-rate instruments to replace fixed-rate instruments in most financial markets, including the NCD market. Today, floating-rate NCDs predominate.

The interest rate offered by most NCDs issued in Hong Kong is pegged either to the inter-bank rate or to the best lending rate, with a margin of between 0.25 per cent and 0.375 per cent over the rate to which it is pegged. The interest rate is adjustable monthly. An NCD is thus similar in some ways to a loan from a depositor to a bank, with a roll-over period of one month. It has become increasingly common to price NCDs according to the Hong Kong Inter-bank Offering Rate (HIBOR), and most of the NCDs issued in 1983 and 1984 were priced with margins of between 0.25 per cent and 0.375 per cent over the one-month HIBOR. The interest rate offered on United States dollar NCDs is usually pegged to the six-month London Inter-bank Offering Rate (LIBOR), with a margin of from 0.1873 per cent to 0.3125 per cent, and it is adjustable every six months.

The Allocation of NCDs

Table 5.7 shows that in 1980, 12.6 per cent of the outstanding Hong Kong dollar NCDs issued by banks and 1.3 per cent of the outstanding Hong Kong dollar NCDs issued by DTCs were held by banks. By 1984, these proportions had increased significantly, to 34.3 per cent for outstanding bank issues and 18.9 per cent for outstanding DTC issues. These proportions are, however, low in comparison with the NCD market in the United Kingdom, where the banking system holds over half of the NCDs issued.

Table 5.7 The Allocation of Hong Kong Dollar NCDs among Different Holders (per cent)

| | End of 1980 | | End of 1984 | |
	HK Dollar	Foreign Currency	HK Dollar	Foreign Currency
Issued by banks in Hong Kong				
Banks	12.6	4.6	34.3	19.9
DTCs	42.5	24.8	39.4	29.3
Public	44.9	70.6	26.3	50.8
Issued by DTCs in Hong Kong				
Banks	1.3	33.0	18.9	3.0
DTCs	35.0	35.9	33.6	29.4
Public	63.7	31.1	47.5	67.6

Source: Hong Kong Monthly Digest of Statistics (Hong Kong, Census and Statistics Department), various issues.

The increase in the NCDs held by banks was perhaps due to the fact that, as from 1983, locally issued NCDs were able to qualify as specified liquid assets, provided that the NCD component of liquid assets held by a bank was not greater than 2 per cent of its deposit liabilities. The proportion of Hong Kong dollar NCDs held by the DTCs remained fairly stable at around 30 to 40 per cent. The relative stability of this sector of the market may have been due to the ability of the DTCs to invest in NCDs for liquidity purposes or to trade actively in NCDs, aiming for capital gains.

Between 1980 and 1984, banks increased their holdings of the foreign currency NCDs issued by banks. These increases may indicate that the banks were employing more foreign currency NCDs to fulfil the minimum liquidity requirement against their deposit liabilities (see Chapter 1). However, the banks also decreased their holdings of DTC issues substantially. The general public held substantial holdings of foreign currency issues. About half of the bank issues and more than half of the DTC issues were held by the public. As the foreign currency issues were all of large denominations, it is very likely that these holdings were mostly held by institutional investors. Again, the share of foreign currency NCDs held by the DTCs was relatively stable at around 30 per cent.

The Secondary Market

The secondary market is a market for the buying and selling of NCDs before they reach maturity. In a secondary market, holders of NCDs can sell, while potential investors can buy, before the NCDs reach maturity. By boosting the liquidity of the NCDs, the secondary market can increase the marketability of newly issued NCDs.

At the time of writing, some 30 institutions have agreed to be the market-makers for NCDs. These institutions consist mainly of the issuing banks, the DTCs, and the dealers who quote the rates to issuers and investors. The market-makers include local institutions as well as foreign institutions. Recently, the Bank of China also participated in the market as an underwriter and market-maker. However, the secondary market is relatively inactive. Very few of the NCDs purchased (about 5 per cent) were traded before maturity.

Several reasons have been put forward to explain the inactive secondary market. One is that local investors have no experience in NCD trading. Another is that dealers are reluctant to hold a large volume of NCDs during periods of volatile interest rates, as they wish to avoid the risk of capital loss. They would rather stay in the more traditional markets such as the inter-bank market and the foreign exchange market. However, this argument is not supported by the stabilization of interest rates in late 1984 and early 1985. Some commentators have also suggested that the 2 per cent liquidity constraint imposed by the Government limits the liquidity of NCDs to some extent and hence the trading activities in the secondary market. The interest rate agreement, which forbids the issue of short-term NCDs (of maturity of less than 15 months), is also cited as one of the factors hindering the development of the secondary market. All the above factors are relevant, but the most important cause is the lack of support by the large banks, which own the bulk of the deposits in Hong Kong.

One way to stimulate the development of the secondary market without the support of the large deposit banks is to develop a discount house similar to that in the United Kingdom and Singapore. A discount house can attract idle short-term funds from banks, DTCs, large corporations, and the Government, and can use these funds to buy short-term financial instruments including NCDs. A discount house can quote 'bid' (buying) and 'ask' (selling) rates for different financial instruments and hence work as a market-maker. By centralizing buying and selling activities in several discount houses, which have expertise in discounting financial instruments, transaction costs can be lowered. By pooling idle funds from various institutions, discount houses can boost secondary market trading activities.

Some Problems and Prospects of the NCD Market

While the interest rate agreement remains in force, small investors will be penalized because they will have to invest in traditional deposit accounts. A further restriction will be imposed on small investors in March 1986, when the minimum deposit per account that registered DTCs can accept will be raised to HK$100,000. Thus small investors with less than HK$100,000 will be prevented from obtaining higher returns through this channel. Given these constraints, NCDs of small denominations will become more attractive to small investors. NCDs of large denominations may not have the same appeal while the secondary market is not well developed, because banks and licensed DTCs can both offer freely competitive rates for deposits of $500,000 or more.

The supply of NCDs may remain small, because of the banks' unwillingness to issue NCDs while the banking sector is highly liquid, as it has been since 1984. However, as the other sectors of the economy experience the rapid economic growth which was initially led by the export sector, the demand for funds will increase, and the banks will then be more willing to attract funds through issuing NCDs.

An Example of an NCD Sale

The above examination of the operation of the NCD market may be complemented by an example illustrating the procedure of buying and selling an NCD. The sale proceeds of an NCD can be calculated by the formula:

$$\text{Proceeds} = \text{Principal} \times \frac{1 + (\text{Issued rate} \times \text{Maturity in days}/365)}{1 + (\text{Quoted yield} \times \text{Days to run}/365)}.$$

Assume that an NCD with a maturity of one year (365 days) is bought for HK\$500,000 and that the interest rate stated on the NCD is 10 per cent per annum. Let an investor sell the NCD after three calendar months (92 days). Thus there are 273 days to maturity (days to run). At the date of sale the interest rate on a nine-month NCD is 8 per cent per annum.

$$\text{Proceeds} = \text{HK\$500,000} \times \frac{1 + (0.10 \times 365/365)}{1 + (0.08 \times 273/365)}$$
$$= \text{HK\$518,948.}$$

Therefore the effective yield from the sale of the NCD is as shown in the following calculation.

$$\text{Effective yield} = \frac{\text{HK\$18,948}}{\text{HK\$500,000}} \times \frac{365}{92} \times 100 \text{ per cent}$$
$$= 15.03 \text{ per cent.}$$

Thus the seller of the NCD will realize a capital gain, with a decrease in the interest rate. On the other hand, the buyer of the NCD will obtain the net proceeds as shown in Table 5.8.

Thus the effective yield for the buyer is as shown below.

$$\text{Effective yield} = \frac{\text{HK\$31,052}}{\text{HK\$518,948}} \times \frac{365}{273} \times 100 \text{ per cent}$$
$$= 8.00 \text{ per cent.}$$

This is exactly the same rate as at the time of the transaction.

Other Financial Instruments

There are other financial markets in which specific negotiable instruments are traded. These instruments take various forms, and include Commercial Paper, Banker's Acceptances and bonds. Although their role in the Hong

Table 5.8 The Net Proceeds of the Purchase of an NCD

	HK$
Principal	500,000
Interest for one year	50,000
Less amount invested	518,948
Net proceeds	31,052

Kong money market is not very important, their development is gaining momentum. Thus a brief discussion of these markets is justified.

Commercial Paper (CP) consists of short-term, unsecured notes. They are issued by large non-financial business firms which have very high credit ratings. The first CP in Hong Kong was issued in 1977 by the Mass Transit Railway Corporation (MTRC), in the form of negotiable bills of exchange to the value of HK$500 million. It had a maturity of 360 days. Since then, the MTRC has dominated the CP market. Recent CP issues by the MTRC had a maturity of 90 days and were sold at a discount from the redemption price. Other companies which have made CP issues include Sun Hung Kai Securities, Cheung Kong (Holdings) Ltd., Hongkong Land, and Jardine Matheson. The outstanding amount of CP in circulation at the time of writing is estimated to be over HK$1,000 million. The minimum denomination of a CP issue usually ranges from HK$500,000 to HK$1 million. Thus institutional investors dominate the market. The interest rate offered on CP is usually close to the HIBOR, which is generally below the best lending rate. The lower interest rate of CP is attractive to large corporations seeking to raise capital, as they are able to obtain funds more cheaply than by borrowing from banks. At the same time, monetary institutions seem to have found CP an attractive investment instrument. (It was reported in the *1984 Economic Background* that holdings of CP by monetary institutions rose by 20 per cent in 1984.)

Prior to 1984, it was thought that the issue of CP violated the DTC Ordinance, because it was considered that taking funds from the general public in the form of a CP issue was quite similar to taking deposits from the public. Corporations wishing to issue CP thus had to apply for exemption from the Ordinance, a process which could take a few weeks, and this could hinder the company from launching an issue at the most favourable time. However, in view of the rapid development of the CP market, the Government announced in November 1984 that it did not regard the issuing of CP as equivalent to taking public deposits, and thus it made the issuing of CP perfectly legal.

Another market that has recently developed is the market in Banker's Acceptances (BAs). A BA is a bill of exchange which is accepted by banks. It is drawn by a party to a transaction and is made payable to the bearer. Traditionally a BA was created in connection with an import or an export. However, a new form of BA was created in July 1979, when Citibank N.A. introduced BAs which were drawn by Citibank's wholly owned subsidiary and accepted by Citibank. This form of BA was thus a paper solely guaranteed by the bank. BAs are usually denominated in multiples of HK$500,000. BAs are sold at a discount which is based on the prevailing money market rate.

An example may help to illustrate the process of purchasing a BA. If an investor wishes to invest HK$500,000 for 30 days, and if the market interest rate is 8 per cent, the purchase price of the BA is as shown in the following calculation.

$$
\begin{aligned}
\text{Purchase price} &= \frac{\text{Face value} \times 365}{365 + (\text{market rate} \times \text{days to maturity})} \\
&= \frac{\text{HK\$500,000} \times 365}{365 + (0.08 \times 30)} \\
&= \text{HK\$496,734.}
\end{aligned}
$$

Unlike the BA market in the United States and the United Kingdom, the secondary market for BAs in Hong Kong is very inactive. The Deputy Secretary for Monetary Affairs suggested, Latter (1984), that this may be because, in the Hong Kong BA market, there are no open-market operations (the buying or selling of securities by monetary authorities for the purpose of controlling the money supply), whereas, in the United States and the United Kingdom markets, there are.

In order to illustrate the procedure of a secondary market deal, an example is given, using the information in the example above, and assuming that the investor decides to sell the BA on the tenth day after purchasing it, and that the market interest rate at the time of the sale is 7.5 per cent. The sale price of the BA and the effective yield are shown in the following calculations.

$$
\begin{aligned}
\text{Sale price} &= \frac{\text{HK\$500,000} \times 365}{365 + (0.075 \times 20)} \\
&= \text{HK\$497,954.}
\end{aligned}
$$

$$
\begin{aligned}
\text{Effective yield} &= \frac{\text{HK\$497,954} - \text{HK\$496,734}}{\text{HK\$496,734}} \times \frac{365}{10} \times 100 \text{ per cent} \\
&= 8.96 \text{ per cent.}
\end{aligned}
$$

The effective yield is higher than the original market interest rate of 8 per cent because the investor has obtained capital gains due to the decrease in the interest rate.

A further financial instrument is a bond. Bonds are debt instruments with relatively long maturities of 5–15 years. Because the Hong Kong Government is financially sound, there are very few government bonds outstanding. The first government bond was issued in 1975. It was a five-year bond in the amount of HK$250 million and was repaid in 1980. The second government bond was issued in 1984 with a maturity of five years in the amount of HK$1,000 million. Public corporations such as the MTRC and private companies such as Hong Kong Electric Co., Hongkong Land, and Hutchison Whampoa Ltd. also floated bonds in the market. It has been estimated that the value of outstanding company bonds in the Hong Kong market at the time of writing is over HK$1,000 million. The secondary market for bonds is not very active. Because of their long maturities it is inappropriate to consider bonds as money market instruments. Money markets are formed with securities that have a year or less remaining until maturity.

The Foreign Exchange Market

Foreign exchange dealing is one of the major operations of commercial banks. Hong Kong has one of the most efficient foreign exchange (FX) markets in the Far East. This is one of the many factors that has attracted foreign banks to Hong Kong and which has strengthened the role of Hong Kong as a financial centre. The final section of this chapter will trace the development of the Hong Kong foreign exchange market, its importance, and its future prospects.

The Development of the Market

In 1941, Hong Kong became a member of the sterling area and maintained a fixed parity of HK$16 to the pound sterling. Until 1972, when the pound sterling was floated, there was an exchange control system, which was intended to prevent a currency drain from the sterling area. However, because of Hong Kong's heavy dependence on foreign trade, through which Hong Kong could earn a large volume of United States dollars, the effect of the exchange control system was not very stringent. Thus, in addition to the formal controlled market, there was also a free market for United States dollars and other convertible currencies.

Before 1973, the foreign exchange market was relatively inactive. Before that year, in order to take part in foreign exchange dealings, banks and brokers had to be authorized by the Exchange Banks Association (now known as the Hong Kong Association of Banks). The foreign exchange rates for selling and buying (ask and bid rates) were jointly determined by the authorized exchange banks and the authorized exchange brokers. The range of 'agreed merchant rates' was very great: the spread of bid offers could sometimes exceed 500 basis points (100 basis points equal 1 per cent). However, rates were also quoted in the free market where they had a more limited range ('a finer spread') than the controlled rate. After 1973, the nominal exchange control scheme was abolished, and the foreign exchange market began to grow.

In 1965, there were only 78 licensed banks and six firms of brokers of local origin in Hong Kong. The first international firm of brokers joined the Hong Kong market in late 1972. The floating of the Hong Kong dollar in late 1974, together with the economic recovery in 1976 which was led by the growth of exports, created a favourable environment for the foreign exchange market. However, the foreign exchange market did not expand greatly until 1978, when the lifting of the moratorium on new bank licences caused an influx of foreign banks.

The newly arrived foreign institutions which came to Hong Kong after 1978 stimulated foreign exchange dealings. There were two main reasons for the foreign banks' interest in foreign exchange dealings. Firstly, they had expertise in such dealings. Secondly, some of these foreign institutions had a weak local currency deposit base at the beginning, so that they could not participate strongly in traditional lending activities, such as trade financing. Foreign exchange dealing enabled these institutions to make profits without committing themselves only to lending.

The Participants in the Market

Foreign exchange dealings take place in the Hong Kong inter-bank foreign exchange market and in trading between the foreign exchange markets of Hong Kong and other financial centres located in the same time zone, such as Tokyo and Singapore. There are also active overnight markets in London, New York, San Francisco and Frankfurt.

The major participants in the foreign exchange market are banks, DTCs, and large corporations. There were 140 banks and 343 DTCs in Hong Kong at the end of 1984, but not all of them were trading in the market. The most active participants included Citibank N.A., the Hongkong and Shanghai Banking Corporation, Morgan Guaranty Trust Company, Bank of Tokyo Ltd., Bank of China, Swiss Bank Corporation, Bankers Trust Company, Chase Manhattan Bank N.A., Bank of America N.T. & S.A., Hang Seng Bank, Midland Bank PLC, Jardine Fleming & Company Ltd., and Wardley Ltd. Foreign banks were among the most active participants.

Table 5.9 provides a breakdown of the most active participants in Hong Kong's foreign exchange market, in terms of the currency traded. The table does not list the United States dollar because all currencies must be traded against the United States dollar and it is, therefore, the most actively traded currency for all participants. Each bank, in general, deals actively in the currency of its home country. The Bank of China is usually a net buyer of United States dollars, because China has to convert her Hong Kong dollar earnings into United States dollars in order to purchase imports.

The foreign exchange participants can deal directly with each other, or indirectly through a broker. Brokers are middlemen between the two parties to a deal. They earn commissions and do not take any position in the market. Brokers provide an important information centre for the foreign exchange market. They collect bid and offer rates from various clients and then channel this information to other participants, enabling them to make the best deal (or 'the finest spread'). Fig. 5.1 shows the relationships among the participating brokers and financial institutions in the Hong Kong foreign exchange market.

There are 11 firms of brokers in Hong Kong, 6 of them from overseas. These 11 firms form the Hong Kong Foreign Exchange and Deposit Brokers' Association. Membership of this association must be officially recognized by the Hong Kong Association of Banks. Brokers in Hong Kong seem to play a

Table 5.9 The Active Market Participants and the Currencies Traded in the Hong Kong Market

Currency	Participants
Deutschmark	Bank of America N.T. & S.A., Bank of Tokyo Ltd., Bankers Trust Company, Chase Manhattan Bank N.A., Citibank N.A., Credit Suisse, Morgan Guaranty Trust Company of New York, Swiss Bank Corporation, Union Bank of Switzerland.
Japanese yen	Bank of Tokyo Ltd., Bankers Trust Company, Fuji Bank Ltd., Mitsubishi Bank Ltd.
Hong Kong dollar	Bank of America N.T. & S.A., Bank of China, Chase Manhattan Bank N.A., Citibank N.A., Hang Lung Bank Ltd., Hang Seng Bank Ltd., Hongkong and Shanghai Banking Corporation, Jardine Fleming & Company Ltd., Ka Wah Bank Ltd., Overseas Trust Bank Ltd., Wardley Ltd.
Sterling	Barclays Bank International Ltd., Citibank N.A., Hongkong and Shanghai Banking Corporation, Midland Bank PLC, Morgan Guaranty Trust Company of New York, other European banks.
Swiss franc	Bankers Trust Company, Citibank N.A., Credit Suisse, Swiss Bank Corporation, Union Bank of Switzerland.

Source: Mak (1983).

less important role in the foreign exchange market than in other financial centres such as London and New York. This is probably because most of the foreign exchange dealings are done directly between the banks. Less than 20 per cent of foreign exchange deals in Hong Kong are done through brokers, and most Hong Kong dollar dealings are done directly. In view of the decreasing volume of business, the Brokers' Association recently lowered its commission charges.

The major benefit of direct dealing, of course, is that no brokerage commission is incurred. An institution wishing to make a deal with another institution must obtain prior credit approval, which is called a credit line, from that institution. Normally the two institutions can deal up to the limit designated by the credit line.

The Mechanics and Activities of the Market

All convertible currencies are traded in the Hong Kong foreign exchange market. All currencies have to be traded against the United States dollar and the broad lot (the minimum trading volume) is US$1 million. Thus, if a bank wants to sell sterling to purchase yen, it must first buy United States dollars and then use the United States dollars to purchase yen. The United States dollar is thus by far the most actively traded currency and all rates are

Fig. 5.1 The Relationships among the Participants in the Hong Kong Foreign Exchange Market

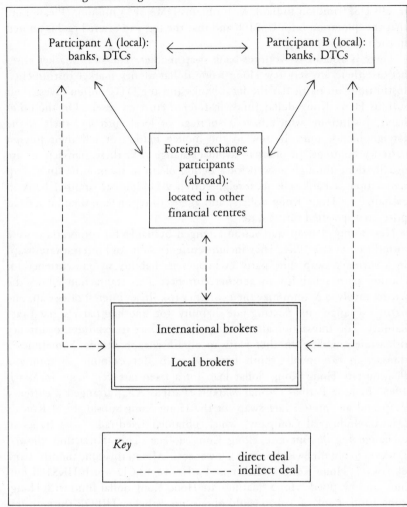

Source: Mak (1983).

quoted against the United States dollar. After the United States dollar, the most actively traded currencies in the market include the Deutschmark, the yen, the Hong Kong dollar, sterling, and the Swiss franc, with the Deutschmark and the yen accounting for the major share of the market. The role of sterling has gradually declined since 1972, when the link between the Hong Kong dollar and sterling was severed. At the time of writing, sterling's market share may be less than 10 per cent.

In the foreign exchange market, the prices of different currencies are usually quoted in the form of 'bid' and 'offered' prices. A bank's 'bid' price is its buying price and the 'offered' price is its selling price. An example illustrates the mechanics of the bid and offer process.

The bid and offer rate for Deutschmarks (DM) given by Bank X are as follows: (a) bid: 3.3255; (b) offered: 3.3275. Therefore if another bank wishes to buy US$1 million from Bank X it must pay DM3.3275 million. If it sells US$1 million to Bank X, it obtains DM3.3255 million. (Please note that the quotation is for US$100 and that the bid and offered rate is quoted in the form 55–75.)

There is also an active inter-bank swap market. The swap market arises because there are very few Hong Kong dollar money market instruments. Institutions, in particular the local banks and the DTCs, often invest their surplus Hong Kong dollar funds in foreign currency assets. On the other hand, institutions which have a shortage of local currency, such as the foreign banks, must borrow in the money market or sell their foreign currency holdings. In order to avoid exchange risk, these transactions are usually done through a swap for a period of up to six months. In a swap transaction, a bank sells its foreign currency holdings to another bank in exchange for Hong Kong dollars, and agrees to repurchase them at a fixed price on a specified future date.

New forms of swap transaction arranged by banks for corporations were introduced in late 1984. They include currency swap and interest rate swap. In a currency swap, one party exchanges its liability in one currency for another party's liability in another currency. This transaction allows the parties involved to minimize their currency risk. In an interest rate swap, one party exchanges its floating-rate liability for another party's fixed-rate liability. This transaction allows one party to reduce its exposure to currency risk while enabling another party to obtain cheaper funds. Sometimes a transaction can involve both types of swap, for example, swapping a floating-rate Hong Kong dollar loan for a fixed-rate yen loan. In March 1985, Banque Paribas Capital Markets (Paribas Asia) arranged a currency swap and an interest rate swap for the Hong Kong subsidiary of Korea's Daewoo Industrial Company, which obtained fixed-rate Swiss francs in exchange for floating-rate Hong Kong dollars. This transaction allowed Daewoo to obtain Swiss francs at a lower cost. Also in the same month, Bank of Tokyo's Hong Kong branch raised a fixed-rate CD worth HK$100 million, and swapped it for a floating-rate Hong Kong dollar fund with Hongkong Land. Bank of Tokyo could obtain funds below HIBOR through this arrangement while Hongkong Land could minimize its interest rate risk. A similar swap transaction was arranged between Dai-Ichi Kangyo Bank's Hong Kong branch and Hongkong Land in April 1985. Although such transactions are new to Hong Kong, they have been received well and are gaining popularity.

In addition to such inter-bank swap transactions, the process of interest arbitrage is constantly taking place in the market. The example below illustrates the arbitrage process. One may assume that an investor has HK$100,000 to invest over a period of three months. He has two options: (a) invest in a three-month Hong Kong dollar deposit which pays 7 per cent; (b) invest in a three-month United States dollar deposit which pays 10 per cent.

There is an interest rate differential of 3 per cent between these options but there is also an exchange rate risk of investing in a United States dollar deposit. The return from the Hong Kong dollar deposit is shown in the following calculation (where 'P' = principal and 'i' = Hong Kong dollar interest rate).

Return on HK$ deposit = P × (1 + i) × (90/360)
    = HK$100,000 × (1 + 0.07) × (90/360)
    = HK$101,750.

Assume that the spot rate (S) is US$1 = HK$8.00. The return in terms of the United States dollar is shown in the following calculation (where 'i*' = United States dollar interest rate).

Return on US$ deposit = (P/S) × (1 + i*) × (90/360)
    = (US$100,000/8) × (1 + 0.10) × (90 × 360)
    = US$12,812.5.

If the Hong Kong dollar appreciates to US$1 = HK$7.90 after three months, the return in terms of Hong Kong dollars is as follows.

Return on US$ deposit = HK$12,812.5 × 7.9
    = HK$101,218.8.

This return is less than is made from a Hong Kong dollar deposit, even if the United States dollar interest rate is higher. One way to protect a United States dollar return is to cover the foreign exchange risk through a forward contract, which guarantees that the investor will be able to sell a given volume of United States dollars for Hong Kong dollars at a fixed rate, called the forward rate (F), three months later. If F = 7.95, the United States dollar return, quoted in terms of Hong Kong dollars, is equal to (HK$12,812.5 × 7.95) = HK$101,859.4. This is higher than the return on a Hong Kong dollar deposit.

The above transaction with a forward cover guarantees a profit of HK$109.4. Such a guarantee may induce more investors to invest in United States dollar deposits. If this should happen, it will raise the interest rate in Hong Kong and will cause the spot United States dollar to appreciate further, as more Hong Kong dollar funds are converted to United States dollars. Moreover, the forward United States dollar rate will depreciate as more forward selling of United States dollars or forward buying of Hong Kong dollars occurs. Therefore the return on United States dollar deposits will be lowered. A state of equilibrium will eventually be reached, since there will be no incentive to shift funds from Hong Kong dollars to United States dollars if returns on both are the same.

Now suppose that the Hong Kong interest rate rises to 8 per cent and that the forward rate changes to 7.961. The return on the Hong Kong dollar deposit will be as follows.

Return on HK$ deposit = HK$100,000 × (1 + 0.08 × 90/360)
    = HK$102,000.

The return on the United States dollar deposit (expressed in Hong Kong dollars) will be as follows.

Return on US$ deposit = (HK$100,000/8) × (1 + 0.10 × 90/360) × 7.961
= HK$102,000.

These calculations are expressed symbolically as follows.

Return on HK$ deposit = P × (1 + i × 90/360)
Return on US$ deposit = P/S × (1 + i* × 90/360).

When a state of equilibrium exists, this may be represented by:

P × (1 + i × 90/360) = P/S × (1 + i* × 90/360) × F.

Rearranging the equation gives a method for calculating the forward rate.

$$F = \frac{(1 + i \times 90/360)}{(1 + i^* \times 90/360)} \times S.$$

If i = 7 per cent, i* = 8 per cent, and S = 8.00, then the calculation of F is as follows.

$$F = \frac{(1 + 0.07 \times 90/360)}{(1 + 0.08 \times 90/360)} \times 8.00$$
$$= 7.98$$

and the 'forward discount' = 8.00 − 7.98 = 0.02. If i = 8 per cent, i* = 7 per cent, and S = 8.00, the calculation gives:

$$F = \frac{(1 + 0.08 \times 90/360)}{(1 + 0.07 \times 90/360)} \times 8.00$$
$$= 8.02$$

and the 'forward premium' = 8.02 − 8.00 = 0.02.

There are no official statistics on the trading volume of the Hong Kong foreign exchange market. Haddon-Cave (1980) mentioned that the average daily turnover of the market was about US$2.5 billion. A study by Mak in early 1983, Mak (1983), revealed that the daily turnover volume was roughly US$10 billion. However, the day-to-day variation may be very large, depending on the activity of the market. In October 1983, the Hong Kong Government abandoned the floating exchange rate system and linked the Hong Kong dollar to the United States dollar, with a fixed parity of US$1 to HK$7.80. Under the new system, the risk of investing in the Hong Kong dollar was vastly reduced. The incentive for people to speculate in Hong Kong dollars became weaker. The turnover volume of Hong Kong dollar dealing, including swap and forward dealings, may therefore be smaller than it would have been if the pegged exchange rate had not been introduced. However, as long as other currencies are still floating against the United States dollar, and as long as the trading volume is increasing, there is still scope for further foreign exchange dealing activities.

Problems and Prospects for the Foreign Exchange Market

The Hong Kong foreign exchange market is an integral part of the network of the world's major markets, which comprises Singapore, Tokyo, Frankfurt, Zurich, London, New York, and San Francisco. This network enables foreign exchange dealings to operate continuously 24 hours a day. The working hours of various markets are given in Table 5.10. One of the major advantages of the Hong Kong market is that, because of its geographical location, its working hours overlap with those of several other markets. Further advantages which favour the Hong Kong market are a highly advanced telecommunication system and a large pool of efficient dealers.

Although the linked exchange rate system is not particularly favourable to foreign exchange dealing, foreign trade is one of the basic forces behind a foreign exchange deal. Hong Kong has a larger volume of trade than Singapore and this gives Hong Kong a competitive edge over Singapore. Furthermore, the gold arbitrage process is always in operation in the gold market, and this process usually involves the foreign exchange market. Interest arbitrage and swap transactions are also constantly being carried out between the money market and the foreign exchange market. Thus the foreign exchange market facilitates an efficient flow of resources and will prosper in the years to come.

The Hong Kong foreign exchange market has undergone very rapid growth since the late 1970s. Because there has been a tremendous growth within such a short time, there have been serious problems caused by the shortage of well-trained and experienced foreign exchange professionals, both on management and operational levels. These problems have been intensified by the trend in the profession towards more sophisticated trading techniques such as swaps and futures. A survey by the Banking Training Board of the Hong Kong Vocational Training Council in 1982 found that 655 people (203 managers and 452 dealers/traders) worked in the area of foreign exchange and that they comprised 1.3 per cent of the total

Table 5.10 The Working Hours of the Foreign Exchange Markets (Hong Kong time)

Market	Open	Close
Tokyo	08.00	15.00
Hong Kong	09.00	16.00
Singapore	09.00	16.00
Frankfurt	15.00	22.00
London	16.00	23.00
New York	22.00	05.00
San Francisco	01.00	08.00

employment in the banking and DTC sector. However the educational level of the foreign exchange staff was lower than that of other staff holding similar ranks in the financial sector. It is therefore necessary to improve the quality and quantity of foreign exchange manpower so that the development of the market is not hindered.

The DTC crisis in 1983 may also have dampened the activity of the market. After this crisis, banks tightened their credit lines to DTCs for fear of bad debts. Thus some DTCs had to reduce their foreign exchange dealings. Some DTCs were forced to withdraw completely from the market. An improvement in the quality of the supervision of the banking and DTC industry is therefore desirable.

References

Dobby, G.C., 'Foreign Exchange and Money Markets in Hong Kong', a paper read to the University of New South Wales Executive Programme, November 1982.

Goodstadt, Leo, '1984 Syndications' Management Score Board', *Asia Banking*, January 1985, pp. 94–100.

Haddon-Cave, C.P., 'The Changing Structure of the Hong Kong Economy', a paper read to the Association Cambiste International Congress, Singapore, XXII, June 1980.

Ho, Y.K., 'Financial Institutions, Markets, and Policies in Hong Kong', in J.Y.S. Cheng (ed.), *Hong Kong in the 1980s* (Hong Kong, Summerson Eastern Publishers Ltd., 1982), Ch. 6, pp. 60–80.

_____'An Analysis of the Hong Kong Money Market', in Y.K. Ho and C.K. Law (eds.), *The Hong Kong Financial Markets: Empirical Evidences* (Hong Kong, University Publishers and Printers, 1983), pp. 39–70.

_____'The Hong Kong Foreign Exchange Market—An Analysis of the Monetary Approach and Market Efficiency', in Y.K. Ho and C.K. Law (eds.), *The Hong Kong Financial Markets: Empirical Evidences* (Hong Kong, University Publishers and Printers, 1983), pp. 235–48.

Hong Kong Government, *1984 Economic Background* (Hong Kong, Government Printer, 1985).

Hong Kong Vocational Training Council, Banking Training Board, *Manpower Survey 1982, Banking Industry* (Hong Kong, Vocational Training Council, 1982).

Jao, Y.C., *Banking and Currency in Hong Kong* (London, Macmillan Press, 1974).

_____'Hong Kong as a Regional Financial Centre: Evolution and Prospects', in C.K. Leung, J.W. Cushman, and Wang Gungwu (eds.), *Hong Kong: Dilemmas of Growth* (Canberra, Australian National University Press, 1980), pp. 161–94.

_____'Financial Structure and Monetary Policy in Hong Kong', in S.Y. Lee and Y.C. Jao (eds.), *Financial Structures and Monetary Policies in Southeast Asia* (London, Macmillan Press, 1982), pp. 7–50.

_____'The Financial Structure', in D.G. Lethbridge (ed.), *The Business Environment in Hong Kong* (Hong Kong, Oxford University Press, second edition, 1984), pp. 124–79.

Latter, A.R., 'The Development of Financial Markets in Hong Kong', paper presented to the conference 'Hong Kong as a Financial Centre in a Rapidly Changing Environment', Hong Kong, 17 February 1984.

Leung, J., 'Hong Kong Interbank Market Draws Notice', *Asian Wall Street Journal*, 10 December 1981.

Mak, N.K., 'The Behaviour of the Hong Kong Foreign Exchange Market', unpublished M. Phil. thesis, The Chinese University of Hong Kong, 1983.

Menezes, Victor, 'Time to Develop Secondary Markets', *Hong Kong Review* (Hong Kong, South China Morning Post, January 1984), pp. 29–32.

Price, Kent, 'Need for an Active Secondary CD Market', *Banking, Finance and Investment Review 1982* (Hong Kong, South China Morning Post, June 1982), pp. 12–13.

6. The Financial Futures Markets

ROBERT HANEY SCOTT

WHEN a person enters into a commercial contract with another person, the contract may require an immediate transaction, called a spot transaction, or it may concern a transaction to take place at a future date. A market is a place where transactions occur. The market in which future transactions are arranged is called a forward market.

Forward markets grow quite naturally in free economies. If parties to a transaction enter into it freely, without coercion, one may presume that all parties benefit from it. For if anyone did not benefit, he or she would simply decline to participate.

People find forward markets beneficial because they reduce risk. For example, a farmer with a crop to harvest next spring does not know what price it will bring. A miller knows that he will want grain to process into flour next spring, but he does not know what price he will have to pay for it. Both the farmer and the miller face the risk that the price of grain may change and cause loss to one and gain to the other. By waiting until next spring to enter into their transaction, both farmer and miller are gambling. By agreeing now on a forward price, both avoid the risks that accompany price fluctuations. A similar situation faces importers, exporters, and everyone in business who plans investments.

But the special forward contracts that individuals often negotiate with each other are cumbersome. Importers and exporters who are active in the forward markets must make complicated arrangements with banks to ensure that foreign exchange is available when it is needed. Because negotiating forward contracts is costly in terms of time and money, futures markets provide valuable services. Futures markets, like forward markets, help reduce risk and, at the same time, futures markets enable traders who wish to reduce risk to do so at a low cost.

Forward Markets and Futures Markets

The difference between a forward market and a futures market for foreign exchange can perhaps best be illustrated by an example. Suppose a Hong Kong importer enters into a contract to pay a trader in England £1,000 next month in exchange for certain goods. Under the current exchange rate of, say, HK$10 = £1, the importer calculates that the transaction will be profitable. But if the price of pounds rises during the month, the importer will have to pay more Hong Kong dollars than he originally anticipated, and the transaction may turn into an unprofitable one. So the importer asks his banker for a contract to buy pounds at the forward price for delivery next month. The banker checks the market by telephone and quotes a price. After completion of formalities, the importer is sure of obtaining the £1,000 he will require. But now the banker has a risk. Other bank customers, however, such as exporters, will wish to sell pounds forward. Banks may find that contracts to sell will approximate contracts to buy. To avoid too much exposure to risk the banker must maintain a balanced position. If buying and selling contracts are not balanced, the bank itself may enter the forward market with other banks or foreign exchange dealers.

Thus the forward market for foreign exchange is comprised of a network of individuals and firms that make contracts directly, or by telephone, for the purchase and sale of foreign exchange at future dates. When the due day arrives the foreign exchange is delivered according to the terms of the contract.

A futures market for foreign exchange is a market in which contracts are written for the purchase or sale of foreign exchange in the future. The contracts themselves are bought and sold. The people who trade contracts usually have no foreign exchange and rarely end up actually delivering or receiving foreign exchange.

A diagram may help to clarify why delivery seldom takes place and may provide a better understanding of how futures markets operate. Fig. 6.1 represents the floor of an exchange, with entries, telephones and desks all around the edges, and a trading floor where many traders communicate (by shouting and signalling to each other) their willingness to trade. Assume that a runner receives a telephone call with an order from an importer who is going to need £1,000 next month. He wants to buy a contract for the delivery of £1,000. The runner goes to trader A with the order, and A begins to shout across the room that he wants to buy a contract. Soon, trader B's attention is caught and B signals that he will sell the contract at the indicated price. Then A jots a note of purchase on a slip of paper and a runner delivers it to the exchange desk. Another runner circulating the room

Fig. 6.1 A Simplified Diagram of a Foreign Exchange Floor

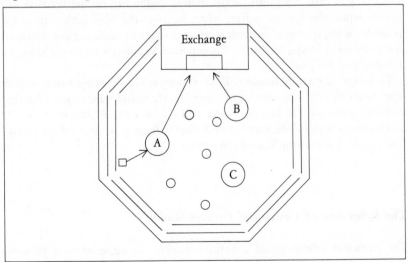

is given a piece of paper by B indicating the sale of a contract, and this runner also delivers the note to the exchange desk. Both A and B have made contracts with the exchange, not with each other.

The exchange has no exposure—its contracts for sale and contracts for purchase will be equal. (Sometimes during hectic trading, some slips of paper denoting purchases and sales are lost on the way to the desk. This happens regularly and, at the end of each trading day, a settlement of positions is carried out according to elaborate rules agreed upon and followed carefully by the members of the exchange.)

The importer who needs £1,000 next month will wait until the day before he needs the money and then order trader A to sell a contract for him. After A sells the contract, perhaps to C, both A and C send notes to the desk. The importer's obligation under the original purchase contract has now been eliminated by the offsetting sale contract. No trader needs to deliver pounds to any other trader so long as offsetting contracts are bought and sold, thereby clearing positions. Delivery is made on very few contracts.

A forward market in foreign exchange is a market in which contracts are made for the purchase or sale of foreign exchange, while a futures market for foreign exchange is a market in which contracts are not only created but also traded.

The importer who needs £1,000 will buy his pounds in the spot market and deliver them to his creditor. The importer has hedged his position. Originally he knew that he would be needing pounds next month. A rise in the price of pounds means that he will have to pay more for them on the spot market. So he buys a contract that states that he agrees to buy pounds at a set price. If the price rises he will make a profit on his contract because he can take delivery of pounds at the original lower price. But he need not take delivery because he can make the same profit merely by selling a contract to offset his original purchase. The difference between the purchase price and the selling price of the contracts will closely approximate the change in the price of pounds that occurred while he held the contract to buy pounds. Thus he will realize a profit on his trading in the futures market that will closely equal the loss he suffers when he pays the now higher price for pounds on the spot market for foreign exchange. By reducing the potential for winning or losing (reducing his exposure to foreign exchange risk), he has attained his goal.

To hedge foreign exchange risk, an exporter, on the other hand, would want to arrange the opposite set of contracts. He would want to sell a foreign exchange contract. He knows that he will be receiving £1,000 next month and wants to 'lock in' the number of dollars that these pounds will give him. The entire process simply works in reverse.

The Relevance of a Financial Futures Market

The principal advantage of a futures market, as opposed to a forward market, is that a trader who wishes to reduce risk can deal with an exchange rather than having to negotiate a specific contract with a specific person or bank. In a stock exchange, when an investor wishes to sell stock he can arrange for his broker to sell it for him on the exchange; it is not necessary for the seller to know who the buyer is. Similarly, a trader wishing to sell wheat on some date in the future may sell a contract to sell wheat on a commodities futures exchange. A stock exchange is a place where stocks are traded and a futures exchange is a place where futures contracts are traded.

An exchange is a clearing house for contracts. It must, however, in the case of futures contracts, establish uniform contracts. It also must establish many specific self-regulatory functions.

When any two people meet to negotiate a forward contract they can set any terms and conditions they like. But for contracts to be traded on an exchange, they must be uniform so that buyers and sellers know what they are trading. Thus contracts must specify selected delivery dates, given amounts of the product, back-up deposits of cash to cover the position, the value of specific price changes, delivery arrangements, and so forth.

Risk Reduction in Futures Markets

Examples describing hedging by farmers and millers are exceedingly old, and therefore commodities futures markets have existed for a very long time. Financial futures exchanges, however, are of recent origin, although well-developed forward markets in foreign exchange have existed for many years.

Financial futures are of two basic types: futures in foreign exchange and futures in selected securities (often called interest rate futures).

1. Foreign Exchange Futures.   As an example from the world of foreign exchange, let us take the case of a Hong Kong fur trader. He will buy skins in Sweden, have them processed into pelts in Germany, import them to Hong Kong to be made into garments, and then sell them in Japan. At each stage there is a risk of loss from changes in foreign exchange rates, from the Swedish kronor to the German Deutschmark, to the Hong Kong dollar, and finally to the Japanese yen. To cover his position he needs to have continuous arrangements with his banker. If the flows of goods across borders are routine, such a trader could maintain a hedged position on a more or less routine arrangement with outstanding futures contracts. This hedging operation does not provide such perfect hedges as those provided by explicit contracts related to specific trades. But the expense of obtaining a high degree of risk reduction is far lower.

2. Interest Rate Futures.   Just as one can write a contract for the future delivery of foreign exchange, one can write a contract for the future delivery of bonds or other financial securities. The price of a bond for delivery at a future date determines the yield that its buyer will realize from holding it. Therefore a futures contract on a financial security will 'lock in' a yield on a security at a future date.

Futures contracts on United States Treasury bills (T-bills) were the subject of serious discussion by a dealer in United States Government securities in the early 1950s. But it was not until 1976 that the International Money Market (IMM) of the Chicago Mercantile Exchange began trading the first interest rate futures contracts on a formal exchange.

An analogy with the farmer and the miller in the examples above is straightforward. Some investors know that they will receive some money within a few months, and that they will want to invest it. They would like to know what interest rate they will receive. Others may be making contingency plans and know that they will be wanting to borrow some money in a few months time. They need to know what interest charges they will have to pay on their future loan. If these borrowers and lenders could be brought together all could reduce their risks by contracting forward with each other. But the possibility of their meeting and knowing each other is unlikely. However, a futures exchange can bring about the same result and enable both borrowers and lenders to reduce risk simultaneously.

An illustration of how an interest return on a future date may be 'locked in' follows. This illustration is adapted from an example given in Drabenstott and McDonaley (1984).

A bank investment manager learns from his current cash flow report in January that US$1 million will be available for investment in March. He knows that the US$1 million will be invested in a 90-day bill. The investment manager expects interest rates to decline between January and March, lowering his rate of return when the US$1 million is actually invested. To preserve the current rate until the cash becomes available to invest, he hedges in the futures market. By buying a T-bill futures contract—by taking a long position—he stands to profit in the futures market if interest rates decline. His cash position and his futures market position in January are as shown in Table 6.1.

In March, the US$1 million becomes available to invest, but interest rates have declined. The cash and futures markets positions are then as shown in the table.

Table 6.1 The Cash and Futures Markets

	Cash Market	Futures Market
January	Notified of cash flow situation. Can purchase a 90-day T-bill at $92.40, at 7.6 per cent interest.	Buys one T-bill contract for March delivery at $91.90, at 8.1 per cent interest.
March	Invests $1 million in a 90-day T-bill at $93.20, a 6.8 per cent rate of return.	Sells one T-bill contract for March delivery at $92.70, at an interest rate of 7.3 per cent.
Result	Target price $92.40 Current price $93.20 Net loss $ 0.80 (80 basis points at $25 per basis point = $2,000 loss.)	Selling price $92.70 Purchase price $91.90 Net profit $ 0.80 (80 basis points at $25 per basis point = $2,000 profit.)

Note: All prices are in United States dollars.
Source: Adapted from Drabenstott and McDonaley (1984).

The final outcome, as shown, is a futures market profit that offsets the cash market loss. The profit made in the futures market exactly offsets the loss in the cash market. The investment manager effectively 'locked in' the interest rate that prevailed in January by hedging in the futures market. In this example, the hedge worked perfectly because the basis risk was zero. In most cases, the basis risk will make the hedge less effective. (Basis is defined below.)

Other Risks in Futures Markets

1. Gambling Elements in Futures Markets.   A broker arranges a contract between two parties for the exchange of an asset. The broker has no stake in the outcome. In contrast, a dealer holds a supply of securities and is prepared either to sell from his stock or to buy and add to it in order to meet his customers' needs on both sides of the market. Because a dealer takes a position and holds a portfolio of the securities in which he trades, he is also assuming an element of risk. That is, he is playing the role of a gambler. The difference between the bid and the asking prices is sufficiently large to induce a dealer to assume this risk-taking position.

All futures markets require that a group of people, who are willing to gamble, participate in making a market by playing the role of dealers in futures contracts. At any particular time, the number (or volume) of people (or money) who wish to hedge their risk positions in one direction may not equal the number on the other side. More farmers than millers may wish to hedge. More investors than borrowers may wish to hedge. The traders on the floor of a futures exchange need to be able and willing to trade contracts even though they do not have definite orders on both sides of the market at the same time. As a result it is always possible for the market to be manipulated. This is something that government regulators fear. The hedge desired by the customer of an exchange may be less than perfect, depending on the extent to which a gambling element dominates the market.

2. Basis Changes in Futures Markets.   The hedger using a futures market may not obtain a perfect hedge for a variety of reasons, but among the most important of these is the possibility that the basis may change. The basis is the difference between the price of the item specified in the futures contract and the price of the item that the hedger deals in. Changes in basis can best be illustrated by an example.

Interest rates generally move up and down together. Assume that a hedger has taken a three-month US$1 million loan from a bank at the prime rate of interest of 12 per cent. He knows that he will want to 'roll over' this loan for another three months. The prime rate may rise to 15 per cent in the meantime, causing his costs to rise. Or it may fall to 10 per cent. But, in order to plan, the hedger wishes to budget for a continuation of the 12 per cent rate. He would like to reduce his risk and 'lock in' the going rate.

So he goes to the futures market for three-month T-bills. Assume that the yield on T-bills is 10 per cent. The difference between the prime rate and the T-bill rate is 2 per cent. This is the basis. If it remains the same for three months, then the hedge will be close to perfect. But if the basis changes, the hedge will be imperfect and the hedger will be taking a gamble.

For example, assume that the hedger sells a US$1 million contract for future delivery of T-bills at 10 per cent. Assume that the prime rate rises from 12 to 15 per cent and that the T-bill rate rises from 10 to 13 per cent. This is illustrated in Fig. 6.2 which shows both rates rising by the same amount. The hedger will have to pay 3 per cent more on the 'roll-over' of his loan. Offsetting this, however, is the gain he can realize by buying T-bills at the current low price (representing a high yield), and delivering them at the contract price previously agreed upon. The contract price is of course higher than the current price and represents a lower yield. Actual delivery is not necessary, as mentioned earlier. All that is required is an offsetting purchase of a contract at the lower price just prior to the delivery date.

Interest rates can fall and, again, if the 2 per cent basis does not change, the hedge will be good—in the sense that the gain from 'rolling over' the loan at a lower interest rate will be offset by losses in the market for futures contracts. If a graph were drawn it would show both yields falling together.

However the basis may become larger. Assume that the prime rate rises as before to 15 per cent, but that the T-bill rate does not change. The hedger still has to pay the higher interest rate when he 'rolls over' his loan, but he makes no profit on the T-bill futures contract to offset the higher costs he faces. This is shown in Fig. 6.3. The hedger is in the same situation as he would have been had he not attempted the hedge.

It should be clear that if the T-bill rate fell while the prime rate rose, the hedger would be in a worse position than he would have been had he not attempted the hedge.

Similarly, even without the aid of a diagram, it is easily appreciated that if the basis narrowed the hedger would make a profit. If, for example, the prime rate remained at 12 per cent while the T-bill rate rose from 10 to 11 per cent, the basis would narrow. The hedger would still pay 12 per cent for his US$1 million loan, but he would make a profit by being able to buy T-bills at a lower price and deliver them at the original contract price.

Fig. 6.2 An Illustration of an Unchanged Basis

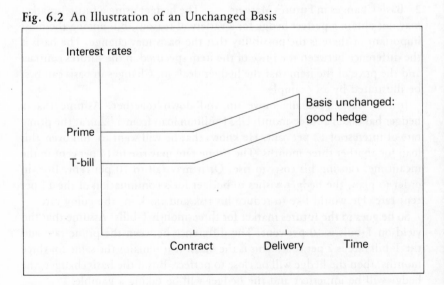

Fig. 6.3 An Illustration of a Larger Basis

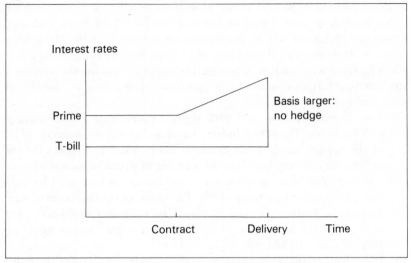

Thus, to the extent that the basis changes over the life of the hedging operation, the hedger is assuming a certain amount of risk. The basis changes only a very small amount if the individual wishes to hedge the interest rate on T-bills and can use the T-bill futures market. But a hedger may wish to hedge the prime rate or some other rate which does not always move closely with the T-bill rate. Thus, in choosing the hedging instrument, a hedger should choose one that is a close substitute for the market instrument with which the hedger operates. This will keep basis changes lower and help reduce risk. (Because investors are sometimes not adequately warned of the risks of loss when ostensibly hedging, such losses prompt law suits. For example, a US$200 million suit was filed in New York for negligence in administration of futures contracts. See *South China Morning Post*, 19 March 1983.)

The Terms Used in Financial Futures Contracts

As explained above, in order for contracts to be traded in large volumes, the 'commodity' being traded—the contract—must be uniform in its characteristics. There must be a specific amount of a specific type of commodity involved in each trade, so that individuals can buy or sell whatever number of contracts they need to hedge their exposure.

The New York Stock Exchange Composite Index

The examples above suggest the types of specifications required for foreign exchange futures and interest rate futures. Space does not permit a list of the specifications of all kinds of financial futures contracts. Details are available from the exchanges. So here we will provide the details of a contract in stock index futures, which is based on those of the New York Stock Exchange Composite Index, by way of illustration. (It is likely that the Hang Seng Index of stock prices in Hong Kong will be the basis of Hong Kong's first financial futures contract, so it is especially useful to examine the terms of a stock-market futures contract.) The specifications required are listed and described below.

(a) Size. The contract size is US$500 times the New York Stock Exchange (NYSE) Index. The NYSE Index is based on the weighted average of all of the approximately 1,520 common stocks listed and traded on the NYSE. Weights are based on the number of shares of each stock outstanding. The prices of stocks on 31 December 1965 are used for base prices (also scaled by a factor of 50). The index is calculated each minute during the trading day and displayed by computer world-wide. For example, if the index were 80 the value of a single contract would be US$500 × 80 = US$40,000.

(b) Price fluctuations. Traders buy and sell the index itself, using the index as a price. As traders raise or lower the price of a contract, the price movements are 5 basis points (0.05). For example, the price might rise from 80.15 to 80.20 to 80.25 and so forth. A movement of 0.05 basis points is equal to US$500 × 0.05 or US$25. So prices move by a minimum of US$25 per contract.

(c) Maturing months. The business day prior to the last business day in the months of March, June, September, and December is the last day of trading in each quarter. The following day is the settlement day for that quarter—the day on which any contracts that happen to remain outstanding are settled.

(d) Trading hours. The trading hours are 10.00 to 16.15 United States Eastern Standard Time.

(e) Settlement. Positions are marked to the market each day. Settlement is made in cash and not in the delivery of any specific securities. Settlement is based upon the difference between yesterday's settlement contract value and today's settlement contract value.

(f) Margins. Outsiders who wish to speculate in contracts must put down US$3,500, while hedgers and members of the exchange need maintain a margin of only US$1,500. These required margins ensure that each trader has provided a cushion to absorb loss should the market turn against him or her.

This list gives only a summary of the detailed provisions needed to establish uniform, and therefore tradable, financial futures contracts. Contracts for foreign exchange provide for final settlement and delivery of foreign exchange. The same is true for T-bill contracts and other bond contracts. However, contracts denominated in Eurodollar bank deposits may also be settled in cash rather than the bank deposit itself. Needless to say, the contract details are numerous, and our purpose here is merely to provide the reader with an outline of the basic types of specifications usually contained in futures contracts.

Trading in similar stock exchange futures contracts takes place on the Chicago Mercantile Exchange (CME) and at the Kansas City Board of Trade (KCBT). Indeed the KCBT was the first institution to offer such contracts. Its contract is based on a geometric average of the prices of 1,700 stocks, each equally weighted and published by Value Line. The CME contract is based upon Standard & Poor's composite index of 500 stock prices weighted by the market value of the components. The Dow Jones Industrial Average is perhaps the most widely publicized stock-market index, but its calculation is less acceptable. This index is the average price of 30 'blue chip' stocks, all of which carry equal weight. Thus it is far less comprehensive as a measure of general market movements. Some observers are also concerned about the manner in which this index is regularly adjusted to accommodate new or expanded issues of stock.

Using the Contract: Speculating and Hedging

Speculators are traders who are prepared to act on the assumption (in other words, to gamble) that the market will generally rise and that this rise will be reflected in the NYSE Index. If the market rises, a speculator will buy ('take a long position in') the index. If the index rises he can sell and realize a profit. He can hold the contract for minutes, hours, days, or weeks. Speculators are needed for a market to operate on a continuous basis—so that there will always be a large volume of trade taking place during trading hours.

In addition, the market provides the opportunity for holders of stocks to hedge against adverse movements in the market. For example, assume that the manager of a diversified portfolio of stocks thinks the market may fall. He could sell the stocks, or he could simply sell the index to establish a 'short' position. If the index fell, he would lose the capital value of his shares but he would gain on his futures contract. If the market rose instead, he would gain on his portfolio but would lose on his futures contract. Thus he could 'lock in', or hedge, his portfolio against swings in capital value.

If the manager plans to liquidate his holdings, he can do so in an orderly fashion, and stabilize the overall value of his portfolio during the liquidation process by adopting a hedging strategy. He takes a short position. Similarly, if he knows that funds will be flowing in at some future date, he can 'lock in' a current average price to pay for his diversified portfolio by a futures hedge. He takes a long position, that is, in this instance, he 'buys' the index.

In general, then, a stock index futures contract enables the holder of a diversified portfolio of stocks to immunize the value of the portfolio from the risk of price fluctuations.

There are two kinds of risk involved in the purchase of a single stock. One is the risk associated with the volatility of that particular stock's price. The other is associated with the volatility of market prices generally. A stock-market futures contract is designed to allow the investor to hedge the general market risk rather than the risk uniquely associated with a particular stock.

Proposals for Futures Markets in Hong Kong

In the past, futures markets were markets where contracts were traded for the delivery of commodities—wheat, coffee, copper, gold, plywood, frozen orange juice, and the like. It is a little strange to think of Deutschmarks, pounds, and yen as 'commodities', but they are now treated as commodities for future delivery in the financial futures markets. It is even more strange to think of United States T-bills, dollar deposits in banks, the index number of a group of stock prices, and so forth, as 'commodities'. Nevertheless, financial futures markets have grown out of the world of commodities, not out of the world of finance, and have taken on the terminology of the traders in the commodity markets.

In Hong Kong in 1980–2, the people active in the commodities exchange put forward proposals for the establishment of futures markets in financial instruments. However the Government did not accept the merits of these proposals. (It was suggested to this author that the banking community in Hong Kong viewed the proposals as a threat to its market for forward contracts in foreign exchange, and that banking interests probably exerted pressure on the Government to refuse to support the development of this innovative market.) Finally the banks decided to 'fight fire with fire' and formed a Steering Committee to develop a proposal for the establishment of their own financial futures market. The Steering Committee submitted its confidential report, 'For the Establishment of the Hong Kong Financial Futures Exchange', to the Commissioner for Securities and Commodities on 15 November 1983.

The Steering Committee consisted of representatives from ten financial institutions in Hong Kong—six American banks, Barclays Bank International Ltd., the Standard Chartered Bank, the Hongkong and Shanghai Banking Corporation, and Wardley Ltd. The Steering Committee appointed a Working Committee of eight. The Working Committee's report proposed the contracts to be traded, the organizational structure of the proposed exchange, the regulations of the exchange—including those covering contract clearings, the system of guaranteeing contracts, the floor plan, training programmes, the legislation required, and the tax rulings relating to trading profits that are needed.

In Table 6.2 there is a brief outline of the terms of the five contracts proposed by the Working Committee and submitted by the Steering Committee to the Commissioner.

The proposed contract listed first in the table—a contract tied to the Hang Seng Index—is similar in most respects to the description given earlier of a stock index futures contract. The Hang Seng Index is an average of the prices of shares of 33 companies each weighted by the number of shares outstanding. The shares of the Hongkong and Shanghai Banking Corporation represent 17 per cent of the index. The 33 companies tend to be tied to banking, land, and utilities, and there is very little representation of manufacturing firms. This is hardly surprising, however, because 95 per cent of the firms in Hong Kong have fewer than 20 employees. Manufacturing firms are, on average, too small to be represented heavily in a stock exchange.

Table 6.2 Proposed Contract Specifications for a Hong Kong Financial Futures Exchange

	Hang Seng Stock Index	Hong Kong Dollar Deposit	Eurodollar Deposit	Japanese Yen	Deutschmark
Trading unit	Hang Seng Index × HK$50	HK$1,000,000 time deposit with 30-day maturity	US$1,000,000 time deposit with 3-month maturity	Y6,250,000	DM62,500
Delivery months*	Mar., June, Sept., Dec.	Mar., June, Sept., Dec.	Mar., June, Sept., Dec.	Mar., June, Sept., Dec.	Mar., June, Sept., Dec.
Price quotation	Quoted in terms of the Hang Seng Index	Index method (100 minus yield based on a 365-day year)	Index method (100 minus yield based on a 360-day year)	US$ per Y	US$ per DM
Minimum price fluctuation	0.5 index points (0.5 pts = HK$25)	0.05 points (5 pts = HK$41.10)	0.01 points (1 pt = US$25)	0.000001 points (1 pt = US$6.25)	0.0001 points (1 pt = US$6.25)
Daily price limits	50 Hang Seng Index points (HK$2,500)	2.50 Futures Index points (HK$2,055)	1.00 Futures Index points (US$2,500)	100 points (US$625)	100 points (US$625)
Delivery method	Cash settlement	Cash settlement	Cash settlement	Physical delivery or cash settlement	Physical delivery or cash settlement

Note: *Trading terminates on the third Wednesday in a trading month.

The Hang Seng Index has shown considerable volatility and has swung from a low of about 150 in 1974 to a high of about 1,800 in 1981. Stock portfolio managers have had an exciting life. A futures contract should enable them to rest with less anxiety if they choose to use it to hedge their position.

Price changes are proposed at 0.50 index points, which amounts to HK$25 per contract and daily limits to trading are placed at 50 index points, or HK$2,500 per contract, above or below the previous day's settlement.

The contracts proposed for Hong Kong dollar deposits and for Eurodollar deposits provide for cash settlements as well. But the proposed contracts in Japanese yen and Deutschmarks provide for either physical delivery or cash settlement.

At the same time that the organization of banks submitted its proposals, the Hong Kong Commodities Exchange also submitted a set of proposals— its second submission. In mid-1984 the Government suggested that the competing groups work out a common agreement.

While Hong Kong business and financial interests were disagreeing over matters of detail, Singapore, Hong Kong's financial competitor, proceeded forthwith. On 7 September 1984, the Singapore International Monetary Exchange, called Simex, formed a trading link in futures with the Chicago Mercantile Exchange. Under this link contracts sold in Chicago can be closed out by offsetting purchases made in Singapore late at night Chicago time. At the time of writing, it is known that futures contracts being traded are denominated in Deutschmarks, Eurodollar deposits, and Japanese yen. Singapore had earlier given serious consideration to forming a link with the Philadelphia Stock Exchange.

The Advantages and Disadvantages of Financial Futures Markets for Hong Kong

An efficiently managed futures market in financial instruments may be able to reduce the risks faced by those who need to borrow and lend, or those who save and invest. It is necessary to ask whether there are alternatives to futures markets. It has already been noted that banks offer an extensive forward market in foreign exchange. While this market will certainly remain as a significant servant of the business community in Hong Kong, a futures market offers a supplementary service. But other alternatives exist. In particular, markets for options have grown extensively in recent years, after lying dormant since they were abandoned in the wake of the Great Depression of the 1930s. The Philadelphia Stock Exchange opened its market for stock options in 1975.

Features of Options Markets

In December 1982 the Philadelphia Stock Exchange opened trading in options in foreign exchange. At the time of writing almost every international bank is represented on the Philadelphia Exchange. The face values of options contracts being traded are £12,500, $50,000 Canadian, DM 62,500, 125,000 French francs, Y6.25 million, and 62,500 Swiss francs.

In 1984 several banks in New York began making a market in options to buy and sell foreign exchange. An options contract may be more suitable than a futures contract in some instances. For example, an importer who knows that he will need to pay his foreign supplier £1,000 next month may buy an option to call for delivery of £1,000 at a fixed price in United States dollars. The purchase price of the option represents a kind of fee. This fee must be paid in order to induce the writer of the option contract (its seller) to assume the risk of loss he will take if the price of pounds rises and he has to deliver high-priced pounds for the lower price specified in the contract.

1. Call and Put Options.   If the price of pounds falls, the buyer of a call option can buy pounds at the lower market price. Therefore his loss is limited to the amount of the price of the option. He should be willing to pay this amount in fees for the privilege of being placed in a limited-loss position.

In America, the call option enables its holders to call for delivery of the foreign exchange at its exercise price at any time up to a given date in the future. In Europe, the options contracts traded enable the holder of the option to exercise his privilege of buying foreign exchange only on a specific future date. That is, in Europe, the call option cannot be called at any time, but only on a given date.

Put options differ from call options. A trader who buys a put option buys the right to sell, say, £1,000 to the option's writer for a given amount of United States dollars at any time between the present and a given future date. Put and call options are traded continuously. They can be sold prior to the delivery date.

2. Multiple Contracts.   A kind of 'pyramiding' of options and futures contracts has begun on some futures exchanges in the United States. As was

Fig. 6.4 Multiple Contracts

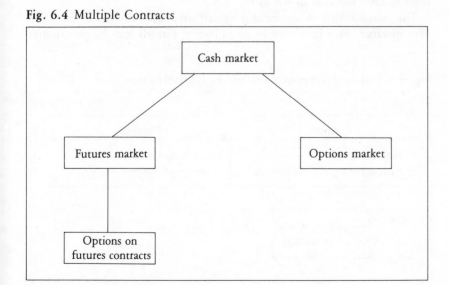

said earlier, there is usually some risk in using futures markets to hedge, because the basis can change. Therefore it is now possible to obtain an option to buy a futures contract. This would enable the buyer of the call option on a future contract to set limits on the loss to which he would otherwise be exposed because of possible changes in the basis.

Options on T-bill futures contracts are available. Put and call options on the Standard & Poor's 500 Stock Index futures contract began trading at the Chicago Mercantile Exchange on 28 January 1983. In early 1985, the Philadelphia Stock Exchange began trading options on the Value Line Stock Index, in which the option is tied to the index itself, and is not an option to buy a futures contract on the index.

From Fig. 6.4 above one can see the possibility that a 'pyramiding' effect could be extended. One could suppose the establishment of a market in futures contracts on options and even a futures contract on options on futures contracts. Needless to say, economics would suggest that the law of diminishing returns would soon be felt in the attempt to reduce risk even more by further 'pyramiding'.

Interest Rate Swap Agreements

The reason for a hedge can be seen in an accounting framework by an examination of an imbalance between the assets and the liabilities of a firm. The importer that we have used as an example so frequently in this chapter has a fixed liability of pounds sterling—£1,000. But if the importer's accounts are kept in Hong Kong dollars, this liability is subject to variation: it may rise or fall to a significant extent. Thus the hedge, in the form of a futures contract, provides the importer with an asset that will rise and fall roughly in line with the rise and fall in the liability.

Applying this general frame of reference, consider the differing asset and liability structure of a pair of firms, A and B. A graphic representation of their balance sheets is shown in Fig. 6.5.

The assets of firm A are steadily valued over time whereas its liabilities vary in value. This firm may be an importer. Firm B may be an exporter

Fig. 6.5 Differing Types of Asset and Liability Structure

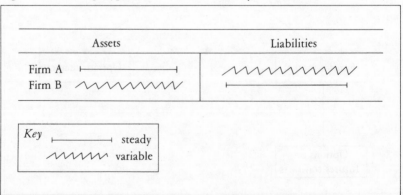

whose claim on forthcoming receipts of pounds is for a given amount in pounds but a varying amount of Hong Kong dollars. In each case the firm's net worth will fluctuate over time.

If these two firms could exchange a steady asset for a variable asset, or a variable liability for a steady liability, they would both benefit from the reduction in risk. The reader may simply imagine a switch of B's jagged line for A's straight line on the asset side. Then A would have two jagged lines indicating simultaneous fluctuations in value, and B would have two matching straight lines. The net worth of each firm would be more stable over time.

The term 'interest rate swap agreement' refers to a situation in which the cash flows of firms A and B are traded to become either steady or subject to variation. For example, assume that firm A is a financial institution that holds mortgages and receives steady monthly payments from its customers, but assume also that it borrows money from the market on a roll-over basis, that is, it has high interest rates to pay at some times, and lower rates at other times. Its periodic cash inflow is steady, while its periodic cash outflow is variable. The opposite situation holds for firm B.

Interest rate swap agreements are arranged by investment bankers. They find firms that have opposite balance sheet problems and arrange for these firms to exchange their interest flows. For example, firm A might receive firm B's variable receipts of interest on its assets, in exchange for which it gives firm B the steady flow of interest earnings it would otherwise have. Usually the investment banker arranges to act as processor and disburser of funds to both entities. That is, the two firms need not necessarily transact with each other. Each has a contract with the bank. For the bank the profit is in the service fees it collects from the two parties to the swap.

Needless to say, the details of interest rate swap agreements become quite complicated quite rapidly, and each case must be treated individually. Thus fees can justifiably be quite high. Nevertheless, the volume of swap agreements has grown dramatically since they were first offered in 1982. These swap agreements act as long-term substitutes for what otherwise would be a demand for interest rate futures contracts.

Gambling, Speculation, and Hedging

One significant problem faced by futures markets and options markets concerns their public image. Many people speculate in stock-, bond, and commodity markets, and futures markets and option markets can be just as speculative—if not more so. But an uninformed public often fails to distinguish between gambling and speculation on the one hand, and risk reduction on the other.

The unique characteristic of gambling is that the risks are purposefully created by the game itself. A horse-race is organized in order that people may bet, in order that there may be a transfer of wealth from one person to another. Speculation, in contrast, involves betting on the outcome when the future course of events is uncertain. All people live with this game. It is not artificially created. Prices of commodities will probably rise or fall tomorrow.

There will be winners and losers. This situation is very unlike gambling where a situation is created to bring about winners and losers.

Thus speculation can, and often does, serve a social purpose. Speculators in futures markets are willing to take bets on both sides of the potential movement of the market. If the price is right they will sell a contract and, if it is also right on the other side, they will buy. If they feel confident that they know in which direction the market will move, they will take a big net position in the direction of the movement they expect. Of course, they can get 'burned'—lose a lot of money in a hurry—when the market moves in the direction they did not expect. But speculators, unlike gamblers, do not create the risks they bet on. Those risks are already there. By speculating, speculators tend in most cases to push prices in the direction of their optimal level, and prices tend to reach the appropriate level for allocation earlier than they would in the absence of speculation. This is true, of course, only if speculators have no monopoly power over prices.

Unlike either speculation or gambling, hedging provides a positive service to all businesses by reducing risk. Therefore hedging is unique and should be viewed as a unique function in support of the economy. The Hong Kong Government has stated that its goal is 'positive non-intervention' in commercial affairs. It would be unfortunate if someone undid the double negative in this phrase and translated it as 'negative intervention'. In any case, although the Government may not wish to support futures markets with cash grants, it should, nevertheless, be prepared to approve applications and provide an appropriate regulatory structure, because futures markets serve legitimate needs.

Futures exchanges have been the subject of some negative publicity. In November 1984 the Kansas City Board of Trade agreed to pay a penalty of US$60,000 in response to charges brought by the Commodity Futures Trading Commission (CFTC). The CFTC had charged eight or nine floor brokers with wash sales in Value Line futures. In wash-sale trading, traders conspire to buy and sell contracts for the express purpose of pushing prices to an artificial level. Furthermore, earlier in 1984 several newspapers had carried reports of widespread drug use among futures traders. The aura of gambling that is associated with the environment in which, for a margin of US$2,500, one can trade commitments in US$1 million T-bills, lends itself to the drug culture. Managers of futures exchanges view these forms of negative publicity as harmful and have acted to police their exchanges appropriately.

But more subtle criticism has come from economists such as Robert J. Samuelson. He viewed futures markets as places in which investors put their money instead of investing in real goods or real bonds and pushing interest rates down and promoting economic growth. He claimed, in the *International Herald Tribune* of 26 January 1983, that real investment and growth would be greater in the absence of futures markets because these markets only act as a drain on capital. But this view is, of course, erroneous. The labour services of traders are diverted to service roles when futures markets are created. But risk reduction, through futures markets, stimulates trade and investment: it acts to promote trade and not to dampen it.

Governments should not allow themselves to be deterred by bad publicity. Instead, they should look at the positive aspects of these new and innovative markets. They should attempt to establish trading regulations that would prevent manipulations of prices and other counter-productive activities that would only serve to damage the image and usefulness of futures markets.

The Hong Kong Government's Position

The Government of Hong Kong received the report of the Steering Committee representing banking interests, and the report of the Hong Kong Commodity Exchange. Proposals made by the two groups differed in detail. It is understandable that the Government would need to examine tax considerations carefully.

The Steering Committee offering the banks' proposal argued that the Inland Revenue Ordinance should be amended to exempt the net profit of futures exchange operations from profit tax. The Committee's principal argument was that such profit is exempt from taxation in Singapore and other countries and that, because of this, the exchange would not be viable in Hong Kong, since traders in Hong Kong would simply move their business elsewhere. Members, brokers, and traders would, however, be subject to tax 'on their commission income derived from business conducted on behalf of clients'. The Hong Kong Commodity Exchange made no request for tax exemption.

The Government's response, at the time of writing, has been to insist that the two groups merge their proposals, on the grounds that if there were two exchanges, neither would be large enough at the outset to provide a profitable volume of trading.

The Government has not looked favourably on foreign exchange futures contracts in United States dollars. It fears that speculation would disturb the foreign exchange value of the Hong Kong dollar. As suggested above, however, an active futures market tends—other things being equal—to stabilize, rather than agitate, prices in the spot markets. It is quite possible that the peg to the United States dollar in September 1983 would have been a less attractive alternative if there had been a well-developed futures market in Hong Kong at the time.

Selected References

Detailed information on their contracts and trading rules are readily available directly from the exchanges upon request. A description of the London International Financial Futures Exchange (LIFFE) is to be found in the article in the *Midland Bank Review* (1982), cited below. For more scholarly articles on various aspects of futures markets see *Journal of Futures Markets* published by Columbia University in New York. Various articles cited below describe hedging in detail and explain the usefulness of hedging to various kinds of financial institutions.

Belongia, Michael T., 'Commodity Options: A New Risk Management Tool for Agricultural Markets', *Review*, Federal Reserve Bank of St. Louis, June/July 1983, pp. 5–15.

_____ and Santoni, G.J., 'Hedging Interest Rate Risk with Financial Futures: Some Basic Principles', *Review*, Federal Reserve Bank of St. Louis, October 1984, pp. 15–25.

_____ and Gregory, Thomas H., 'Are Options on Treasury Bond Futures Priced Efficiently?', *Review*, Federal Reserve Bank of St. Louis, January 1984, pp. 5–13.

Berger, Lawrence W., 'The Booming Market in Financial Futures', *The Morgan Guaranty Survey*, New York, December 1982, pp. 6–9.

Chalupa, Karel V., 'Foreign Currency Futures: Reducing Foreign Exchange Risk', *Economic Perspectives*, Federal Reserve Bank of Chicago, Winter 1982, pp. 3–11.

Chan Suk Han, Lui Man Chi, and Sum Mei Lin, 'Financial Futures', *Business Administration Academic Bulletin*, New Asia College, Chinese University of Hong Kong, 1984, pp. 47–56.

Drabenstott, M. and McDonaley, A. O'm., 'Futures Markets: a Primer for Financial Institutions', *Economic Review*, Federal Reserve Bank of Kansas City, November 1984, pp. 17–33.

'Financial Futures: A New Market for London', *Midland Bank Review*, Autumn/Winter 1982.

Geraghty, Lawrence J., Jr., 'Hedge Programs Demand Involvement at the Top', *Savings Institutions*, September 1983, pp. 76–8.

Goodman, Laurie S., 'The New Options Markets', *Quarterly Review*, Federal Reserve Bank of New York, Autumn 1982, pp. 35–47.

Hilliard, Jimmy E. and Verbrugge, James A., 'Savings Institutions Must Manage Risk', *Savings Institutions*, September 1983, pp. 68–72.

'How Financial Futures Trading Works', *Asian Money Manager*, August 1982, pp. 27–9.

Journal of Futures Markets, Center for the Study of Futures Markets, Columbia University, New York.

Koch, Donald L., Steinhauser, Delores W., and Whigham, Pamela, 'Financial Futures as a Tool for Banks and S & Ls', *Economic Review*, Federal Reserve Bank of Atlanta, September 1982, pp. 4–23.

Kopprasch, Robert W., 'Exchange Traded Options on Fixed Income Securities' (New York, Salomon Brothers Incorporated), February 1982.

_____ 'Introduction to Interest Rate Hedging' (New York, Salomon Brothers Incorporated), November 1982.

Leibowitz, Martin L., 'The Analysis of Value and Volatility in Financial Futures' (Salomon Brothers Center for the Study of Financial Institutions, Graduate School of Business Administration, New York University), 1981, No. 3.

Potter, Howard, 'Hedging Liabilities Can Cut Costs and Risks', *Savings Institutions*, September 1983, pp. 90–1.

Rosenberg, Joel, 'Effective Hedging Depends on Proper Hedge Ratios', *Savings Institutions*, September 1983, pp. 82–9.

Waldman, Michael and Lupo, Thomas B., 'Risk-Controlled Arbitrage for Thrift Institutions' (New York, Salomon Brothers Incorporated), October 1983.

7. Unit Trusts and Insurance Companies

ROBERT HANEY SCOTT

In line with Hong Kong's growth as a financial centre there has been a rapid expansion in recent years of both unit trusts and insurance companies. This chapter contains a description of unit trusts and their functions and a brief report on the growth of insurance companies.

It may be noted that unit trusts and insurance both appeal to investors who want to reduce the risks associated with their investments. As is well known, a person who buys insurance absorbs a small cost in the form of a premium in exchange for protection from the risk or possibility of a large loss. Similarly, someone who invests in a unit trust is contributing to a pool of funds that will be used to purchase a diversified portfolio of financial assets such as shares of stock, bonds, certificates of deposits in banks, and so forth. The idea that an investor should diversify a portfolio is as time honoured and true as the ancient adage that you should 'never put all your eggs in one basket'. Diversification reduces risk and therein lies the value of a unit trust as an investment medium.

The Unit Trust: a Pool of Funds

The mean of a sample of items will be very near the mean of the population of items from which the sample is drawn, provided, of course, that the sample is large and is selected at random. If a sample of only one is selected it would be very risky to assume that this sample item represents the population. However thirty items, carefully drawn at random, can be presumed with great confidence to have a mean that approximates the mean of the population of items.

Bearing in mind the above considerations regarding samples, one may imagine an investor with HK$10,000 to invest. This amount is not sufficient to be divided into 30 parts in order to purchase a random sample of shares in 30 different companies. Investing this amount in the shares of a single company means accepting the risks associated with that company's investment programme—putting all one's eggs in one basket.

It is simply impractical for an individual investor to attempt to diversify his small portfolio of investments adequately by purchasing shares in several different companies. However, if this individual could pool his HK$10,000 with the funds of 1,000 other people, the total amount available for investment would be HK$10 million. This sum could be used to purchase a diversified portfolio of assets and the individual could, with HK$10,000, own a share of this portfolio.

The pooling of funds to achieve a goal is as old as the idea of partnerships in ventures and shares of stock in an enterprise. But the idea of investing in a pool of funds to be used to invest in various financial instruments came to fruition in the middle of this century. In the United States pools of funds to be invested in shares of stock or bonds are called mutual funds.

Managers of open-ended mutual funds will buy and sell shares or bonds in response to changing market conditions. That is, the pool of funds is managed. In contrast, unit investment trusts retain a more or less fixed portfolio that is subject to change only when a bond or other security is in difficulty.

Many different types of institution exist for the pooling of funds. In America, legislation in the late 1960s permitted the establishment of Real Estate Investment Trusts (REITs). These institutions sold shares to small investors and purchased income-producing properties such as apartment buildings, office buildings, and shopping centres. These were called equity trusts. Thus a shareholder in the trust could own a piece of a large real estate project and could deduct depreciation and accounting expenses from trust income for tax purposes. Many REITs also invested in firms engaged in property development, as opposed to existing property. These were called mortgage trusts, as distinct from equity trusts. Many of these trusts failed in the early 1970s in the wake of the oil crisis because expenditure on energy supplies and the costs of heating buildings rose precipitously.

More recently in the United States there has been a huge growth in Money Market Mutual Funds (MMMFs). These funds are placed in short-term financial assets such as bank certificates of deposit, commercial paper, United Stated Treasury bills (T-bills), and so forth. They now total some US$125 billion. A special feature of these funds is that most of them permit investors to withdraw funds in minimum amounts of about US$500, up to three times each month, by simply writing a cheque. Legislation passed in 1982 permitted banks to operate similar funds for their customers. These are called Money Market Deposit accounts (MMDs) and are covered by federal deposit insurance up to US$100,000. The MMMFs are regulated by the Securities and Exchange Commission, whereas the MMDs are regulated by the banking authorities. The different characteristics of these funds and the different authorities responsible for them tend to cause regulatory confusion from time to time.

Pooled funds have provided for various types of investment, one of which, the so-called unit trust, has shown remarkable growth over the past few years. The first unit trust was put together in the City of London in 1868. It was called the Foreign and Colonial Government Trust. The provisions of this trust may be summarized briefly. There were to be five trustees. No more than £100,000 was to be invested in any one foreign stock. A list of 16 stocks was selected. The sum of £2 10s was to be deducted from each £100 par value certificate for expenses. The goal of this trust was to reduce risk and to provide a stable dividend income.[1]

The first unit trust in Hong Kong was established in 1960, with the Hongkong and Shanghai Banking Corporation as trustee. It was to have a life of 10 years, an initial service charge of no more than 10 per cent, and a 'half-yearly administration charge of one-half of one per cent. . .'.[2] The development of unit trusts in Hong Kong was slow until 1980.

Closed-end and Open-ended Funds

A closed-end fund has a basic capitalization of perhaps HK$50 million. Shares in the fund may be sold and the funds will then be invested as provided by the fund's prospectus. Shares in the fund may be traded in a market, but the number of shares remains unchanged until or unless the fund formalizes an expansion programme.

Shares in an open-ended fund, by contrast, can be traded—bought and sold—with the fund itself. An investor can purchase units of the fund at any time at a price that fluctuates with the average value of the underlying securities. As the cash flows to the fund, its managers purchase more underlying securities. When holders of units decide to sell, they sell to the fund, the managers of which then liquidate some portion of the underlying securities in order to have the funds to redeem the investors' shares. Thus the size of the asset structure of an open-ended fund will vary from day to day.

The Operating Characteristics of Unit Trusts

A unit trust differs from a company and is regulated differently. It must have a clearly stated investment policy. Some trusts aim at stocks that promise long-term growth and some at assets that are highly liquid. Others specify diversification over geographical regions in firms engaged in similar types of activities, or diversification over types of activities. They may attempt to balance growth and income distribution or they may aim for good current income yields. Indeed, units may be income units or accumulation units.

Trustees in Hong Kong are usually banks, whereas in the United States they are not. In their fiduciary capacity the trustees are legally responsible. Trust accounts are subject to specific rules and the authorities are entitled to conduct investigations into the activities of trusts, if they consider it necessary to do so.

Trust deeds usually spell out in some detail the mechanism for setting the price for subscription units being sold to the investing public, and for the redemption price that unit-holders receive when they sell units back to the trust. Some funds are willing to buy and sell units each business day, while others limit trading to once a week or even once a month. There are also limits placed on the number of units that can be redeemed by one holder on one day, and a request for redemption must be presented in advance of the trading day.

Investment Restrictions

Unit trusts usually require that no more than perhaps 5 or 10 per cent of a fund's total assets can be invested in the assets of any one company. Similarly, a trust may not buy more than 10 per cent of the assets of a given company. There are also restrictions on the extent of a trust's purchases of securities that are not regularly traded in a market-place. In some instances the managers of a unit trust are permitted to borrow in order to be able to make timely purchases of securities on behalf of the investors, but such borrowing is limited in extent.

Unit Trusts in Hong Kong

The number of unit trusts authorized to conduct business in Hong Kong exceeded 100 in 1983. Over 50 of these were constituted under Hong Kong laws, while the remainder were introduced by foreign financial firms with offices in Hong Kong.

Local financial management companies have generated most of the local trusts. A few examples from the many that exist will suffice. In 1983 one company, Wardley Ltd., managed several funds, each with special terms and goals. The Wardley Trust holds Hong Kong bank stock and has investments in shares of oil firms in Australia, retail firms in Belgium, beverage firms in France, chemical firms and shipping firms in Holland, and in property companies, utilities, and other investments in Japan, the Philippines, Sweden, the United Kingdom, and the United States. The Wardley Nikko Asia Fund has holdings in Hong Kong, Singapore, Malaysia, and the Philippines. The Wardley Bond Trust holds sterling assets, Swiss francs, Deutschmark bonds, United States Treasury bonds and other assets denominated in United States dollars, and assets denominated in Japanese yen. Wardley Ltd. also has a specialized trust devoted to holding a diversified portfolio of shares in Japanese companies. Another company, G.T. Management Ltd., operates a large number of unit trust funds. Table 7.1 provides a profile of some of these funds, indicating their areas of investment and their performance. Table 7.2 provides details of the investment portfolio of one of these funds—GT Global Technology Fund. A full list of all the trust funds in Hong Kong may be obtained from the Securities Commission's Committee on Unit Trusts.

The Regulation of Unit Trusts

In Hong Kong the operations of unit trusts are subject to a number of ordinances: the Securities Ordinance, the Protection of Investors Ordinance, and the Trustee Ordinance. All unit trusts are required to be authorized by the Securities Commission. A Code on Unit Trusts and Mutual Funds was established by the Securities Commission in line with its authority. The Code came into force in 1978.

A five-member Committee on Unit Trusts administers the Code and may amend it. The Secretary of the Committee performs the administrative functions appropriate to the position. The Committee approves applications for the establishment of trusts subject to the final approval of the Securities Commission.

The Code is comprised of 78 articles and is a comprehensive framework for

Table 7.1 A Profile of Some GT United States Dollar Offshore Funds (as at 1 April 1985)

	Berry Pacific Fund	GT ASEAN Hong Kong Growth Fund	GT Asia Fund	GT Australia Fund	GT Dollar Fund	GT Europe Fund	GT Global Technology Fund	GT South China Fund
Area of investment	Japanese equities	Hong Kong Singapore Malaysia Thailand Philippines Indonesia	Japan SE Asia Australia	Australian equities	US equities	European equities	Technology stocks world-wide	Hong Kong equities
Launch date	1970	1980	1975	1978	1970	1984	1982	1984
Estimated yield	0.77	1.35	1.24	1.21	0.87	–	–	–
Minimum investment	Nil	Nil	Nil	Nil	Nil	Nil	Nil	Nil
Placing fee	5%	5%	5%	5%	5%	5%	5%	5%
Management fee	0.75%	1%	0.75%	1%	1%	1%	1.5%	1%
Size of fund in US$m. at 29/3/85	196.8	18.1	64.9	16.7	98.3	13.6	18.9	12.6
Cumulative performance in US$m. over one year*	–13.7	–3.3	–16.9	–37.6	+8.0	–4.1	–2.7	+16.0
Cumulative performance in US$ since launch*	+1,010.9	+56.4	+290.0	+117.2	+62.5	–1.3	+29.2	+40.7
Compound annual rate increase % p.a. since launch*	+17.7	+10.2	+15.5	+12.8	+3.5	–1.0	+10.1	+31.4

Notes: *Calculated to 29 March 1985, with dividends reinvested.
Dealing in all funds is daily, except GT Dollar Fund.

Source: G.T. Management Ltd., Hong Kong.

Table 7.2 The Investment Portfolio of the GT Global Technology Fund (in US dollars as at 31 December 1984)

	Market Value	Per cent of Net Assets
Teledata communications equipment	2,512,894	21.6
Information processing systems	2,332,562	19.9
Information processing software	2,203,373	18.9
Biotechnology	1,506,045	12.9
Semiconductors and manufacturing	1,018,045	8.6
Information processing CAD/CAM	672,525	5.8
Electronics	624,545	5.4
Office equipment	231,533	2.0
Private placement	35,849	0.3
Net cash and accounts receivable	542,173	4.6
Total net assets	11,679,544	100.0

Source: G.T. Management Ltd., Hong Kong.

the formation, operation, and promotion of unit trusts. In many ways the Committee depends on the managers and trustees of unit trusts to comply with the regulations. In other words, regulation is provided for, but government officials do not actively oversee the trusts' operations. In cases of fraud and/or negligence the body of unit trust holders may hold the trustees liable for damages. Thus active supervision may not be necessary.

The Code contains provisions and definitions of terms that must be used in a trust deed. It requires that the trustees provide explanatory memoranda that include a clear and concise statement of investment objectives and policies. The composition of a trust fund and the restrictions to be made on investments must be outlined.

Provisions for expanding a fund, and also for redeeming units for cash, must be stipulated. Special conditions may be made for the temporary sale of units at a fixed price, whereas usually an offer price is calculated on the basis of the prices of a fund's underlying assets during the previous 24 hours. Details in the Code also provide for the issue of unit trust certificates, either in registered or bearer form.

The basis for calculating the manager's remuneration, that is, the fees to be paid to the management company, must be stated clearly, as must the manner and method of the distribution of trust receipts to unit holders.

Auditing provisions must be complied with, and at least two reports must be published each year. The contents of the reports are specified.

The relations between the trustees and the management company are subject to scrutiny. In general, trustees and management must not be connected, but the Committee may waive this requirement if it is satisfied that both management and trustees will behave professionally, that is, as if they were independent of each other. Trustees may, in some circumstances, replace the management company, and may also retire and replace themselves.

Regulations over the Sale of Units

The promotional activities associated with the sale of units in the trust are severely limited.

No forecasts of the trust's performance may be made to the public or to non-unit holders. No radio, television, cinema or poster advertising of the trust is permitted in Hong Kong, nor is door-to-door canvassing for sales . . . any advertisement or other invitation to the public to invest in a unit trust requires the Commission's prior approval. . .[3]

These restraints on the marketing of unit trusts are supposedly designed to protect the investing public, but it is difficult to understand how restrictions on the distribution of information to the public can help. The adage is sometimes true that 'What he doesn't know won't hurt him'. But surely it is just as often true that what he does know can help him. The restrictions appear to be designed to reduce the competition among financial institutions rather than to prevent the fraudulent misrepresentation of the returns that are available on pools of invested funds.

Many trusts doing business in Hong Kong are, of course, regulated by supervisory agencies operating in their home countries as well as by Hong Kong laws. For example the regulatory agency in the United States is the Securities and Exchange Commission—an agency that imposes stringent regulations, most of which require the extensive provision of information and disclosure to the public. Heavy fines and penalties are imposed in cases of misrepresentation. Other countries, including Hong Kong, have regulations that are more lenient.

Restrictions on the promotion of sales in unit trusts among the general public mean that units are sold principally to institutional investors. Among the most important institutional investors are pension funds.

The Insurance Market

Insurance companies and unit trusts represent a large group of non-deposit-taking financial institutions. Unit trusts and insurance companies both accept an investor's money and use it to reinvest in interest-earning assets, in order to be able to repay the investor at a future time. But of course insurance is unique in that a person paying an insurance premium only receives a return when certain losses are incurred. This is true in the case of pure insurance, in which a small premium is paid in order to protect the insured from suffering a large loss. (One could say perhaps that the insured person is betting the insurance company that he will have a big loss—a bet against himself—while the company is betting that the insured will avoid loss.)

But many insurance policies are not of this 'pure' type. Many, especially life insurance policies, contain not only provisions for reimbursements for losses, but also provisions for the building up of savings. Thus many life insurance policies represent a combination of a savings programme and insurance protection.

Table 7.3 The Principal Financial Performance Statistics of the Insurance Sector in 1982 (HK$ million)

	General Insurers	Life Insurers	Insurance Agents, Brokers and Other Insurance Services	Total
Compensation of employees	217.9	92.5	174.0	484.4
Operating expenses	234.5	86.3	150.7	471.5
Net claims	988.6	332.4	n/a	1,321.0
Expenditure	2,818.0	560.1	324.7	3,702.8
Retained premiums	2,337.3	873.2	n/a	3,210.5
Gross premiums	4,771.6	896.5	n/a	5,668.1
Income and receipts	3,589.0	1,196.9	460.7	5,246.6
Technical reserves	1,812.8	3,606.7	n/a	5,419.5
Investment	3,053.4	3,656.2	n/a	6,709.6
Gross additions to fixed assets	47.7	29.5	27.1	104.3

Notes: n/a = not applicable.
The term 'insurers' refers to both insurers and reinsurers.

Source: Economic Report, Economic Research Department, Hongkong and Shanghai Banking Corporation, November 1984.

The Size of the Hong Kong Insurance Industry

In 1984 the Hongkong and Shanghai Banking Corporation analysed the published financial statements of 25 insurance companies incorporated in Hong Kong. This sample was drawn from a population of just under 200 companies. The data related to the year 1982.

The findings of the survey were that premiums had increased over the previous year by 16 per cent, but that profits had increased by 52 per cent. Since claims did not grow to the same degree, the average rate of return to shareholders rose from 15.7 per cent to 18.9 per cent.[4] The total assets had also increased in that year, by an astounding 26 per cent. Gross premium receipts had risen by 16 per cent.

Portfolios of stocks and bonds accounted for about 33 per cent of all assets, cash and bank balances formed about 20 per cent of assets, and mortgages formed 15 per cent. The total value of the investments administered by the insurers was HK$3,853 million in 1980 and HK$6,710 million in 1982. Approximately 96 per cent of these investments were in financial assets, with only the remaining 4 per cent being held in fixed assets.

Such rapid rates of growth by one sector of the economy can occur over several periods when an industry is expanding from a small and limited base. But it is obvious that such rates of expansion cannot be sustained over longer periods, because this could lead to a situation in which insurance business became larger than all other business.

Table 7.4 The Principal Personnel Statistics of the Insurance Sector in 1982

	General Insurers	Life Insurers	Insurance Agents, Brokers and Other Insurance Services	Total
Establishments	152	30	677	859
Persons engaged	3,897	1,649	3,188	8,735

Note: The term 'insurers' refers to both insurers and reinsurers.

Source: Economic Report, Economic Research Department, Hongkong and Shanghai Banking Corporation, November 1984.

The Hongkong and Shanghai Banking Corporation analysis estimates that

[the] insurance services consumed by the domestic economy, in terms of gross premiums, should be in the neighbourhood of HK$6.3 billion in 1982—consisting of HK$5.4 billion of general insurance premiums and HK$910 million of life insurance premiums. The corresponding estimates of retained premiums were HK$4.6 billion, HK$3.8 billion and HK$890 million respectively.[5]

Tables 7.3 and 7.4 provide a general summary of data on the insurance industry in Hong Kong in 1982.

Notes

1. This information was presented in an excellent unpublished term paper by Ong Ying and Ng Kim Sing, 'Unit Trust Business in Hong Kong', December 1983, in the Department of Accounting and Finance, the Chinese University of Hong Kong, Course Finance 401B, Financial Markets and Institutions. The author is extremely grateful for this source of information and relies on it on many occasions throughout this chapter.
2. See Ong Ying and Ng Kim Sing (1983), p. 9.
3. See Ong Ying and Ng Kim Sing (1983), p. 28.
4. Data are reported in *Economic Report* (the monthly newsletter of the Hongkong and Shanghai Banking Corporation), November 1984.
5. See note 4.

References

Persons interested in the current status of unit trusts in Hong Kong should contact the office of the Secretary of the Committee on Unit Trusts of the Securities Commission. This office will provide a potential investor with a list of trusts that are available. Since each trust has its unique qualities, the investor should obtain brochures from the trust officers. The brochures should contain all the information that is relevant.

The author is unaware, at the time of writing, of any comprehensive study of the unit trust business in Hong Kong, with the sole exception of the reference cited in note 1 of this chapter.

With regard to the insurance business, the Economic Research Department of the Hongkong and Shanghai Banking Corporation prepared a report entitled 'Recent Developments and the Performance of the Insurance Industry'. This report is available upon request by writing to GPO Box 64, Hong Kong.

Data on the performance of the insurance sector are also available from the Census and Statistics Department.

8. International Financial Relations

ELBERT Y.C. SHIH

ALTHOUGH the subject of international finance encompasses a large variety of topics, this chapter focuses on two of them: an analysis of the balance of payments in Hong Kong, and an examination of exchange rate regimes in Hong Kong. In considering the exchange rate system, we emphasize its effect on the balance of payments, trade, and other macro-economic variables.

The Balance of Payments

A country's balance of payments is a set of accounts that summarize international transactions, including exchanges of goods and services and transfers of capital. Transactions are classified as debits or credits and are grouped into different accounts. A line is drawn to separate autonomous transactions (items in the balance of payments that take place for their own sake) from accommodating transactions (compensatory items that are viewed as financing the balance of payments deficit or surplus). This is done in order to determine whether there is a payments surplus or deficit for a specified time period.

Hong Kong's Balance of Payments

It is not possible to evaluate Hong Kong's balance of payments performance on basic balance or on official settlements balance, because the published data cover the balance of trade in goods and services only. The method of presenting Hong Kong's international payments accounts does not indicate an assumption that only the exchange of goods and services between countries is autonomous and that other transactions are accommodating. Rather, it is simply that in Hong Kong no systematic record is kept of capital movements and transfer payments, and data on official reserves assets are not published and, therefore, are not available to the public. Hence, the overall payments position can only be inferred from indicators such as the movements of exchange rates. Exchange rate regimes are discussed in the second part of this chapter.

Table 8.1 shows the total volume of Hong Kong's exports and imports of goods and services from 1973 to 1984 and the balance between them. Throughout these years, Hong Kong had a deficit in its merchandise account and a surplus in its services account. There was an overall trade surplus until 1978, when the surplus in services failed to cover the deficit in the merchandise trade. In subsequent years the trade deficit has continued as Hong Kong's merchandise performance has deteriorated. A measure of

Table 8.1 The Imports and Exports of Goods and Services 1973–84 (at current market prices, HK$ million)

	1973	1974	1975	1976	1977	1978	1979	1980	1981	1982	1983	1984
Goods												
Exports (f.o.b.)	25,999	30,036	29,833	41,557	44,833	53,908	75,934	98,242	122,163	127,385	160,699	221,440
Imports (c.i.f.)	29,049	34,142	33,532	43,520	48,796	63,263	86,339	111,794	139,246	143,769	176,581	224,812
Balance on goods	−3,053	−4,106	−3,699	−1,963	−3,963	−9,335	−10,405	−13,552	−17,083	−16,384	−15,882	3,372
Services												
Exports	7,287	8,486	8,674	11,599	12,281	14,737	19,258	22,203	27,218	30,088	35,106	44,455
Imports	3,278	4,064	4,491	5,590	6,718	8,278	11,968	14,912	19,234	20,796	24,655	29,440
Balance on services	4,009	4,422	4,183	6,009	5,563	6,459	7,290	7,291	7,984	9,292	10,451	15,015
Total exports of goods and services	33,286	38,522	38,507	53,156	57,114	68,645	95,192	120,445	149,381	157,473	195,805	265,895
Total imports of goods and services	32,327	38,206	38,023	49,110	55,514	71,541	98,307	126,706	158,480	164,565	201,236	254,252
Balance on goods and services	959	316	484	4,046	1,600	−2,896	−3,115	−6,261	−9,099	−7,092	−5,431	11,643

Source: *Hong Kong Monthly Digest of Statistics* (Hong Kong, Census and Statistics Department), various issues, and *Estimate of Gross Domestic Product* (Hong Kong, Census and Statistics Department), various issues.

the trade gap is the ratio of trade deficit to total imports, and this is shown in Table 8.2. The gap reached its highest level in 1981 and has narrowed since then, suggesting that effective trade adjustments have been under way. To obtain a better understanding of Hong Kong's trade performance, it is useful to examine more closely the pattern of Hong Kong's trading activities.

Hong Kong's Trade

Hong Kong is congested with people and scarce in natural resources and foodstuffs, and therefore needs to import a great variety of items for its ever-growing economy and population. To pay for its imports, Hong Kong must earn foreign exchange through exports. In broad terms, Hong Kong imports raw materials and capital goods (accounting for more than half of its total imports) to use in manufacturing products. These products are sold abroad and, together with various services provided by Hong Kong, constitute the major sources of the foreign exchange earnings that are needed to pay for Hong Kong's imports.

The importance of foreign trade to Hong Kong's economy can also be seen from the ratio of trade to national product. From 1973 to 1983, total trade (comprising imports, domestic exports, and re-exports) averaged 150 per cent of Hong Kong's Gross Domestic Product (GDP), and in 1984 was 178 per cent. The average annual growth rate of trade for the same period was about 21 per cent.[1] This explains why Hong Kong is one of the most open economies in the world and why international trade is crucial in shaping its economy and its growth.

The success and sustained growth in the volume of Hong Kong's trade may be attributed to numerous factors, which include the following.
(a) Geographic location. Hong Kong is located at a strategic position in South-east Asia, a region that has been characterized by a series of economic recoveries and 'miracles' and which has maintained its economic growth at a more rapid pace than other areas during the past two decades. Hong Kong and other countries have thrived on competition

Table 8.2 The Trade Gap 1978–84 (trade deficit as a percentage of total imports)

	Visible Trade Gap	Total Trade Gap
1978	14.79	4.04
1979	12.05	3.17
1980	12.12	4.94
1981	12.27	5.74
1982	11.40	4.31
1983	8.99	2.70
1984	1.50	*

Note: *Total exports exceed imports.
Source: Calculated from Table 8.1.

and interaction within the region, and trade expansion is expected to continue.

(b) Business environment. As a *laissez-faire* economy, Hong Kong mostly follows a policy of free enterprise and free trade. The market adjusts itself to changes in underlying factors, and the economy adapts itself to the market adjustment. Furthermore, with comparatively low tax rates and few restrictions on trade, Hong Kong provides an environment which is conducive to efficient production and competitive trading.

(c) Facilities. Hong Kong is equipped with an advanced communications network and adequate transportation facilities. Hong Kong is also endowed with one of the world's finest harbours and has the third largest container port in the world.

All of these factors contribute to Hong Kong's development as a major international trade centre.

Imports

During the period 1973–84, the value of total imports increased steadily, except for 1975 when world trade in general slowed down as a result of a world-wide recession. Services maintained their level of about 11 per cent of total imports throughout the period. As a percentage of GDP, imports rose from 65.7 per cent in 1977 to 87.7 per cent in 1984, suggesting a substantial increase in the propensity to import.

Imports classified by end use are presented in Fig. 8.1 which shows changes in the relative importance of each category over selected years. Raw materials and semi-manufactured goods are always the largest category of Hong Kong's imports. The second largest import item is consumer goods, such as electrical appliances, clothing, diamonds, and watches. Electrical and other industrial machinery, parts, and fuel are imported for use in industrialization and development. The percentage of foodstuffs decreased from 24.7 per cent of total imports in 1964 to 11.2 per cent in 1983.

Hong Kong imports its merchandise mainly from China, Japan, the United States, Taiwan, Singapore, and the United Kingdom—and, in terms of the value of imports in 1983, in that order. Japan is the major source of fabrics made of man-made fibres, of iron and steel, and of semi-manufactured goods, and in 1976 Japan replaced the United States as the largest supplier of capital goods to Hong Kong. China emerged as the most important supplier of consumer goods in 1980. Half of Hong Kong's food is imported from China.

Since China launched its modernization movement in the post-Mao Zedong era, its economic transactions with the rest of the world have increased substantially. China's final exports to Hong Kong and re-exports through Hong Kong as an entrepôt have both grown rapidly. Consequently, China surpassed Japan in 1982 to become the largest supplier (by value) to Hong Kong. On the other hand, the United Kingdom, after losing its market share to Asian industrialized countries such as Taiwan and Singapore, has, since 1975, been at the bottom of the list of Hong Kong's major suppliers.

Fig. 8.1 Imports Classified by End Use 1970–83 (per cent)

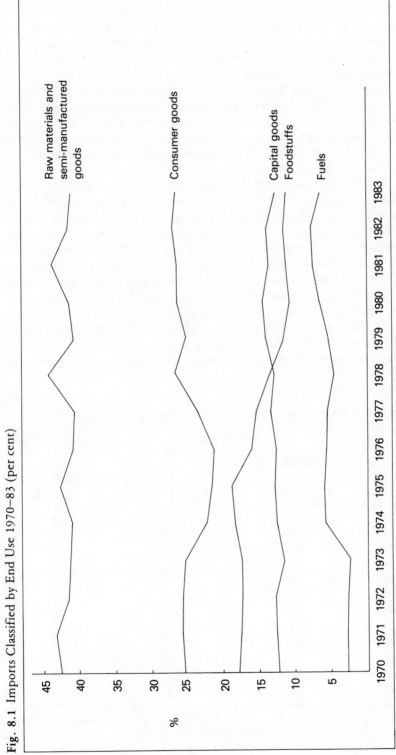

Source: *Hong Kong Monthly Digest of Statistics* (Hong Kong, Census and Statistics Department), various issues.

Exports

Hong Kong's industries are primarily export-oriented. Exports not only enable Hong Kong to pay for imports, but also create job opportunities and markets to absorb domestic products. For the period 1973–84, exports averaged about 70 per cent of GDP.

Since 1973 Hong Kong has exported more clothing than any other country. It is also one of the major exporters of radios, watches, toys, dolls, electrical fans, and plastic flowers. Because of its high export–GDP ratio, Hong Kong's export performance usually has a significant impact on its employment, especially in basic industries such as textiles and clothing, watches, and plastic products.

Hong Kong exports most of its goods to a limited number of countries. Over the past decade, Hong Kong has found its major export markets in the United States, the United Kingdom, China, and West Germany. Concentration ratios of export markets provide a measure of the degree of concentration, either in geographical terms or in one product category. (The higher the ratio, the larger is the concentration of exports in one market or in the one category of product for which data are provided.) Table 8.3 shows selected concentration ratios for Hong Kong's exports, for the period 1973–84. Clothing and other articles of apparel, Hong Kong's major export, varied from 33 per cent to 45 per cent of total domestic exports during this 12-year period. Mainly as a result of a rapid increase in the export of watches, toys, and electronic components for computers, this concentration

Table 8.3 The Concentration Ratios of Exports 1973–84 (per cent)

	Export Market		Category of Export
	United States, United Kingdom, and West Germany	United States	Clothing and Other Apparel
1973	59	35	38
1974	55	32	38
1975	57	32	45
1976	57	34	44
1977	58	39	40
1978	58	37	39
1979	56	34	36
1980	54	33	34
1981	55	36	35
1982	55	38	35
1983	58	42	33
1984	59	44	34

Source: Calculated from *Kong Kong Monthly Digest of Statistics* (Hong Kong, Census and Statistics Department), various issues.

ratio has decreased since 1975, thus showing a reduction in the relative importance of clothing as a source of export earnings. However, geographically, the concentration ratio does not show any highly significant change, although exports to the United States increased from 33 per cent of total exports in 1980 to 44 per cent in 1984. To lessen its dependence on one or a few countries for its exports, Hong Kong needs greater market diversification. This would help to reduce the instability of exchange earnings.

Services

With rapid economic growth and the development of its financial sector, the export services rendered by Hong Kong have improved greatly and have increased by about five times over the past decade. In 1983, they amounted to about 20 per cent of Hong Kong's total exports.

Hong Kong has one of the largest container ports in the world, and more than 90 per cent of its exports are transported by sea. Air carriers have also grown steadily and brought in much business. Altogether transportation provides more than 50 per cent of the total income from export services.

Tourism is another of Hong Kong's important export services. Partly because of aggressive promotion by the Hong Kong Tourist Association, the expenditure by visitors to Hong Kong has almost quadrupled over the last ten years. Furthermore, the rise in the number of visitors has increased hotel occupancy rates and contributed to the growth of the hotel industry.

Over the past decade, other services, including insurance and banking, have also increased but are minor in terms of the total value of export services.

Accompanying the growth of exports has been a growth in the imports of services, but they constitute only about 11 per cent of total imports. Overall, the excess of exports of services over imports of services has helped Hong Kong to finance the deficit in its merchandise account.

Exchange Regimes and Economic Performance in Hong Kong

There are differing views of the present world exchange regime. Proponents highlight the advantages of the flexible exchange rates that are presumed to be inherent in the present system. Critics tend to attribute a variety of economic problems to the inadequacy of the prevailing exchange rate arrangements. The purpose of this section of this chapter is to discuss the Hong Kong exchange regimes and to assess their impact on economic performance in Hong Kong.[2]

We first review the changes in exchange regimes which Hong Kong has experienced, and then examine economic performance and trade in Hong Kong under different exchange systems. Finally, in the third part of this chapter, we analyse the linked exchange rate implemented in 1983.

Exchange Regimes in Hong Kong

Hong Kong has undergone several major exchange rate reforms during the past two decades. After abandoning the silver standard in 1935, it pegged its currency to the pound sterling and retained this peg throughout the Bretton Woods era until 1972, when it switched the link to the United States dollar. A short time later, Hong Kong broke the link with the United States dollar and began floating the Hong Kong dollar, in November 1974. After the currency weakened and a major crisis occurred, in 1983 Hong Kong adopted a 'guided' exchange rate system (which will be examined later in this chapter).

During the period of fixed exchange rates, the Hong Kong dollar currency was fully backed by foreign exchange reserves, and notes were issued for sterling at a fixed exchange rate. The Hong Kong money supply was, therefore, tied to its balance of payments performance, and to the world value of the currency to which it was fixed.

In the absence of a central bank in Hong Kong to take stabilization measures, the free-market economy regulated itself through the self-adjusting mechanism inherent in the sterling exchange standard. For instance, when the economy was booming, total expenditures increased, and imports rose in relation to exports, resulting in a trade deficit. As the Government did not counteract this trend, exchange reserves and the money supply decreased, helping to curb the import demand and to reduce the deficit.

Smooth and effective adjustment under the fixed exchange rates enabled the Hong Kong economy to adapt to the state of the global business cycle without sacrificing domestic economic objectives. The economy maintained a steady growth of real GDP, averaging about 9 per cent per annum from 1961 to 1972.[3] The effectiveness of the domestic automatic adjustment and the stability and growth of the economies of Hong Kong's major trading partners contributed to the steady growth of Hong Kong's imports and exports during this period. The close movements of the annual growth rates of exports and imports shown in Fig. 8.2 may reflect to an extent the adaptability and resilience of the economy. As a result, the fixed exchange rate was never under severe pressure to make adjustment changes.

Nevertheless, a small open economy like Hong Kong found it difficult to insulate itself from the repercussions of the world-wide currency realignments in the early 1970s. After a series of devaluations, the pound sterling began to float in 1972 and Hong Kong pegged its currency to the United States dollar before letting it float in 1974.

As Hong Kong is one of the most open free-market economies, and there is minimal government intervention, the Hong Kong dollar was virtually 'clean floating' between 1975 and 1983. In Fig. 8.3 the movements of the Effective Exchange Rate Index (EERI) and the Consumer Price Index (CPI) for Hong Kong display a close inverse relationship. Statistics also indicate that in the years when the CPI increase rate was low, exports exceeded imports and the EERI remained relatively high. After 1978, as the inflation rate increased and the excess of imports over exports grew, the EERI declined steadily.[4] The variation in exchange rates thus provided a channel through which a payments imbalance was adjusted during the 'floating rate' period.

Fig. 8.2 The Growth Rates of Hong Kong Imports and Exports 1960–72

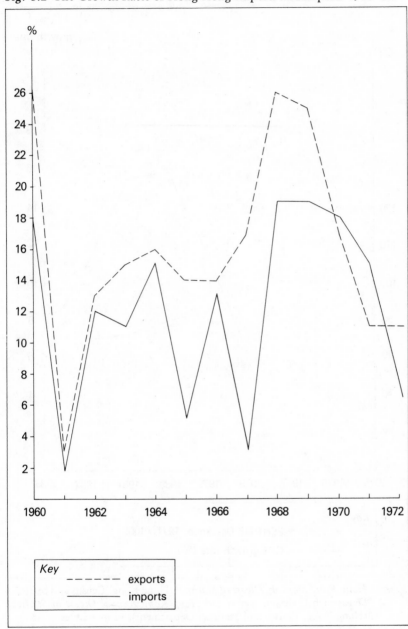

Source: *Hong Kong Annual Digest of Statistics* (Hong Kong, Census and Statistics Department), various issues.

Exchange Rates and Economic Performance

The proponents of floating exchange rates tend to argue that when the exchange rate is determined by market demand and supply, a country's balance of payments can be adjusted through rate variations.[5] In this way,

Fig. 8.3 The Hong Kong EERI and CPI Growth Rate 1975–83

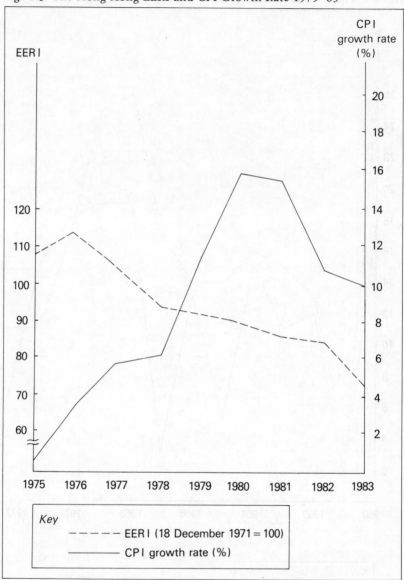

Source: *Hong Kong Monthly Digest of Statistics* (Hong Kong, Census and Statistics
Department), various issues; and *Hong Kong Annual Digest of Statistics*
(Hong Kong, Census and Statistics Department), various issues.

they argue, its economy can be considerably insulated from external disturbances and its economic policy can be more independent and more effective
in achieving domestic goals. With fixed exchange rates, however, business
fluctuations are transmitted between economies without the buffer which
exchange rate variations provide. Stable exchange rates reduce the insulation
of the domestic economy from the repercussions of foreign events.

The results of a study of price movements (the CPI), real income (GDP), and the money supply (M1) in Hong Kong over the period 1965–83 do not entirely support the above argument. Table 8.4 shows that the average inflation rate rose from 4.5 to 8.8 per cent, and that the real GDP growth rate fell from 9.3 to 8.7 per cent in the period of floating rates. However, the dispersion of M1 growth rates (as measured by the standard deviation) decreased from 15.3 to 8.8 per cent after Hong Kong floated its currency in late 1974, possibly as a result of greater exchange flexibility, which reduced the impact of the repercussions of foreign events on exchange reserves and the money supply.

Exchange regimes have often been assessed in terms of their impact on international trade. Floating rates are sometimes blamed for impeding trade, since some uncertainty is associated with exchange rate fluctuations. We will also consider changes in the value of trade and in the relationship between trade and exchange rate variability, in order to analyse the effect of exchange flexibility on Hong Kong's trade.

If a floating exchange system has an adverse impact on trade, it might be expected that the value of trade compared with national income (trade/GDP) should fall during a period of floating rates. Although, in Hong Kong, this ratio has been more volatile since 1974, it does not show any significant sign of decline.

Table 8.5 compares the average annual growth rates of imports with the total trade of Hong Kong, for the periods of fixed exchange rates (1961–74) and flexible exchange rates (1975–83). The nominal growth rates of both imports and total trade are higher during the years of floating rates than in the earlier years. But, as inflation rates were higher in the period 1975–83, there is little difference in real growth rates in the two periods. In short, statistics do not suggest that a change in the exchange rate system has generated any significant impact on trade in Hong Kong.

Table 8.4 The Growth Rates of the CPI, the GDP, and M1 in Hong Kong during Periods of Fixed and Flexible Exchange Rates

Time Period	Average Growth Rates (%)	Standard Deviation
CPI		
1965–72	4.5	1.8
1975–83	8.8	4.9
Real GDP		
1961–73	9.3	4.5
1975–83	8.7	5.1
M1		
1967–74	11.4	15.3
1975–83	14.4	8.8

Source: Calculated from *Hong Kong Monthly Digest of Statistics* (Hong Kong, Census and Statistics Department), various issues, and *Hong Kong Annual Digest of Statistics* (Hong Kong, Census and Statistics Department), various issues.

Table 8.5 The Average Growth Rates of Imports and Trade in Hong Kong 1961–83 (per cent)

	1961–74	1975–83
Average growth rates of imports	14.3	20.3
Average growth rates of trade	15.9	20.6

Source: Calculated from *Hong Kong Monthly Digest of Statistics* (Hong Kong, Census and Statistics Department), various issues; and *Hong Kong Annual Digest of Statistics* (Hong Kong, Census and Statistics Department), various issues.

Traders generally take uncertainties into account when making decisions. One of the sources of uncertainty relates to exchange rates, yet there is no agreement on the effect of exchange rate variability on trade. Although exchange rate variability does not necessarily increase the uncertainties facing traders, it has been widely used as an observable measure of uncertainty. We have calculated the standard deviation of the monthly Hong Kong dollar–United States dollar exchange rates for two time periods: 1962–9, while Hong Kong was on the sterling exchange standard; and from 1974 to 1983, when Hong Kong had floating exchange rates. As expected, Fig. 8.4 shows that the exchange rate variability was greater in the later years.

Did fluctuations in the exchange rates have an adverse impact on trade? How did Hong Kong's trade react to a greater exchange rate variability? The author has undertaken an empirical analysis to find the answer to these questions.[6] The standard deviation of the daily EERI over every three-month period from the beginning of 1977 to the beginning of 1984 was calculated, as a measure of the exchange rate uncertainty faced by the Hong Kong economy. (This is shown in Fig. 8.5.) In order to explain the movements of imports and exports in Hong Kong, this analysis also examined incomes and prices.[7] The results of this analysis indicate that both imports and exports moved in the way that would theoretically be expected, that is, they were positively related to income but were inversely related to relative prices and to exchange rate variability. However the effect of the EERI was statistically insignificant. In other words, these data show that greater fluctuations in exchange rates during the years of floating rates did not have a significant impact on Hong Kong's trade.

An Analysis of the Linked Exchange Rate System

Background

The exchange value of the Hong Kong dollar, as measured by the trade-weighted EERI, began to move down in 1978. In that year, the EERI fell below 100 (18 December 1971 = 100) for the first time since Hong Kong had switched to floating rates in 1974, and continued to decline rather slowly in the following years. As Hong Kong's trade balance turned from surplus to

Fig. 8.4 The Standard Deviation of the Monthly Hong Kong Dollar–
United States Dollar Exchange Rates 1962–9 and 1974–84

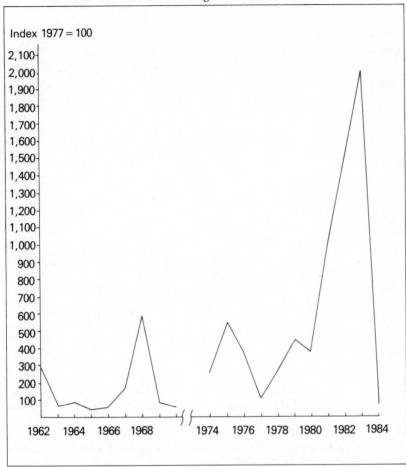

Source: *Hong Kong Monthly Digest of Statistics* (Hong Kong, Census and Statistics
Department), various issues.

deficit, and inflation increased, a small currency depreciation helped the
adjustment of trade. However, since October 1982, the rate of depreciation
has accelerated. In spite of a decrease in inflation and a narrowing of the
deficit gap the Hong Kong EERI fell to a record low figure of 57.2 on 24
September 1983, and the exchange rate with the United States dollar was
HK$9.60. An estimate based on economic factors alone, which was made at
about this time, indicated that the Hong Kong dollar was undervalued by
about 30 per cent.[8] The reason for this is believed to have been primarily
political. Uncertainties about the outcome of the talks between Britain and
China over the future of Hong Kong after 1997 caused speculation against
the Hong Kong dollar in the years 1982 and 1983. Large shifts in currency
demand from the Hong Kong dollar to other currencies, especially the United
States dollar, occurred during 1983.

Fig. 8.5 The Standard Deviation of the Daily Hong Kong Dollar–United States Dollar Exchange Rates 1977–84

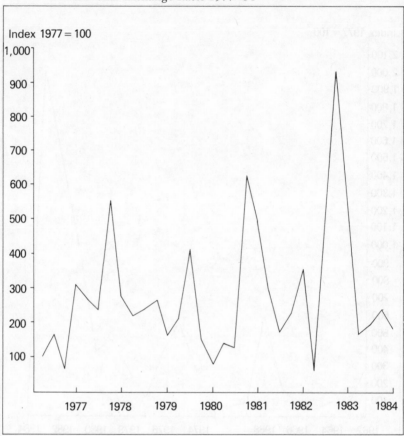

Source: *Hong Kong Monthly Digest of Statistics* (Hong Kong, Census and Statistics Department), various issues.

Dual Exchange Rates

To prevent further deterioration in the economy, measures were taken to stabilize the exchange value of the currency. The Financial Secretary of Hong Kong announced on 15 October 1983 that, in future, when the note-issuing banks wished to issue notes, they would be required to deposit US$1 with the Exchange Fund in order to obtain a Certificate of Indebtedness (CI) worth HK$7.80; and the Fund would also be required to give US$1 for every CI worth HK$7.80 turned in to it. The same conversion rate was applied to other commercial banks, while the price of the United States dollar for the general public would have to be determined by the exchange market. (Therefore this price may or may not be HK$7.80.) As a result a two-tier market was created in Hong Kong and, since that time, there have been two exchange rates between the local currency and the United States dollar—a pegged rate between the banking sector and the Exchange Fund and a free-market rate for the rest of the economy.

The Stability of the Market Rate and Arbitrage

Though a free-market rate of exchange could be at any level determined by market forces, the rate in Hong Kong has shown remarkable stability since dual rates were brought into effect. Most of the time it has fluctuated within the range of 1 per cent above or below the 'linked' rate of US$1 = HK$7.80. Thus the Government has achieved exactly the result it intended—that the market rate should stay in line with the peg. Thus the dual exchange rate system is also termed a 'guided' exchange rate system. But how is it possible for the freely fluctuating market rate to stay so close to the peg? The explanation lies in the arbitrage process (defined as the simultaneous purchase and sale of a currency to take advantage of different prices in different markets). Under arbitrage, the competition of market participants holds the market rate close to the rate set by the Government.

In the Hong Kong exchange market, which is known for its keen competition and efficiency, well-informed exchange dealers always take prompt action when they observe opportunities to improve their position. With dual exchange rates, price differences in a given foreign currency provide them with opportunities for exchange arbitrage. For example, when the market price of the United States dollar exceeds the pegged exchange rate value, commercial banks use Hong Kong currency to buy United States dollars from the note-issuing banks (which in turn may obtain United States dollars from the Exchange Fund), and sell the United States dollars on the exchange market. When the market price of the United States dollar falls below the pegged rate, the banks buy United States dollars on the market and sell them to the Exchange Fund for a higher price. The banks gain on either type of transaction and can continue to do so until the market rate approaches the pegged exchange rate.

Assuming that there are no transaction costs, the condition for profitable arbitrage when the market rate is higher than the peg may be stated quite simply, by means of the equation:

$$(P - 7.80)/7.80 < i,$$

where 'P' is the market price of the United States dollar and 'i' is the interest rate required for the use of funds for arbitrage.

For example, this equation shows that, when the market exchange rate value of the United States dollar is HK$7.83, each Hong Kong dollar used for arbitrage would earn (7.83 − 7.80)/7.80, that is, HK$0.003846. The rate of return depends on the length of time involved in the arbitrage process. If only one day is needed, the annual rate would be 138 per cent. In other words, arbitrage is expected to occur as long as the required interest rate and the transaction costs are less than 138 per cent.

Arbitrage in the exchange market not only keeps the free-market rate close to the linked rate of US$1 = HK$7.80, but also affects the Hong Kong money supply. As the position of the Hong Kong dollar strengthens, more United States dollars are presented to the Exchange Fund by banks for Hong Kong dollars, and the money supply increases. On the other hand, a deterioration in the value of the Hong Kong dollar tends to decrease the money supply. Since the money supply and credit conditions usually affect interest rates, the movements of interest rates may reflect, to a certain extent, the exchange value of the Hong Kong dollar.

The Linked Exchange Rate and Interest Rates

When the linked rate and the market exchange rate are equal, arbitrage does not take place and, of course, has no effect on interest rates. When these two exchange rates are different, the size of the difference between them significantly affects interest rates. Because arbitrage provides banks with an outlet for excess funds, an individual who wishes to obtain a short-term loan from a bank must pay an interest rate which is not less than the profit that might be realized from arbitrage. Suppose that 'd' is the number of days needed in the arbitrage process and that 'P' is the market exchange rate, the minimum interest rate ('r') that one must pay to the bank is given in the following equation.[9]

$$r = [(P - 7.80)/7.80] \times 360/d.$$

Thus $r = (46.154P - 360)d$.

The equation indicates that the higher the market exchange rate and the shorter the period for arbitrage, the higher the interest rate one needs to pay to the bank. In practice, however, 'r' should be considerably lower than the value shown in this equation because transaction costs in the market must be taken into account. Provided that the market exchange rate is US\$1 = HK\$7.80, arbitrage does not exist, and therefore arbitrage profit would not be a factor in determining the interest rate charged by the banks.

It is important to note that arbitrage may not take place when the market interest rate is higher than the difference between the market exchange rate and the linked rate. Funds are used for purposes other than arbitrage. Consequently, the exchange rate moves freely in the market, and the linked rate is ineffective in bringing the market rate in line with the peg, until the interest rate falls below 'r', or until the differential between the market exchange rate and the peg grows larger than the interest rate.

Adjustment Mechanisms

Since Hong Kong has no central bank, adjustment of the economy is mainly self-regulating. A payments deficit, for instance, may cause the market exchange rate to increase, and arbitrage is likely to follow. Credit may contract and interest rates may rise. All these changes may lead to decreases in investment and other expenditures, including imports. Besides, more capital may flow in to earn higher interest rates. Consequently, deficits may be reduced or even eliminated. Conversely, when surpluses occur, adjustment in the opposite direction occurs.

Under conditions of floating exchange rates, exchange rate variations generally tend to reduce the impact on exchange reserves and interest rates of the performance of the balance of payments. Under the current linked exchange rate system in Hong Kong, the internal economy is more subject to the influence of external adjustments. Table 8.6 shows that Hong Kong had more and greater changes in interest rates during the nine-month period immediately following the introduction of dual exchange rates in October 1983 than in any of the preceding periods from 1980. An additional aspect of a linked exchange rate system is that interest rate variability is also larger than under a system of floating exchange rates.

During the period of floating rates (1974 to 1983), the supply of money and credit conditions were independent of Hong Kong's external payments position, and a rapid expansion of credit was held to be responsible for an increase in inflation and a weakening in the value of the currency. Following the creation of dual exchange rates in October 1983, monetary growth was largely dependent on the performance of Hong Kong's balance of payments.

The new currency arrangement established in 1983 was made in the wake of a massive flight of capital and a precipitous fall in the exchange value of the Hong Kong dollar during the year 1983. Political uncertainties and a floating exchange rate were the factors which were blamed for the dollar crisis. It was generally believed at that time that stability in the exchange rate between the currencies of Hong Kong and the United States was necessary, in order to achieve one of the Government's primary long-term goals—a stable economy with an inflation rate corresponding to that in the United States.[10]

As a consequence of the pegging of the Hong Kong dollar to the value of the United States dollar, economic conditions in the United States could directly affect Hong Kong's exports. For a highly open economy like Hong Kong, the effect would be far-reaching, in particular because the United States is the largest importer of Hong Kong's goods. The influence of economic trends in other countries might be less. If the exchange value of the United States dollar were to change, the Hong Kong dollar would fluctuate in relation to other currencies also. Of course the changes in the

Table 8.6 The Frequency and Size of Changes in Interest Rates 1980–July 1984*

	1980	1981	1982	Jan.–Sept. 1983	Oct. 1983–July 1984
Frequency of changes	11	7	6	6	12
Largest margin of change (% points)	2	2	1.5	3	3.25
Coefficient of variation	0.16	0.07	0.05	0.12	0.18

Note: *Prime rates set by the Hong Kong Association of Banks.

Source: Calculated from Hong Kong Monthly Digest of Statistics (Hong Kong, Census and Statistics Department), various issues.

United States dollar might not be of benefit to the Hong Kong economy. Therefore exchange rate variations can not be relied on as a means of adjustment in the event of external disturbances.

If imported instability intensifies, pressure for adjusting the linked rate increases. But changing the peg may lead to other problems. First of all, it is not easy to determine an appropriate rate. Further, as expected from adjustable peg arrangements, any change tends to be large. Trade, investment, and the exchange market might thus be affected significantly. In view of the decrease in inflation in 1984 and the goals set by the Government to achieve price stability and to regulate the money supply, it seems likely that the linked exchange rate system will be maintained as it is.

Summary and Conclusions

Because it lacks arable land and other natural resources, Hong Kong relies heavily on imports of foodstuffs, raw materials, and capital goods. Exports are equally essential because foreign exchange earnings are needed to pay for imports. Consequently, Hong Kong has had a remarkable sustained growth of foreign trade and has become one of the most open economies in the world, partially because of its free-trade and free-enterprise economy.

During the period of observation (1973–84), raw materials and semi-manufactured goods have been the largest category of imports, while the importance of foodstuffs, measured as a percentage of total imports, has declined steadily. On the export side, Hong Kong specializes primarily in labour-intensive manufactured goods. Textile products account for more than one-third of Hong Kong's exports. More than one-third of Hong Kong's merchandise has been exported to the United States. To reduce its dependence on only a few countries for its exports, Hong Kong needs to make greater efforts to diversify its export markets. Besides, in the course of industrialization, Hong Kong is expected to move away from specialization in labour-intensive manufactured goods towards high-technology products which will require more highly skilled labour.

Hong Kong has been characterized by its free-market economy, which regulates itself through the self-adjusting mechanism that is inherent in the sterling exchange standard and a system of floating exchange rates. Effective adjustments under fixed exchange rates helped Hong Kong to maintain a balanced growth of trade and a steady increase in real GDP from 1961 to 1972. However we find that, after turning to floating rates in 1974, Hong Kong had lower rates of growth and higher rates of inflation, while the pattern of trade was not significantly affected by the changes in the exchange regime. Although greater exchange rate flexibility was expected to benefit the economy of Hong Kong, the fact that this did not happen does not mean that the alleged advantages of floating rates do not exist. Rather, it suggests that the exchange rate is only one of many factors that help to shape the state of the economy. The effectiveness of an exchange rate depends very much on other factors such as the domestic monetary system and external disturbances. The impact of the exchange rate alone is relatively limited.

The viability of the dual exchange rate arrangement introduced in 1983 hinges to a large extent on the economies of the United States and Hong Kong. Disregarding political considerations, close economic co-operation between these two countries would greatly reduce the costs of linking the currencies—costs which include changes in money supply, interest rate adjustments, and investment decisions in Hong Kong.

Notes

1. Calculated from various issues of the *Hong Kong Monthly Digest of Statistics* (Hong Kong, Census and Statistics Department).
2. This section is based primarily on a paper presented by the author at the Annual Meeting of the Southwestern Society of Economists in New Orleans, 1985.
3. See *Hong Kong Monthly Digest of Statistics*.
4. *Hong Kong Monthly Digest of Statistics*.
5. See Friedman (1953), Johnson (1969).
6. Unpublished. This research is reported in the paper referred to in note 2.
7. Volume equations for Hong Kong's exports and imports were estimated. The results are given below:

$$X = -5.73 + 3.83FY - 1.58RPX - 0.007SD$$
$$\quad\quad (4.66) \quad\quad (-1.46) \quad\quad (-0.19)$$
$$M = 3.59 + 1.09DY - 0.87RPM - 0.008SD$$
$$\quad\quad (8.71) \quad\quad (-1.00) \quad\quad (-0.28)$$

where

    X = volume of exports
    M = volume of imports
    FY = trade-weighted income average of the United States, Japan, the United Kingdom, and West Germany
    DY = domestic income
    RPX = relative price of exports to imports
    RPM = relative price of imports to exports
    SD = standard deviation of daily EERI within each quarter.

8. 'Anatomy of the Hong Kong Dollar's Recent Weakness', *Hang Seng Economic Quarterly*, July 1983, pp. 9–21.
9. This equation is applicable when P>7.80. For P<7.80, $r = [360(7.80/P-1)]/d$.
10. *South China Morning Post*, 25 November 1983.

References

Akhtar, M. and Hilton, R., 'Effects of Exchange Rate Uncertainty on German and U.S. Trade', *Quarterly Review*, Federal Reserve Bank of New York, Spring 1984, pp. 7–16.
'Anatomy of the Hong Kong Dollar's Recent Weakness', *Hang Seng Economic Quarterly* (Hong Kong), July 1983, pp.9–21.
Batten, D.S. and Ott, M., 'Five Common Myths About Floating Exchange Rates', *Review*, Federal Reserve Bank of St. Louis, Nov. 1983, pp. 5–15.
De Grauwe, P., 'What Are the Scope and Limits of Fruitful International Monetary Cooperation in the 1980s?', in G.M. von Furstenberg (ed.), *International*

Money and Credit: The Policy Roles (Washington, DC, International Monetary Fund, 1983), pp. 375–405.

Dunn R., Jr., *The Many Disappointments of Flexible Exchange Rates* (New Jersey, Princeton University, Dec. 1983).

Friedman, M., *Essays in Positive Economics* (Chicago, University of Chicago Press, 1953), pp. 157–203.

Goldstein, M., 'Downward Price Inflexibility, Ratchet Effects and the Inflationary Impact of Import Price Changes', *IMF Staff Papers*, Nov. 1977, pp. 569–612.

_____ *Have Flexible Exchange Rates Handicapped Macroeconomic Policy?* (New Jersey, Princeton University, June 1983).

Hong Kong Government, Census and Statistics Department, *Estimate of Gross Domestic Product* (various issues).

_____ *Hong Kong Annual Digest of Statistics* (various issues).

_____ *Hong Kong Monthly Digest of Statistics* (various issues).

International Monetary Fund, *Exchange Rate Volatility and World Trade* (Washington, DC, International Monetary Fund, July 1984).

_____ *International Financial Statistics* (Washington, DC, International Monetary Fund, various issues).

Johnson, H.G., 'The Case for Flexible Exchange Rates—1969', in H.G. Johnson and J. Nash, *U.K. and Floating Exchanges* (London, International Economic Association, 1969) pp. 9–37.

Lethbridge, D.G. (ed.), *The Business Environment in Hong Kong* (Hong Kong, Oxford University Press, second edition, 1984).

South China Morning Post, 25 November 1983.

9. Electronic Fund Transfer Systems

Simon S.M. Ho

Money is merely information, and as such can reside in computer storages with payments consisting of data transfer between one machine and another.

(James Martin[1])

Hong Kong became a major international financial centre in the 1970s, and the banking industry has developed rapidly since then. One of the major contributing factors to this rapid development is the fact that Information Technology (which is commonly referred to as IT) has been used extensively and intensively. Among all businesses, banks comprise the largest group of computer users. They were therefore the first group in Hong Kong to experience the large savings in costs and the various other benefits which the efficient introduction of computerization brings.

The most vital operation of any banking business is the handling of financial data. Technological developments have led to the gradual installation of Electronic Fund Transfer Systems (EFTSs) that are used to process financial data and to transfer funds among financial institutions electronically. The development of EFTSs has been a popular subject of discussion within banking circles over the past decade. Today it is the centre of attention.

While recent electronic fund transfer innovations offer a new array of computerized electronic banking products and services, such as Automated Teller Machines (ATMs) and Point-Of-Sale (POS) systems, the technology on which these innovations rest is still in its infancy. EFTSs currently account for only a small portion of fund transfers in Hong Kong. For many reasons, the early prediction that the new technology would soon lead to a cashless and chequeless society has not been borne out, but EFTS services now exist and financial institutions are moving steadily towards an information society that will use less cash and fewer cheques.

This chapter discusses the nature of these developments, and some of the issues that must be resolved as these systems become more common. Some of the material in this chapter is based on a mailed questionnaire survey and informal discussions with professionals in financial institutions and the Electronic Data Processing (EDP) industry.

The Application of Information Technology in Banks

The computerization of banking operations in Hong Kong began in 1966 when the Chartered Bank (now known as the Standard Chartered Bank) installed a centralized mainframe computer and developed the batch processing of routine banking transactions. Since then, like their counterparts in the West, the major banks in Hong Kong have gradually introduced computerized operations in order to save costs and to compete in the highly competitive banking market. Since 1969 Magnetic Ink Character Recognition (MICR) characters have been printed on cheques, enabling the use of cheque readers/sorters, which have reduced the cost of processing cheques and the time required to do so.

Once cheque processing was electronically automated, bankers realized the benefits to be gained by automating many other large-volume functions. Thus the computer has had a revolutionary effect on the banking industry. In the late 1960s and early 1970s numerous computer applications were developed and launched to automate internal accounting and marketing information systems. (Batch-oriented applications include loan analysis, account reconciliation, foreign trade and exchange dealings, the issue of capital stock, the payment of utilities bills, the handling of payrolls, and money management. Most of these batch systems aim to automate internal operations. Many are designed to provide information which is necessary to improve managerial decision making.) During these years, bank account transactions continued to be processed in an off-line manner, and few efforts were made to upgrade direct computerized banking services for the banks' clients.

In the mid-1970s, some revolutionary changes occurred. Although banks first employed computers to automate routine internal tasks, they gradually moved into on-line data processing. (As it pertains to banking, the on-line concept refers to a process for 'capturing' data as close to the point of transaction as possible, for example at the teller's window.) Still using a centralized mainframe computer, the banks established on-line distributed processing networks in all their branches. In an effort to reduce rising costs and paper handling, on-line savings accounts were introduced. These enabled customers to make deposits, transfer funds, withdraw cash, and obtain up-to-date account information at any on-line teller terminal. By using these terminals it became possible for an account holder to conduct his banking business at any branch of a bank instead of being restricted to one branch.

An examination of the development of modern banking practices indicates that banks in general initially adopted an inward-looking approach to their computerization. It was necessary first to find answers to internal operational problems, before turning towards computer systems aimed at developing new profitable self-service electronic banking for customers, typified today by Automated Teller Machines (ATMs).

At the time of writing, about 80 per cent of banks in Hong Kong have well-established data processing departments and are using sophisticated IT to assist them in speeding up operations, in providing better management information, and in improving services to their customers. Perhaps the most significant impact of IT on banks and their customers is in the introduction of new payment methods.

The EFTS and the Evolution of the Payments Mechanism

Payment systems have evolved from a barter system to today's diverse range that includes cash, cheques, credit cards, and electronic fund transfers. With the exception of cash payments, fund transfers are now largely made by means of written instructions requesting one financial institution to transfer funds to another financial institution. Through the banking system, paper cheques may be utilized without the need for currency. Cheques came into widespread use because they offered considerable advantages over cash: they were easily transported in any amount; they were easily transferred between parties; they involved much less danger of loss or theft than cash;and they served as proof of payment.

In Hong Kong fundamental changes have occurred over the last decade in the way individuals and businesses make and receive payments. Although cash remains the most convenient means of making small payments, the increase in the use of cheques and credit cards has been rapid. During the period 1977–84 the volume of banking transactions in Hong Kong, as represented by the value of cheques cleared annually through the cheque clearing house, rose by almost 100 per cent. (See Table 9.1.) In 1984, for example, 82,346,706 cheques were processed by the banking system. Although the annual growth rate of cheques dropped to below 10 per cent in 1981, it cannot be assumed that the use of cheques will reach a peak within the next few years. Cheque volume will certainly continue to increase. The growth in the use of cheques in the period 1977–84 also imposed a substantial cost burden on the banks as further employees and machines were required just to process these paper documents.

Although some automated facilities, such as MICR readers/sorters, have been utilized, not all cheque processing functions have been amenable to automation. Cheques are still handled by tellers, the encoding process requires human handling, and cheques must still be physically transported from one financial institution to another. In cheque processing, the average

Table 9.1 Hong Kong Bank Cheque Transactions 1977–84

	Number of Items Cleared	Increase (%)	Total Value (HK$ million)	Increase %	Average Value per Item (HK$ thousand)
1977	41,450,772	–	647,487	–	15.62
1978	49,621,611	19.7	1,006,598	55.50	20.29
1979	56,958,063	14.8	1,605,812	59.50	28.19
1980	67,669,491	18.8	3,019,546	88.00	44.62
1981	73,536,630	8.7	4,807,863	59.20	65.38
1982	74,832,800	1.8	5,792,607	20.50	77.41
1983	77,252,000	3.2	6,040,255	4.28	78.19
1984	82,346,706	6.5	7,099,064	17.53	86.21

Source: Hong Kong Monthly Digest of Statistics (Hong Kong, Census and Statistics Department), January 1985.

cheque is handled more than 10 times within the whole banking system. It is estimated that the processing cost per cheque is about HK$3.[2] This results in huge costs for the entire banking system. Furthermore, because of the indirect nature of the cheque clearing process, there are often delays before payees receive their funds.

To reduce physical processing costs, radical changes in payment methods are desirable. If the paper document which carries payment data could be replaced by an electronic signal and transferred through speedy telecommunications, the cost and amount of manual handling could be substantially reduced. It is for this reason that the banks are extremely interested in pursuing the new payment transaction system known as the Electronic Fund Transfer System (EFTS).

Five major factors have accelerated the development of the EFTS.

(a) The banking industry has found the existing payment systems increasingly inefficient and costly.

(b) Financial institutions have started to use IT to protect and increase their market share, as well as to generate new revenues.

(c) The importance of speed in financial transactions has caused many financial controllers and fund managers to demand fast, accurate, and accessible accounts information for global fund transfers.

(d) The advent of micro-electronics and telecommunications technology has resulted in the gradual installation of electronic systems.

(e) In general, individual and corporate customers have sought greater control over their financial affairs and more convenient services.

The EFTS revolution began in the United States, and this method of payment has affected banking and shopping habits, wage payment methods, and other regular payments throughout the world. The first sign of these changes in Hong Kong occurred in 1980 when ATMs were first installed by Hong Kong's two largest banks—the Hongkong and Shanghai Banking Corporation and the Standard Chartered Bank. Since 1980 various EFTS services have been developed in Hong Kong through the combined efforts of financial institutions, computer suppliers, merchants, employers, the government, systems auditors, and the general public.

Although an EFTS is often considered a revolutionary development with far-reaching effects, it can also be viewed as just another step in the evolution of the payments mechanism. While cash and cheques have coexisted for many years, the EFTS has now joined them as another medium of transaction. Some observers have predicted that an EFTS could bring about a cashless, chequeless transaction system in the future. This evolution reflects the continuing efforts being made to improve the efficiency of trading and the payments mechanism.

The Concepts and Components of an EFTS

The United States National Commission on Electronic Fund Transfer (NCEFT) defined an EFTS as 'a payments system in which the processing and communications necessary to effect economic exchange and the processing and communications necessary for the production and distribution of services incidental or related to economical exchange are dependent wholly or in large part on the use of electronics'.[3] The American Institute of Certified Public Accountants (AICPA) defined an EFTS as 'a computer-based network that enables payment system transactions to be initiated, approved, executed, and recorded with electronic impulses and machine-sensible data rather than with paper'.[4]

Thus an EFTS allows financial institutions to transfer funds instantaneously, internally and with other financial institutions. It also provides faster, more efficient services to customers by processing items electronically. By bringing together the point of initiation of a transaction and the point of posting it, an EFTS can reduce many paper processing and teller costs.

However, to speak of 'the EFTS' is an oversimplification. Many people view an EFTS as a monolithic integrated system in which all computer systems, remote terminals, telephone systems, and switching centres are interconnected. In fact, such an integrated national system does not exist and it may be at least another 25 years before it will exist.

Therefore 'EFTS' can be viewed as a generic term referring to various computer-based technologies for delivering electronic banking services. At the time of writing, there are a number of transitional fragmented EFTS components, which will eventually form a full EFTS. In fact, EFTS developments are proceeding in several directions and in various phases. Generally, the development of an EFTS can be classified into the following four phases.

(a) Phase 1 aims at computerizing standard internal operations of banks: current accounts, savings accounts, bills and loans, foreign exchange dealings, general ledger, payroll, and administration. These early applications are limited to back-office functions and offer little direct service to customers.

(b) Phase 2 seeks to introduce improved customer sevices: an Automated Clearing House (ACH), on-line ATMs, POS terminals, a regional inter-bank EFTS, and message transmission systems.

(c) Phase 3 provides home and office banking, sophisticated Cash Management Services (CMSs), and Decision Support Systems (DSSs).

(d) Phase 4 is a totally integrated nation-wide system with all of the above features.

It is estimated that Japan, Hong Kong, and Singapore are closer to Phase 2 than other South-east Asian countries. But of course, when compared with EFTS developments in the United States and some European countries, progress to date in many Asian countries is still several years behind.

For the sake of clarity, most EFTS components can be grouped into six major categories.

(a) The Automated Clearing House (ACH) and preauthorized payments.

(b) A payment system wire network.

(c) Corporate Cash Management Services (CMSs).

(d) Automated Teller Machines (ATMs).

(e) Electronic Fund Transfer at Point of Sale (EFTPOS).

(f) Home banking systems.

The first three are generally used for business or commercial fund transfers and involve large sums. The last three are used for individual retail transactions. These EFTS components are driving the Hong Kong financial system from a paper base to an electronic foundation. Fig. 9.1 depicts the general structure and components of a relatively integrated comprehensive EFTS. The following pages focus on the operations and implications of the major EFTS elements in Hong Kong in greater detail.

The ACH and Preauthorized Payments

The corner-stone of the EFTS is the Automated Clearing House (ACH) system. It is part of the back-office inter-bank clearing system to transmit debit and credit items among financial institutions electronically rather than manually. The ACH processes payments or credits that have been prearranged by the payer and payee; such preauthorized items are made automatically according to the agreed procedure and schedule. Thus an ACH is likely to replace the often burdensome physical processing of a paper cheque, and may make funds available to the receiving party more quickly.

Typical preauthorized banking or 'autopay' applications include the following.

(a) The direct deposit of funds such as salary, welfare payments, and stock dividends into a recipient's bank account. The traditional paper-based payroll system which is shown in Fig. 9.2 may be compared with the direct deposit cycle shown in Fig. 9.3. To process direct payroll deposits, an employee first signs an authorization form. Before each pay-day, an employer produces a list or magnetic tape with the appropriate payroll data for each employee. The list or magnetic tape is sent to the employer's bank, which, on the pay-day, debits his account for the entire payroll amount and credits the account of each employee who holds an account at that bank. The remaining credits on the list or magnetic tape are transmitted to the ACH for distribution to the banks at which other employees have accounts. Parties involved in these systems receive a descriptive statement showing the payment.

(b) The direct payment by the bank of regular recurrent expenses such as utilities bills, mortgage, car, and insurance payments. To process these payments, the payee signs an authorization form for a specific recurring amount or the amount billed by a specific creditor to the payee's bank. The creditor company creates a list recording a routing number and account number for each customer participating, with the amount owed and the date due. Following a similar procedure to that of the direct deposit system, the creditor company sends the list to its bank, which processes and distributes output tapes to receiving banks through the ACH. When the bank receives the magnetic tape, it matches an incoming debit transaction from a creditor with a customer debit authorization which is retained on file. If the debit is proper, a transfer is initiated automatically. The payee's bank statement serves as a receipt of payment.

Preauthorized payment or 'autopay' services were spearheaded in Hong

Fig. 9.1 The Structure and Components of a Full EFTS

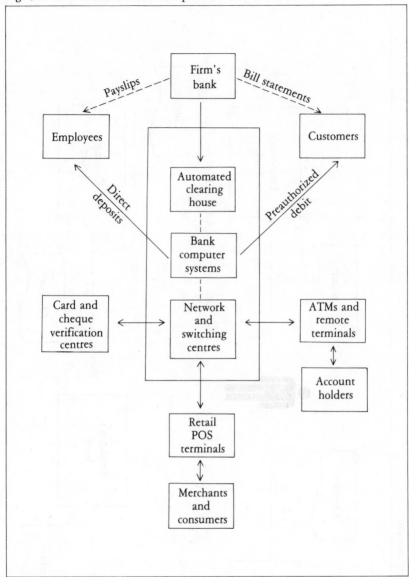

Kong by the Hongkong and Shanghai Banking Corporation in the early 1970s. At the time of writing, an average of 120,000 'autopay' transactions are processed each day.[5] Although the preauthorized payment system offers customers convenience and a saving of the time taken to write and mail cheques, many customers consider that the advantages are often offset by disadvantages such as a perceived loss of control over payments, errors in payments, fears of overdraft, and the loss of cheque 'float' (the time between the writing and clearing of a cheque). If a memorandum bill could be sent to a payee in advance, it would allow him to ensure that enough funds

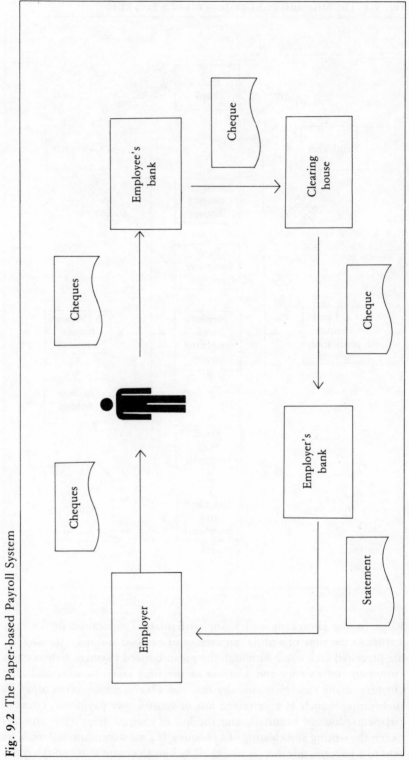

Fig. 9.2 The Paper-based Payroll System

Fig. 9.3 The Direct Deposit Cycle

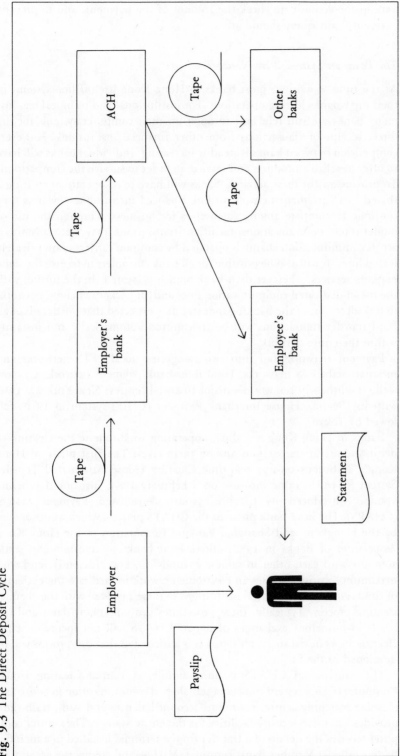

were in the account, to check the amount of the payment, and to prevent payment if any query should arise.

The Payment System Wire Network

At the time of writing, most banks in Hong Kong use off-line systems in their inter-bank clearing operations. For institutional and technical reasons, many banks are still reluctant to open up their computer systems for the direct receipt of transactions from other financial institutions. However, competition between banks is steadily increasing. Individual banks will have to offer new EFTS products and services in order to survive the competition. To provide any of these services, banks will have to co-operate in creating a shared EFTS payment network to link financial institutions—even as they continue to compete among themselves for business. Through the use of modern telecommunications facilities, transactions may be transmitted across communication channels operated by common carriers or on privately leased lines. It will also be possible for all bank customers to receive the same banking services, wherever their bank branch is located. In the future, with the use of dedicated communication lines and/or packet switching networks to link all sectors of the banking industry, it is expected that the details of all fund transfer transactions will be transmitted automatically and instantly within the entire network.

Payment networks fall into two categories: local EFTS networks and international EFTS networks. Local inter-bank payment networks are now well established in the world's major financial centres: New York was first, with its Clearing House Interbank Payment (CHIP) system in 1970, followed by Tokyo.

Banks in Hong Kong are also co-operating to automate the clearing of debit and credit transactions among themselves. The first phase of Hong Kong's ambitious on-line real-time Clearing House Automated Transfer System (CHATS) came into use on 8 February 1984, just one day before London introduced its Clearing House Automated Payment System (CHAPS). The inter-bank phase of the CHATS project, which was proposed by the Hongkong and Shanghai Banking Corporation to the Hong Kong Association of Banks in 1982, allows local banks to transmit and settle accounts with each other in same-day funds quickly, efficiently, and with maximum security.[6] It uses an electronic network to facilitate the exchange of funds among the financial institutions that are involved with the cheque-clearing process. Typically, these procedures can take many days, and can result in numerous exchanges of paper. CHATS will not include cheque clearing in its initial stage, although it is anticipated that this process will be developed in the future.

The structure of CHATS is quite simple. A central Clearing House Computer (CHC) system controls a star-shaped communication network and message switching centre, maintains account balances and audit trails, and provides extensive security facilities for the entire system. The central computer receives the details of a transfer from a terminal installed in a member bank—called a Member Bank Terminal (MBT)—and credits the account of the receiver bank, debits that of the sender, and dispatches a report to the receiver bank's MBT.

The process may be illustrated by an example. A bank may wish to lend funds to another bank requiring short-term funds, or may need to send a large payment to another bank for buying foreign currency. Traditionally the transfer of such funds from one bank to another would be by means of some form of paper such as a cashier's order which would be carried by messenger from the sending bank to the beneficiary bank. It could take several days to clear the cheque and this could cause unnecessary delay. CHATS, however, enables the funds to be transferred in seconds and provides same-day value to the beneficiary bank.

A net settlement position report is sent to each MBT at the end of the day, and the total debits and credits are incorporated into a statement of clearing from the central computer. The system also allows next-day payment, which will lighten the burden of banks dealing with large volumes on single days, for instance at the end of a financial year. In such cases, the central computer accepts the payment, and delays crediting it to the receiving bank until the following day.

The wire transfer system is characterized by a large volume of transactions, large monetary values, and the immediate availability of the funds transferred. These features make the system vulnerable to fraud and costly errors. Since CHATS is designed to handle payments worth millions of dollars between banks, the design of the system includes extensive security facilities and checking systems, to ensure that any transfer entered into the system is not corrupted or lost. Banks and customers cannot afford to have a system which can break down in the middle of a transfer. It is important that this local EFTS network be secure, fast, efficient, error-free, and able to route transactions to any member bank.

Similarly, international networks are used in the transfer of large amounts between financial institutions in different countries. An electronic bank message switching network operated by the Society for Worldwide Interbank Financial Telecommunication (SWIFT) has been providing an efficient and fast way of transferring funds and transmitting banking instructions between banks around the world since 1978. The SWIFT network was designed to replace the services previously performed by telex and mail, and it can reduce tedious and burdensome manual processing and clerical errors.

The SWIFT network also maintains a complex security and control system in order to maintain very reliable and convenient services to the participating financial institutions. The SWIFT network has proved to be a success and is in use by more than 1,000 member banks in about 40 countries. However, several countries have expressed concern over the flow of data across national boundaries, and this may provoke restrictions on international fund transfers and exchanges of data.

In February 1980, 13 of Hong Kong's major banks joined the SWIFT network, and this marked an important milestone in the development of the EFTS. SWIFT enables these banks to keep pace with the most advanced European and North American banks in their handling of international money transfers in the field of corporate and international banking.[7] This service should reduce the problems encountered by the banking community in handling international payments. In the future, the international Visa and Mastercharge Card networks may even link with the SWIFT network for the quick authorization and processing of transactions.

Corporate Cash Management Services

Many corporate customers of financial institutions wish to have all their data on cash balances in one location, so that they can mobilize their funds more effectively. They wish to access their account status in the bank, make on-line transfers, and retrieve a range of financial quotations and services directly.

Bank managers also want all the information on their corporate customers in one place so that they can make better loan or investment decisions. While some banks have been concentrating on automating retail operations, other have been studying the feasibility of offering electronic banking services to international corporate customers.

Asian banks are lagging behind the international American banks, many of which have developed highly comprehensive electronic corporate Cash Management Services (CMSs). American banks which have taken a very aggressive role in technology-based banking services include Merrill Lynch, Pierce, Fenner & Smith, which offers a 'Cash Management Account', Chase Manhattan, which offers Infocash, Citibank, with its Citicash Manager, and Chemical Bank, which offers the Chemlink System. Some of these services have been introduced to Hong Kong and provide a level of global cash management that few other bank products can match.

By linking a bank's local network to a global switching network, it is possible to place a CMS terminal in a customer's premises. Typical CMSs include the following:

(a) facilities to enable corporate customers to make world-wide account balance enquiries directly, to establish the identity of payers and the currency and location of outstanding receivables;

(b) 'lock-box' services which immediately pool all of a customer's deposits into one single account;

(c) world-wide electronic fund transfer between accounts directly through customers' terminals;

(d) international banking services such as money market investment, foreign exchange, and fund accounting;

(e) decision support and information products which allow customers to manage their foreign exchange exposure, analyse historical informaion, and make future projections.

Before the advent of these cash management services, companies had to collect their world-wide balances by themselves. Through world-wide data integration, it should now be possible for bank customers to do business with other banks almost anywhere in the world. Withdrawals are automatically debited against the lowest-yielding fund and idle funds are transferred regularly into a high-yield investment fund. Customers not only improve their payment efficiency, but also operate their business more effectively.

In Hong Kong, the Bank of America recently announced plans to invest in and develop a major data processing centre known as the International Banking System (IBS), which will offer a range of international fund transfer services, and will computerize the bank's banking business globally. The Hongkong and Shanghai Banking Corporation has also been installing a Hong Kong-based electronic cash management system, named Hong-link.[8] This electronic banking system is expected to compete vigorously with those already being offered in Asia by the large American banks. Since Hong-link's major clients are mainly based in Asia, the bank decided to develop its own system rather than to use proprietary products from the United States. The bank's Asian customers were involved in the design of the system and consequently the system suits local conditions and users' needs.

As some business spills over from the bigger banks to the smaller, the pressure will grow on the smaller bankers to provide similar services to meet their own customers' cash management needs. The trend towards cash management is, therefore, unavoidable, and alert financial institutions will need to plan to co-operate with their corporate clients in automating cash management operations. Some smaller banks in Asia are already making useful progress in this sphere. At present these systems are quite expensive but, as the number of subscribers increases, costs will drop accordingly.

Experience to date has shown that the demand for CMSs in Hong Kong is gradually increasing. One of the major problems that the corporate cash management concept has encountered is that many managers lack experience or confidence in operating their computer terminals directly. There is some concern also about the security of these systems. Firms require a system that is secure, flexible, easy to operate, and under their own control. It will take several years for corporate customers to accept CMS concepts completely, but bankers are confident that their clients will find such services invaluable and cost-effective. To promote the use of CMSs, banks will probably offer free or low-cost terminals to their corporate customers. In return, customers will be required to maintain a minimum balance or to pay a fee according to the level of use of the service.

Banking can no longer depend solely upon traditional channels to generate deposits and profits. Instead, as automated cash management services become more popular, corporate customers will increasingly manage their own funds, and banks will have to turn increasingly to technical and fee-charging services for revenue and profit.

Automated Teller Machines

The introduction of ATMs marked the first major move of banks in Hong Kong towards the development of an EFTS. For customers, ATMs are the most direct and visible of the electronic banking products which banks offer. In the recent ATM boom, Hong Kong quickly caught up with other advanced countries in its provision of EFTS services. In fact, Hong Kong was among the first in South-east Asia to provide widespread self-service banking. Unattended and remotely controlled ATMs which provide 24-hour retail banking services are being installed by about 35 banks. At the time of writing, over 1,200 ATMs are operating and about two million ATM cards are in use in Hong Kong. These machines function as minibranches of banks in bank buildings, department stores, railway stations, housing estates, and other busy non-bank sites. Continuous service is more convenient for customers and increases the utilization of equipment.

The growth of the ATM market has been extremely rapid since the first installation of an ATM by the Standard Chartered Bank in 1979. As a result of vigorous marketing, ATM services have been widely accepted by customers, despite the consequent reduction of personal banking services. The Hongkong and Shanghai Banking Corporation's ATM network (known as the Electronic Teller Card or ETC system) is probably the most heavily utilized system in the world, in terms of the number of transactions performed each day. Customers can use ATMs to make cash withdrawals and off-line deposits, transfer funds between accounts, order cheque books and statements, make account status enquiries, and draw against some credit card accounts or overdraft facilities. The current ATMs are used primarily as cash dispensers. It is estimated that over 75 per cent of all ATM transactions are cash withdrawals and that other transactions, such as deposits and transfers, account for only a small percentage. Future innovations in ATM design could offer faster and more flexible features. It is expected that a second generation, multifunctional ATM will offer a much greater range of services, the only criterion being that they can be presented in a form which may be included in the menu of options offered to ATM customers. Such facilities may include accepting cash deposits, displaying detailed account statements, counting notes for immediate deposit, dispensing retail negotiable certificates of deposit, gift cheques, and traveller's cheques, transferring funds to third-party accounts, processing loan applications, and other banking activities. However, not all of these advanced facilities are likely to be available in the near future in Hong Kong. How banks in Hong Kong will exploit the use of ATM systems depends on their customers' needs and the level of risk they are willing to bear.

Many people expect that greater competition between banks and among types of financial institution will result from further development of the EFTS. Large banks attempt to gain customers by setting up more branches as well as a proprietary ATM network. Because of the huge initial costs and the subsequent operating costs, the smaller banks will not be able to compete with the larger banks in this way. However smaller banks might find it advantageous to join a shared ATM network and expand their market area at a much lower cost than with a conventional branch. Therefore smaller banks will continue to use ATMs as an economical outlet for their services and as a means of competing with the far larger branch network of the major banks.

Co-operation among banks to form a joint ATM network, such as the joint network between the Hongkong and Shanghai Banking Corporation and the Hang Seng Bank, and the JETCO network, is one way of sharing the expensive installation cost and provides customers with many more machines for use at more locations. The Joint Electronic Teller Services Co. Ltd.

(JETCO) was formed in 1982 by four independent local banks, the Bank of East Asia, Chekiang First Bank, Shanghai Commercial Bank, and Wing Lung Bank. The Bank of China Group, Chase Manhattan Bank, Nan Tung Bank, and Tai Fung Bank of Macau later joined the network, resulting in a total of 20 member banks.[9] All the ATMs in this large shared network are accessible via one card and all the switching and settlement of accounts between member banks is handled by a centralized Joint Electronic Teller Services (JETS) data processing centre. (See Figure 9.4.) Undoubtedly, the success of the network system will depend very much on co-operation among the member banks.

ATMs will never totally replace human tellers, but they have helped banks to expand their market without the need to employ additional tellers. The long-term future of ATMs seems assured, because they are able to offer the convenience of 24-hour service and an expanded range of services. Some economic problems relating to ATMs have yet to be resolved. These will be discussed in more detail later.

Electronic Fund Transfer at Point of Sale

The Electronic Fund Transfer at Point of Sale (EFTPOS) system is one EFTS service that has grown significantly in recent years, causing marked changes in the relationships among financial institutions, retailers, and consumers. An EFTPOS system allows a customer to pay for goods and services at the merchant's location (for example, a supermarket) by transferring funds from the customer's account to the shop's account either immediately or at the end of the day. By entering transaction data into the electronic payment network at the time and place of sale, the system promotes the paperless transfer of funds in transactions between customers and businesses.

For retailers, the POS terminals will range from an ordinary telephone for a verbal check, to a full electronic cash register linked with a central computer. Generally, POS systems can offer several types of service, either individually or in combination: cheque verification, credit card referral, data capture, and fund transfer. Therefore the POS system may be viewed as a delivery system rather than a specific service. The POS terminal for data capture is well established, and present interest focuses on how POS terminals with direct debit capability function, the economics of direct debiting, the acceptance of these terminals by consumers, and the payment transactions that they will displace.

Such retail EFTPOS systems are being tried in France, Canada, the United States, Belgium, and Holland. The EFTPOS system was introduced in Hong Kong for a pilot test with more than 200 POS terminals installed in retail stores in June 1985. The Electronic Payment Services (EPS) system was developed mainly by the Hong Kong Association of Banks in conjunction with the Hongkong and Shanghai Banking Corporation, and will be supported by the CHATS network system. A group of 29 Hong Kong banks which issue ATM cards formed a company, Electronic Payment Service Co. (HK) Limited, to launch the EPS system in Hong Kong. The system enables authorized banks to connect their computers to a shared network of POS terminals at shops, through a POS central switching computer.

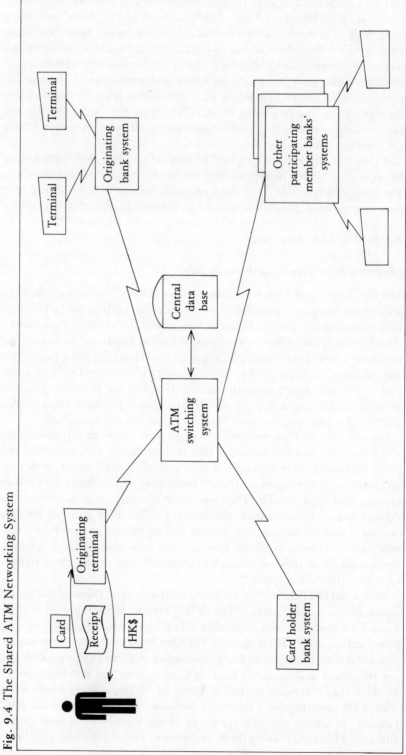

Fig. 9.4 The Shared ATM Networking System

The primary aim of the EPS system is to allow retailers to accept about two million local ATM-type debit cards. For the 400,000 credit card holders, credit card checking and over-credit limit referrals will also be accepted by the same terminal, to be sent to a POS central computer for routing to the card-issuing institution for approval.

The POS system provides similar automatic verification of all transactions using ATM-type debit cards, by referral to the card holder's bank. At the time of purchase, a customer's card is inserted into and read by a card reader in the POS terminal. As with ATMs, the customer must first key in his Personal Identification Number (PIN) via a compact keypad. The salesman then enters other necessary transaction data (such as product codes, quantity, prices) through the terminal keyboard or a scanner. If the customer's account has sufficient funds, it is debited for the amount of the purchase in favour of the merchant. The retailer must maintain an account with one authorized bank which issues debit cards and with one member of a credit institution, in order to collect the proceeds of all its card transactions.

The primary advantage of this system may be that it enables inter-bank money transfers to be electronically cleared without cash or paper transactions. Under such a system, merchants require less cash for daily transactions and they can speed up the check-out process. Merchants can also reduce handling costs, cheque float, bad debts, losses through bad cheques, and the risk of credit extension or excessive use. Detailed accounting and inventory data can also be recorded instantly, thus allowing the merchant to maximize the efficiency of the sales force, increase control over inventories, and monitor the characteristics of the store's clientele.

On the other hand, customers seem to derive fewer benefits from the system. The EFTPOS system does offer some advantages and convenience to customers. Customers will have direct access to their bank accounts at retailers' counters, they will not need to carry large amounts of cash, and they will write fewer cheques. By using debit cards, they will not have to risk over-reaching their credit limit each time they purchase or require cash from an ATM. At the same time there is the disadvantage that their accounts are debited immediately.

The technology used in POS systems is not new. Some pilot experiments conducted in the United States failed, while others achieved a measure of success. However, given the convenience that POS systems offer, it is certain that financial institutions, in conjunction with retailers, will eventually provide such services. If the pilot test of the Hong Kong EPS system proves successful, Hong Kong will have a large-scale operational EFTPOS while many other countries are still in the experimental stage. Nevertheless, the handling of the issues of pricing, ownership, security, and customer acceptance will determine how fast debit cards become popular. These issues will be discussed in more detail later in this chapter.

Remote Home Banking

Remote banking by ATMs and POS systems is achieving popularity, and these products may provide a significant impetus for the future development of home banking services in Hong Kong. Remote banking systems that use telephones rather than terminals to enter transaction data are being used in several Asian countries. Fox example, the United Overseas Bank in Singapore reported that its 'Telebank' system is quite successful. Chase Manhattan Bank in Hong Kong started a similar telephone banking service in Hong Kong in 1982. These systems are normally limited to the paying of bills, transfers between accounts, and account status enquiries. Given the high cost of telephone operators, telephone banking will sustain considerable pressure in the future as the customer base becomes larger. A further step in the development of EFTS services is home banking that uses microcomputer terminals; this is likely to be introduced in Hong Kong soon. By linking the bank's computer systems with the telephone line and microcomputer of individual customers, direct access to the bank can provide customers with the services that an ATM offers, except for cash deposits and withdrawals. The customers may use touch-tone telephones or terminal keyboards in their own homes to enter passwords, account numbers, and the amount of the transfer. Home banking may be brought to customers through the Hong Kong Telephone Company's Viewdata system, which will also provide services such as home bill-paying and shopping, the display of news and other financial information.

In some countries a home banking system is attractive because a relatively small investment is required in order to offer regular banking services to distant households. Chemical Bank, for example, has installed several hundred 'Pronto' home banking systems, which offer a wide range of facilities, in some major American cities. But many people doubt whether home banking will be successful in Hong Kong. At the time of writing, there seems to be little interest in or need for home banking in Hong Kong.

Home banking may not be appropriate in Hong Kong at present because the system does not fit in with the existing life-styles of Hong Kong people, and the infrastructure is not available. Home banking may not suit the demands and requirements of the dense local population. At present, there seems to be little incentive for customers to change to home banking, as ATMs or bank branches are readily accessible to the whole population. Similarly, the Viewdata system is unlikely to emerge as a primary shopping aid since there are numerous shops and retail stores throughout Hong Kong. Furthermore, many people in Hong Kong have accounts with several banks. Since many terminals are usable with only one bank, people cannot use such terminals to transfer funds between their accounts with different banks. At the time of writing, it seems unlikely that all banks and financial institutions will eventually be totally integrated into one system in Hong Kong.

Terminals in homes are not nearly as common as televisions and telephones. In addition, telecommunications devices will continue to be expensive in the near future. Consumers are unwilling to pay significant amounts for these services; certainly few would buy a microcomputer or special terminal when they can walk to a bank or ATM and obtain banking services for little or no charge.

It seems that the educated, wealthier section of the population is most likely to use home banking, in order to obtain an overdraft or a cash management account. However, these people are likely to use or pay for home banking only if new, high value-added financial services could be made available through home banking, such as financial planning, current financial position analysis, security trading, various automatic fund transfer opportunities, and a range of other financial services beyond the regular services currently offered.

Home banking will probably be available for trial in Hong Kong by 1987. After a few years of the trial period, it will be clear whether such a system is likely to be offered as a normal banking service. The adoption process will certainly take time and education. A market survey based on experience in the United States predicted 3 per cent market penetration initially, growing to 27 per cent over five years.[10] Other factors which will determine the future development of home banking include the availability of proper and cost-effective delivery systems for telecommunications, the willingness of banks to innovate, and acceptance by customers. Nevertheless, the pace of change in financial and banking business is now so rapid that few financial institutions in Hong Kong can afford to delay strategic decisions regarding home banking.

Implications for Financial Systems

As EFTS services spread throughout the financial sector it is instructive to watch the development of electronic transaction activity in other countries. In the United States, the structure of financial institutions is undergoing rapid changes. In particular, the traditional role of banks as commercial lenders and creators of deposit money is breaking down. Banks are expanding their operations into other forms of commercial activity, and other institutions are taking over some of the roles formerly played by banks.

In the United States, the legal definition of a bank is a firm that both accepts deposits and makes commercial loans. Thus, a department store chain could accept deposits, but instead of making commercial loans it would only invest in securities, and would therefore be called a 'non-bank bank'. Or a stock brokerage firm might make commercial loans but might not accept deposits. It, too, would be described as a 'non-bank bank'. In this way, the markets that banks formerly controlled are facing competition from outsiders. Public sector and private bodies concerned about the regulation of banks and the United States Congress are still debating whether or not banks should be protected from these inroads into their markets.

Whatever the eventual outcome, it is clear that the rapid development of EFTS facilities has provided an efficient technological base for the evolving competitive structure.

It is possible to view EFTS services as a means to effect the instantaneous transfer of the ownership of assets. For example, United States Treasury securities are now usually sold only on a book-entry basis—that is, the bills or bonds are not printed and issued to the lender, but are only registered, and numbered, and kept on record in the memory of a computer. When a lender sells a bond, numbers are transferred—not pieces of paper. More and more individuals and firms are moving toward the ownership of various divisible and indivisible financial and non-financial assets that can be exchanged by debits and credits to computerized accounts.

For example, assume that a person places his or her house up for mortgage with a lender (not necessarily a bank). Instead of receiving the mortgage funds and starting a system of repayments, the borrower could accept a line of credit against the mortgaged property. He could then essentially 'sell' a part of his house by drawing against the line of credit offered by the lender. Eventually the borrower would be able to exchange a part of a house for a package of securities owned by some other person with similarly computerized facilities. This would be a form of barter by electronic transfer. It would not be necessary to use money as a medium of exchange, although money would still be used as a unit of account.

The eventual possibility of direct barter transactions by electronic transfer of asset ownership causes concern among the authorities who regulate banks and control the money supply. The widespread use of electronic barter may weaken the constraining effect on inflationary and deflationary pressures which the control over money at present exerts. This is a problem that bears watching in the future.

The Economics of Alternative Payment Systems

When the idea of an EFTS was first conceived in the 1960s, many experts predicted that the technology would have profound effects on the economy and ultimately lead to a cashless and chequeless society. By the early 1970s, there were predictions that electronic payments would become the main form of payment within a decade. Yet only a small fraction of payment volume today is electronic. These early predictions have not been borne out in any society using an EFTS. In fact, many of the related questions could not be solved easily, since they depend on many technological, economic, social, and institutional factors for which there are few data. One of the main reasons that customers have been reluctant to accept an EFTS is that there is no economic incentive to offset the loss of credit card and cheque 'float' (the time between the writing of a cheque and its clearance), and consumers are unwilling to pay an extra cost to use EFTS services.

While there is a formal and reliable source of data on the number, monetary value, and transaction cost of cheques, there is no such source of data on cash, credit, and EFTS payments in Hong Kong. Since many banks are not willing to disclose EFTS transaction data, which they classify as confidential, data on the growth of different retail banking services are also largely unavailable. It is therefore difficult to evaluate the potential savings or benefits in using the EFTS instead of traditional paper payment methods. In fact, some banks in Hong Kong have not formulated a proper strategy in retail banking. They have an extensive and inefficient cheque handling system, as well as a very expensive EFTS which is insufficiently utilized, in that it is used mostly for balance enquiries and low-value cash withdrawals. Because there are no reliable data on the cost of alternative payment systems, some EFTSs are likely to be implemented without a valid assessment of whether they are profitable and justifiable. EFTS services are also likely to be priced without an adequate understanding of their costs. Some EFTS installations have been defended on the grounds of long-term market competition. Some banks have enjoyed gains while others have experienced large losses.

In general, payments in Hong Kong are still largely made with cash, especially transactions with a value of less than HK$100. Currency in circulation has grown at an average rate of 15 per cent per year in the last 10 years. In spite of the enormous number of cash transactions and their low transaction cost, it is estimated that they account for only a small percentage of the monetary value of total payments. The number of cheque transactions grew from 41,450,772 in 1977 to 82,346,706 in 1984, and these account for the greater part of the monetary value of transactions in Hong Kong (see Table 9.1). The huge cost of processing paper cheques is at present largely subsidized by the banking system, and the cost to account holders of writing an additional cheque is usually less than the marginal cost of handling a cheque. As a result, too many cheques are written, and more resources than is desirable are allocated to cheque processing. Not until banks start to charge full fees for cheque services will it be easy to induce customers to convert to EFTS services.

Credit card activity has been expanding rapidly over the last few years and there are currently about 400,000 cards in use in Hong Kong. A survey conducted by the author reveals that credit card operations are considered marginal or only slightly profitable, because they incur high administrative and processing costs. Card-issuing institutions have begun to ask card holders to share part of the cost by levying an annual charge.

On the other hand, the anticipated costs for EFTS services are immense. A foreign bank in Hong Kong recently projected that an ATM transaction would cost about HK$25 as compared with HK$3 per transaction by a human teller. In addition, this bank estimated that ATMs generated only about 15 per cent of the total volume of retail banking transactions in 1983. It is important to understand the cost characteristics of EFTS equipment. It is obvious that an EFTS involves a large fixed cost for expensive computer resources but relatively small variable costs. Because of the size of the fixed cost, it is estimated that the average cost of an EFTS transaction will fall below the average cost of a cheque or cash transaction only if a sufficiently large volume of use is attained. Some banks which have installed ATMs have had a large increase in retail activities, but many accounts are very small. It is expensive for banks to run many small accounts. To justify the huge capital investment which an EFTS installation requires, a minimum value per EFTS transaction must be set. Banks also find it advantageous to join a shared ATM network, and to expand their market area at a much lower cost than they would incur by setting up conventional branches. Therefore bankers should exercise considerable care in looking at the economics of ATM installation and future market trends.

Similarly, the cost is the most important aspect of the EFTPOS system. Given the huge cost of an on-line communication network and real-time processing, direct debiting has little economic advantage over the conventional systems it is intended to replace. One reason for the slow development of the EFTPOS system is the need to apportion its cost among financial institutions, retailers, and customers. The system developers and investors expect a return on their investment. The issue of who pays for the EFTPOS system cannot be ignored, because the system will essentially be a joint effort between banks and merchants. Consumers will only use the EFTPOS system if they are assured that they will not be asked to contribute to the large capital investment which the system requires. Indeed, consumers expect the EFTPOS system to reduce bank charges or prices eventually. Since banks will be the major beneficiaries, it is therefore reasonable that banks should absorb a large portion of the cost, although retailers should be responsible for part of the installation fee and the operating costs. Under the EPS charge scheme, the EPS company will charge the retailers for every ATM transaction on a sliding scale according to the value of the transaction.[11] The company will also charge the card-issuing institutions for credit card purchases, so that consumers may not have to pay any charge for using EPS services.

Whatever the overall cost of the EFTPOS system, banks will probably change their traditional policy on charging customers for banking services. Banks will begin to charge more for the less profitable retail banking services they provide as soon as they believe that their retail customers can absorb part of the visible costs. The Hongkong and Shanghai Banking Corporation group and the Standard Chartered Bank have been levying an annual charge for credit card holders since 1983. Some banks also charge a fee for current accounts with an average balance below a minimum level. Other banks are currently reviewing their fee structure and pricing decisions on retail banking and are likely to follow suit. EFT services, such as ATM transactions, are also likely to be priced at a figure that will, in the long term, favour EFTS transactions over teller-assisted or paper transactions.

It is therefore crucial to provide a long-term economic justification for EFTS services which combines cost savings with greater value and convenience. It seems that an adjustment of the banking fee schedule is inevitable, and a differential pricing strategy is likely to be used in order to encourage EFTS usage. In addition, fee income from other new EFTS services will be an important source of bank revenue, especially since interest margins can be expected to remain small because of competition. As automated cash management services become more popular, corporate customers will increasingly manage their own funds, and banks will have to turn increasingly to technical and fee-related services for revenue and profit.

Banks expect that high utilization of other ATM services can be achieved, and that the marginal costs of making an EFTS transaction will be lower than those of cheque transactions. If costs can be reduced, financial institutions will offer more EFTS services. It is expected that appropriate pricing policies will provide economic incentives for the continuing growth of EFTS services during the 1980s.

Social and Legal Aspects and Consumer Acceptance

The emergence of EFTS technology does not necessarily mean that people will accept it or will be able to take advantage of it, and it is worth noting some of the constraints to change. A key question is whether consumers really want EFTS. What will happen, for instance, if we create a sophisticated EFTS and customers do not want it? Are customers willing to pay for the value added? If the majority of consumers do not accept the service, it will never be cost effective and will probably fail. It is for this reason that many financial institutions have proceeded very slowly and carefully in installing ATMs and EFTPOS terminals.

Until recently experts considered EFTS services to be highly desirable and inevitable, but research has revealed that EFTS development has slowed, because of soaring costs, consumer resistance, and some legal constraints. Consumers do not want to lose control over certain financial decisions but they may do so, as a result of preauthorized payments, costly errors, lack of proof of payment, and the elimination of floating cheques. To most businesses and individual consumers, having control over their finances still means using conventional cheques for payment. While one of the objectives of an EFTS has been to eliminate the inconvenience of cheques, most consumers do not regard cheques as inconvenient and costly. A survey conducted by the author has revealed that individuals are generally satisfied with the present payment system and do not want the total displacement of cash and cheques. Thus, in many cases, it may require considerable incentives for customers to change their method of payment totally from cheques to direct debiting or other electronic means.

EFTPOS systems must also compete with cash in both convenience and costs. Consumers are not likely to be enthusiastic about an EFTPOS terminal which is available to the customers of some banks and not others. They would prefer existing procedures and will resist using POS terminals if they feel that the systems are too complicated. Technology and product design need to be upgraded, and only services that are fast, convenient, easy to use, and reliable will accelerate EFTPOS activities.

Another issue, personal privacy and system security, is increasingly important in an EFTS installation. An EFTS can capture details of an individual's financial transactions instantaneously. A large volume of important and sensitive personal data, such as financial transactions, property owned, and buying habits, is stored in the system. Unauthorized entry to the system could enable the creation of a black market in confidential information and mailing lists. A major concern is the protection of consumer privacy and the need to prevent unauthorized access to and storage of informaion. Legislation needs to be revised so that no government or private sector agency can obtain access to an individual's financial information without the prior approval of the individual.

Research has revealed that there is no clear definition of responsibilities and liabilities for EFTS fraud, errors, or irregularities. The embezzlement and manipulation of electronic financial records could be more difficult to detect, unless proper controls can be developed for EFTSs. Possible failures or irregularities in the security or reliability of EFTS services could cause serious damage to participants in the system and the operation of a shared EFT network could cause further complications.

There is no legislation in Hong Kong to regulate EFTS services. To protect the public interest, regulations are needed that, at the very least, specify clearly the kind of information which providers of the services must give to their customers. Such information includes the liabilities and responsibilities associated with the improper use of plastic cards; the means of stopping a payment or reversing a transaction; and the methods used to calculate interest charges or other fees for using the services. Financial institutions offering EFTS services should not only emphasize the positive aspects of these services, but also inform the user about negative aspects such as liabilities, the risk of loss, and the inconvenience that might occur. When regulations and laws governing EFTS services are introduced, they will influence the form of the system developed, the speed of its adoption, and consumers' acceptance of the new payment system.

While the future of EFTS services seems assured, businesses and consumers at present lack an adequate knowledge of EFTS capabilities, the options for different types of EFTS development, and their economic and social implications. The volume of EFTS services is limited not only by consumers' acceptance but also by consumers' awareness. A well-co-ordinated public education programme is needed, involving the financial institutions, the Government, the Consumer Council, and the mass media, to ensure the protection of the public. Moreover, the development of EFTS services should not be left to technical experts and computer vendors. EFTS developments deserve attention at the highest policy-making level within the financial institutions and the regulatory agencies (such as the Consumer Council, the Banking Commission, and the Banking Advisory Committee).

The Outlook for EFTSs

As EFTSs become more widely adopted, their impact will be felt by all sections of the population. An EFTS offers both benefits and costs to users. An EFTS can eliminate unnecessary delays in fund transfers and can reduce transaction costs. Reducing such costs sometimes helps not only financial institutions but also consumers and business firms. EFTSs are destined to have a dramatic impact on the physical structure of the financial industry as well as on the manner in which the institutions' services are offered to their customers. EFTSs are also altering traditional payment mechanisms. Instead of the usual few days of cheque 'float', payments will be made more quickly, and changes in money balances will occur promptly. A substantial increase in the transaction flow of money will significantly affect local financial markets and the economy of Hong Kong.

It seems safe to predict that, by the early 1990s, Hong Kong will have a relatively sophisticated shared electronic payment network, as well as the traditional paper-based systems. The payment network system will enable a high proportion of large inter-bank payments to be handled automatically. The development of EFTPOS, CMS and home banking projects will require greater co-operation between the banks which share the network system. Individual customers will be able to have access to a wide variety of electronic banking facilities with a microprocessor memory card. The growth rate of currency and cheques will thus gradually decline. The number of bank branches will be more stable, and a large proportion of banking transactions will be initiated by customers away from bank premises. Non-financial firms will start to consider installing ATMs in order to provide better services to their clients.

The changes in bank operations that will accompany the growth of EFTSs are likely to lead indirectly to some changes in the business of financial institutions. For instance, some banks have considered amalgamating current accounts and savings accounts into single interest-bearing accounts. An increasing proportion of consumer lending will probably be in the form of low-cost overdrafts made available by the use of an ATM card. Using the large volume of local and international financial data stored in a bank's computer system, financial institutions may begin to offer profitable information services to their customers, either through a link with, or in direct competition with, the Viewdata service. Bankers expect that their income will in the future be derived more from fees for specialist services. We have already seen how information technology was at first used to reduce the volume of transactions and the cost of operations, and how more recently financial institutions have come to regard themselves as being in the information business. Information technology is now used as a basis for the provision of new services which enable institutions to stay ahead of their competitors and to generate new revenue. It will become more difficult in the future to differentiate the service provided by one bank from that of another.

Finally, it should be stressed that financial institutions must be cautious in their approach to EFTSs and should not be blindly led by technology or market forces. An EFTS should be introduced only as a part of an institution's long-term corporate business strategy. Banks should carefully analyse their markets and provide products tailored to meet the needs of selected consumer groups. Innovations to the financial system must be made slowly and carefully, if they are to be successful. The manner in which the issues of pricing, ownership, security, and customer acceptance are handled will determine how quickly EFTS services are widely adopted. Despite all the difficulties associated with the development of EFTS services, information technology has been vital to the successful growth of financial institutions in Hong Kong. A great deal remains to be done before the information technology revolution is a reality.

Notes

1. Martin (1978), p. 89.
2. The estimate of the cost of processing a cheque is based on an informal discussion with a local banker.

3. See National Commission on Electronic Fund Transfer (1977).
4. American Institute of Certified Public Accountants (1978), p. 1.
5. Lee (1984), p. 36.6.
6. Borland (1983), pp. 22–4.
7. Wild (1982), p. 33.
8. Nicholls (1984), p. 8.
9. Kan (1984), pp. 35.1–35.12.
10. DeCotiis (1984), p. 42.
11. Retailers or institutions which issue credit cards will have to pay EPS according to the charge scheme shown below:

Transaction Amount	Charge
less than HK$100	HK$0.50
HK$100–HK$300	HK$1.00
HK$300–HK$500	HK$1.50
more than HK$500	HK$2.00

The minimum charge for each POS terminal is HK$900 per month.

References

Altschul, J., 'No Real Need for Home Banking', *Asian Banking*, May 1984, pp. 96–8.
American Institute of Certified Public Accountants, *Audit Considerations in Electronic Funds Transfer Systems* (New York, AICPA, 1978).
Armstrong, N., 'The Headlong Invasion of Electronic Banking', *Asian Finance*, 15 September 1983, pp. 58–62.
Asian Finance, 'Electronic Banking: Technology Creates a Class Apart', 15 March 1984, pp. 73–86.
Bedwell, D.E., 'Payments in the Financial Services Industry of the 1980s', *Economic Review*, Federal Reserve Bank of Atlanta, December 1983, pp. 4–10.
Benton, J.B., 'Electronic Fund Transfer: Pitfalls and Payoffs', *Harvard Business Review*, July–August 1977, pp. 16–32.
Borland, A.G., 'CHATS—Clearing House Automated Transfer System', *Hong Kong Computer Society Yearbook 1983* (Hong Kong, Hong Kong Computer Society, 1983).
Communications of the ACM, Special Issue on EFT Symposium, Vol. 22, No. 12, December 1979, pp. 639–71.
Computer—Asia, 'The Retail Revolution', July 1984, pp. 34–6.
DeCotiis, A.R., 'The Business Plan for Home Banking', *Economic Review*, Federal Reserve Bank of Atlanta, July/August 1984, p. 42.
Economic Review, Special Issue: Displacing the Check (Federal Reserve Bank of Atlanta, August 1983).
Economic Review, Special Issue on the Revolution in Retail Payment (Federal Reserve Bank of Atlanta, July/August 1984).
Ho, S.S.M., 'The Computerization of the Bank Industry in Hong Kong: Implications and Prospects', *The Hong Kong Economic Journal Monthly*, Vol. 8, No. 10, January 1984, pp. 24–7.
—— 'Electronic Funds Transfer Systems: Special Problems in Hong Kong', *Asian Banking*, May 1984, pp. 91–2, 101.
Jones, D., 'Leading the World in Cash Management Systems', *Banking World*, August 1983, pp. 40–1.
Kan, M., 'JETCO—The Banking Network in Hong Kong', *Proceedings of SEARCC 84 Conference* (Hong Kong, Hong Kong Computer Society, September 1984), pp. 35.1–35.13.

Lau, A.K., 'Computer Operations in Banking', *Proceedings of Hong Kong Computer Conference 1979* (Hong Kong, Hong Kong Computer Society, 1979), pp. 2.6.1–2.6.3.

Lee, A., 'Information Technology Development in Banking', *Proceedings of SEARCC 84 Conference* (Hong Kong, Hong Kong Computer Society, September 1984), pp. 36.1–36.11.

Martin, J., *The Wired Society* (Englewood Cliffs, NJ, Prentice-Hall, 1978), pp. 89–103.

Metzker, P.F., 'Future Payments System Technology: Can Small Financial Institutions Compete?', *Economic Review*, Federal Reserve Bank of Atlanta, November 1982, pp. 58–67.

National Commission on Electronic Fund Transfer, *EFT in the United States: Policy Recommendations and the Public Interest* (Washington, DC, NCEFT, 28 October 1977).

Niblack, W.C., 'Development of Electronic Funds Transfer Systems', *Economic Review*, Federal Reserve Bank of St. Louis, September 1976, pp. 10–18.

Nicholls L., 'High-tech Forcing Specialization', *Banking, Finance and Investment Review* (Hong Kong, South China Morning Post, June 1984), pp. 7–8.

Schaller, C.A., 'The Revolution of EFTS', *Journal of Accountancy* (New York, The American Institute of Certified Public Accountants, October 1978), pp. 74–80.

Todd, P.C., 'Technology will Change Face of Banking', *Asian Money Manager*, October 1981, pp. 25–6.

Wild, R.J., 'Electronic Banking: the Only Way Out', *Hong Kong Review* (Hong Kong, South China Morning Post, January 1982), pp. 32–3.

Witt, H.J., 'Trends in Banking', *Data Processing*, Vol. 25, No. 2, March 1983, pp. 24–6.

Index